READING CULTURE
THEORY, PRAXIS, POLITICS

Pramod K. Nayar

SAGE Publications
New Delhi / Thousand Oaks / London

First published in 2006 by

Sage Publications India Pvt Ltd
B-42, Panchsheel Enclave
New Delhi 110 017
www.indiasage.com

Sage Publications Inc
2455 Teller Road
Thousand Oaks, California 91320

Sage Publications Ltd
1 Oliver's Yard, 55 City Road
London EC1Y 1SP

Published by Tejeshwar Singh for Sage Publications India Pvt Ltd, phototypeset in 10/12 Minion by C&M Digital, Chennai and printed at Chaman Enterprises, New Delhi.

Library of Congress Cataloging-in-Publication Data

Nayar, Pramod K.
  Reading culture: theory, praxis, politics / Pramod K. Nayar.
    p. cm.
  Includes bibliographical references and index.
    1. Popular culture—India. 2. India—Social life and customs. I. Title.

DS428.2.N39   306.0954—dc22   2006   2006002703

ISBN: 0–7619–3474–X (PB)   81–7829–621–7 (India-PB)

Sage Production Team: Proteeti Banerjee, Rrishi Raote, Rajib Chatterjee and Santosh Rawat

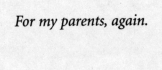

For my parents, again.

CONTENTS

LIST OF BOXES

PREFACE

This book maps the discipline of Cultural Studies through a study of select genres. *Reading Culture* is interested in the ways in which public culture, an integral component of civil society, generates meanings. Since public culture reflects the prevalent power relations between identities, races, genders and classes, meanings generated seek to retain, contest or invert these relations. This process of meaning-generation and contestation informs public cultural forms in subtle ways.

Culture works its strategies of inclusion and exclusion so that certain identities, norms, values, modes of thinking and knowledge are marginalized in the meaning-game. Such strategies take recourse to certain rhetorical-narrative modes, which conceal an oppressive, marginalizing *politics* beneath their surface aesthetics and 'obvious' meanings. Cultural genres such as comics, cinema, museums and tourism—the four genres that this book explores—are primarily narratives, and each genre has its own narrative form and modes of representation. *Reading Culture* explores these narratives to demonstrate how their representational strategies naturalize dominant ideologies and hegemonic discourses.

The opening chapter situates the terms of the debate, the tools of analysis and the locations in which contemporary Cultural Studies 'works'. Individual chapters devoted to cinema, comics, museums and tourist brochures explore the discourses within each genre and analyse the politics that constitute latent subtexts to the manifest rhetoric.

A section of the museums chapter appeared as 'The Politics of Optics: Museums and Public Culture' in *Seva Bharati Journal of English Studies* 1 (2005), pp. 10–31. 'DestiNations: The Poetics and Politics of Travel Culture', from Chapter 5, 'Brochure Culture', appeared in ANVES 1, 1 (2006), pp. 18–31. A part of this chapter was also delivered as a talk, 'Travel/Writing', at the workshop on 'Travel Writing and Culture

Reporting' organized by the Tourism and Hospitality Training Centre, Hyderabad (August 2004).

Pramod K. Nayar
Hyderabad

ACKNOWLEDGEMENTS

I owe a huge debt to several people—quite a few of whom I have annoyed considerably, consistently, but who were generous enough to forgive me—who have contributed to this book.

My parents, for their support, affection and prayers—they keep me going. Ai and Baba, for their affectionate support, and for ensuring that my Nagpur visits were really *vacations*.

Dr Anna Kurian, that miraculous combination of colleague *and* friend, who reads my work closely, and offers (apologetically) suggestions and advice that I have come to value so highly.

My mentors over the years: Professor Mohan Ramanan, Professor Sudhakar Marathe, Professor Narayana Chandran and Professor Probal Dasgupta.

Professor Narayana Chandran: for his insights into the operations of the English language in India, and for his concept-that-threatens-to-become-a-refrain, 'the social life of English in India', a special 'thank you'.

Venumaman, who bought me my first comic book, *Amar Chitra Katha*'s *Krishna*, several years ago—with no foreknowledge of what he was setting me out on!

The referee of the manuscript for perceptive comments and suggestions.

C. Arnold, Visitor Services, the British Museum, London, for sending me brochures and newsletters.

M.K. Jagadish, American Information and Research Centre, Chennai, for supplying books and articles.

Lakshmi Jyoti of the Tourism and Hospitality Training Centre, Hyderabad, for inviting me to talk at her training programme on 'Travel/Writing', and for procuring generally unavailable documents on central and state government tourism policies.

M. Balamani of MS University, Baroda, for allowing me to look at her work-in-progress on household rituals in India.

Shrenik Avlani for supplying museum brochures and a heap of comic books.

Dr Anita Mannur of Wesleyan University, for sending me her own and others' writings on *Amar Chitra Katha*.

Professor Frances Pritchett of Columbia University, for sending me her essay on *Amar Chitra Katha*.

Jihasa Vachcharajani, for procuring books from CIEFL, and for her insistence on carefully reading everything I write.

Niyati Dhuldhoya, for her (extended, fragmented) phone calls from Mumbai, frantic emails, and comments on the comics and museum chapters.

Ajit and Panikkar for sustained affection and friendship.

Debjani Dutta, then at Sage India, for first discovering potential in the proposal.

Mimi Choudhury, then at Sage India, for advice and encouragement as the project moved on.

Anamika Mukharji at Sage India, for smoothening the final stages with her efficiency.

Proteeti Banerjee, for cleaning up the manuscript with some 'routine' felicity (and trying not to ask embarrassing questions about awkward syntax).

Rrishi Raote for an efficient production job and his 'designs' on the book!

Nandini, who negotiates my catastrophic work schedules with equal parts worry and aplomb.

Pranav, having moved on from my last book—when, at 1½ years, he was trying to switch off the PC—to a stage where he directs the cursor to the 'correct' (*'yeh theek hai'*, in his lexicon) point.

The work of art is the product of a negotiation between a creator or class of creators, equipped with a complex, communally shared repertoire of conventions, and the institutions and practices of society. In order to achieve the negotiation, artists need to create a currency that is valid for a meaningful, mutually profitable exchange. It is important to emphasize that the process involves not simply appropriation but exchange, since the existence of art always implies a return, a return normally measured in pleasure and interest .... Society's dominant currencies, money and prestige, are invariably involved, but I am here using the term 'currency' metaphorically to designate the systematic adjustments, symbolizations and lines of credit necessary to enable such an exchange to take place.

Stephen Greenblatt, 'Towards a Poetics of Culture' (1989)

Introduction

READING CULTURE

Cultural Studies is a resolutely interdisciplinary 'field'. Its often bewildering alchemy of methodologies—its praxis—from literary studies, sociology, political theory and political economy, art history, media and image studies, philosophy and discourse analysis is informed by theoretical insights from poststructuralism, feminism, Marxism, queer studies and postcolonialism. This eclecticism contributes to Cultural Studies' analytical rigour, its politics and, not infrequently, its incomprehensibility.[1] This book sets out the contours of this politically informed, theoretically inflected and analytically rigorous discipline of Cultural Studies through a study of select genres in public culture.

'Culture', Raymond Williams informs us, is one of the most complex words in the English language (1976: 76). It includes both material things and symbols. The bourgeois class in the modern state has to

---

Box 1.1: Cultural studies

It is concerned with practices, institutions and modes of classification through which cultural values and norms are instilled in a population. It analyses the forms and representational strategies of social and cultural power through which certain groups dominate other sections of the population and control the dissemination of meanings and values. This cultural and interpretive domination is often coterminous with maintaining political and economic power over the dispossessed and the disempowered. Cultural Studies offers its methodologies and resources to agents of social change—such as women's movements—and establishes relations with specific cultural institutions and fields of cultural management.

govern with the actual consent of the governed. For this consent to 'happen', the class becomes an 'educator', as it seeks to raise the mass of the population to a moral–cultural level that suits its own interests (Gramsci 1971: 258–60).[2] Cultural mechanisms of the arts, religion and education are the means through which consent is secured and power effected. The state itself divides into political society and the cultural-ideological apparatus of civil society. The relation *between* these levels is the arena of Cultural Studies.

Box 1.2: Culture

'Culture' derives from the words 'cultura' and the Latin 'colere', meaning to inhabit, cultivate, protect and honour with worship. In 19th-century Europe the term began to be associated with the elite: the idea of 'high' culture was implicit in the very term. Culture can be defined as ideas, knowledge and modes of doing things. Cultural Studies reveals what we assume to be natural and immanent in 'culture' as being rooted in complex *negotiations* of power over meanings. During the course of this negotiation, some elements of the cluster are closed off and marginalized. Soon the valorized elements become established as 'true' ('high') culture, while the other elements are 'lost'. Finally, once this hierarchy of 'high' and 'low' is in place, it becomes 'naturalized'.

Public culture is a component of this civil society, a realm of social meanings and pleasures, the globalized, hybridized spaces where elite/non-elite, urban/non-urban, literary/oral, cosmopolitan/local, metropolitan/folk elements mix messily. Public culture is a space where meanings are contested, distorted and revived in a continuous process. Public culture includes cinema, advertisements, television, celebrity gossip in magazines and newspapers, autobiographies and biographies of public figures, websites and web-pages of institutions, tourist guides and leaflets, museums, comic strips consumed—sometimes literally—by children, state iconography (remember the 'India Shining' ads which provided a textual preface to the 2004 elections?), city maps and guides, etc. In public culture private and state interests, low and high cultural media, and different classes and groups formulate, represent and debate what culture is, or should be.[3]

A phrase that supplies Cultural Studies with its scope, definition and agenda would be: *culture and power*. Cultural Studies is interested in the ways in which culture works its strategies of inclusion and exclusion. It is interested in the process by which power relations between and within groups of human beings organize cultural codes, forms of knowledge and identities located in the realities of race, gender, class and caste.

Glenn Jordan and Chris Weedon compile a set of questions that cogently summarize the various issues within Cultural Studies. Each of these questions has to do with 'culture'.

Whose culture shall be the official one and whose shall be subordinated? What cultures shall be regarded as worthy of display and which shall be hidden? Whose history shall be remembered and whose marginalized? What images of social life shall be projected and which shall be marginalized? What voices shall be heard and on what basis? This is the realm of cultural politics. (1995: 4)

An emphasis on discourse and textuality is central to Cultural Studies. Subjects, identities and relationships are constructed out of

---

Box 1.3: Power

Cultural Studies is concerned with the dispossessed, those oppressed, marginalized and silenced in the power relations between people, classes, races, sexual preferences, ethnicities and genders. Power, which is intimately linked to knowledge, is negotiated out of social relations and constitutes individuals and bodies. Thus the human body is an object of study in medicine, law, biology, philosophy, and the arts. Each of these 'disciplines' attains its status *as* discipline by developing a set of analytical practices that create objects of inquiry and knowledge. These analytical practices are acts of power, since knowledge about an object leads quickly to control—through legislation by law or the prescription of medication by physicians—over the object. Finally, these practices find expression in representations.

---

discourse. Cultural Studies asks questions about the process through which the understanding and reading of cultural texts is effected. What is the subject position—teacher or student, informed reader or an untrained one? What are the modes of representation of the subject for analysis? Cultural Studies analyses modes of representation in popular/mass culture, while locating both within political economy. It thus pays particular attention to the material conditions of cultural production, such as the printing and publishing industry, the advertisements and forms of media publicity, reviewing and the politics of institutional teaching. It shifts focus from the author as the transcendent authority to *social* contexts of the production of texts and meanings.

Cultural Studies is chiefly concerned with the question of the Other. It argues that the dominant class has maintained its power through

---

Box 1.4: Discourse

In Cultural Studies language and interpretation are treated as intimately connected to issues of class, power, ideology and the material conditions in which the speech-act or interpretation occurs. Discourse defines and produces the objects of knowledge in an intelligible way. Discourse is the regulated and regulatory context in which knowledge is produced; it is the very terrain of thought and expression. Culture itself is treated as a *text* with representational codes, symbols and metaphors, all of which are rooted in the power relations and struggles in the material world.

---

processes of Othering, classifying social groups as philistines, savage and 'uncultured', treating them as objects of knowledge and, therefore, subject to power and control. Thus Cultural Studies is interested in the socio-cultural process through which women, the differently abled, the working classes, the non-white races and queers become 'othered' or marginalized. As an example of the process of power-negotiations within a society, let us look at the marginalization of the Dalitbahujan culture in India. Kancha Ilaiah (1996) demonstrates how Hindu Brahminism kept Dalitbahujan culture separate from Hinduism itself, as its 'other'. Ilaiah writes:

They [Hindu Brahmins] decisively thrust us aside ... treated us as the vulgar 'working mass' having no dignity, no self-respect. Our history, our language, our philosophy, our skills, our knowledge of science and technology were all rendered invisible ... the very idea of caste negated the idea of history. Our history, therefore, became non-history. (p. 166)

Ilaiah notes that no Dalitbahujan gods figured in stories studied at school. For the Brahmin or the bania, the 'prescribed' stories were familiar because Rama and Krishna were the gods they worshipped, while the Dalitbahujan knew only Pochamma, Potaraju and Beerappa.

What difference did it make to us whether we had an English textbook that talked about Milton's *Paradise Lost* or *Paradise Regained* ... or Wordsworth's poetry about English nature, or a Telugu textbook that talks about Kalidasa's *Meghasandesham....* We do not share the contents of either; we do not find our lives reflected in their narratives. (ibid.: 177)

Sanskrit and English both functioned as controlling devices—they established 'national cultures' by ignoring and deliberately silencing other

---

Box 1.5: Representation and stereotyping

'Representation' means the norms of signifying (meaning-generating) practices. Representation in Cultural Studies is intimately linked to power, the practices of ideological domination and selective marginalization. Representations derive their common base of understanding from larger cultural ideas regarding women and minorities. Advertisements depicting women in conjunction with a specific product reflect a cultural condition where women's bodies and the product are both objects to be displayed, possessed and controlled by aggressive masculine power. Stereotypes 'order' the world through particular categorizations of persons. The stereotype maintains sharp boundaries, and also renders otherwise invisible identities (such as the gay or the working-class man) visible through specific 'codes' (the gay man's 'effeminate' walk, the working-class man's smell). It reduces the Other to a set of unchanging attributes. Race, gender, sexual preference, class are all coded into specific stereotypes prior to control. By reducing the Other to one set of knowable features—the 'criminal' working class, the rebellious youth—society preserves its 'self' from ambivalence. Their rhetorical power proceeds from the fact that they are regarded as common-places in everyday life. Rapid social and cultural change leads to stereotyping as a source of stability and unchanging meaning.

cultural forms and languages. Culture is thus about power: who wields it and who controls the narrative-interpretive acts.

Cultural Studies cathects political economy, politics, language and history into the realm of culture and identity where differential power relations have their greatest impact. This emancipatory drive in Cultural Studies draws upon, as noted earlier, critiques of 'high' culture such as Marxism and feminism. It locates cultural themes firmly within political culture and political economy through a combination of sociological inquiry and discourse analysis—praxis—while seeking a politically informed pedagogic presence (Giroux 2000).

In India, with its own systems of domination, reading culture involves 'interfacing' the intracultural and the intercultural (Bharucha 2001). We need to radically *contextualize* local (folk, tribal, gender-specific, caste-linked) cultures. This requires: (*i*) access to the native languages and dialects where the articulation of culture occurs; and (*ii*) an understanding of the political economy within which that particular culture 'operates'. To speak of a 'tribal culture' without also addressing the economic conditions and political contexts in which the tribe lives/works de-links culture from everyday life and economy.

Box 1.6: Identity

Identities are not immanent but *constructed* through processes of negotiations and discourses. Cultural Studies is interested, as the definitions of power and discourse have shown, in those processes by which individual/social (racial, gendered, ethnic, sexual, communal) identities are constructed. Particular identity categories are built around their presumed 'unique' conditions—such as of being black, or being a woman. Reducing all experience to a collective one (as a woman, as gay, as a Dalit) takes away the sheer singularity of individual suffering. Thus rape or violence against a particular individual can be explained as the result of a racist/classed/patriarchal/casteist discourse, but it cannot take away the fact that the pain is unique to the body that suffers.

Thus public culture studies in India must take into account literacy, class, caste, gender, sexuality, migration (both within and outside the Indian nation-state), languages and dialects, political culture, the role of democracy, oral/folk cultures, the role of English in India—what Narayana Chandran appositely terms 'the social life of English in India' (personal communication)—as an empowering language (where even defences of vernacular and regional literature are conducted in *English* by highly-paid professors of *English* who, of course, will not teach in a Telugu or Urdu university because the social and economic capital lies in English), mass culture, the multiple 'isms' (nationalism, communalism, secularism and regionalism), translation and adaptation. Cultural Studies situates each of the above within political economy (colonialism, neo-colonialism, the MNC and global capital presence, NRI investment). Material conditions of everyday existence need to be foregrounded before any discussion of the cultural artifact.

Cultural Studies' analytics is thus a praxis and pedagogic practice heavily informed by contemporary critical theory, and it embeds a politics that seeks to be egalitarian and emancipatory.

Box 1.7: Ideology

Ideology can be defined as a coherent set of beliefs and attitudes. Karl Marx suggested that the ideas of the ruling class become the ideas of the entire society. It masks the actual conditions of exploitation and uneven power relations between classes and people. Ideologies are negotiated between classes. An individual is 'interpellated'—inserted into the social system—through ideology. Religious institutions, the law, the education system, the media and the family instill the dominant ideology and allocate particular roles to individuals within the system of production.

❏ LOCATIONS

This section sets out, very briefly, the locations within which the analysis of contemporary public culture is sited. It is worth repeating the informing assumption here: that the realms of economics (from production to markets and shopping), politics (from local bodies to nation-states) and technology (from the domestic appliance to space engineering) have manifestations and intersections with/in the domain of cultural practice.

Modernity

The term 'modernity' comes from the Latin 'modernus', which was used to distinguish the Christian present from the 'pagan' past. However, 'modern' is associated with the definitive epistemological break that occurs with the European Enlightenment in the 17th and 18th centuries. On the one hand it ushered in science, medicine and new forms of knowledge ostensibly seeking the emancipation of humankind. On the other, it developed exploitative socio-economic modes of 'development'.

European modernity helped define the West against the non-European (Asian, South American, African). Modernity is closely aligned with colonialism and slave labour. Notions of taste, style and manners evolved during modernity because of Europe's construction of these other non-white cultures as primitive, pagan and undeveloped. (This, of course, by no means suggests that all of Europe was a homogeneous mass—the distinct class differences in European societies meant that several of these stereotypes were equally applicable to the underclass.) Modernity evolved new styles of art, generated images of human alienation, and set in motion a train of ideas about the human condition, helped by both philosophies of the mind and scientific discoveries.

Box 1.8: Modernity

Modernity is linked to the rise of capitalist economy, the emergence of the nation-state (with the Treaty of Westphalia, 1648), the increasingly global information and military systems, and the rationalization of work and time in industrial, urbanized conditions. It is linked to the beginnings of globalization, the emphasis on the 'human' as an object of discourse and study, the subordination of instinct to medicine, religion and the law. The prison, the hospital, the asylum became sites of regulation of the 'criminal', the old (and therefore economically non-productive), the sick and the insane. Modernity has also been instrumental in 'facilitating' excessive military interventions, poverty and severe class distinctions.

Postmodernity

Postmodernity, associated with the post-industrial scenario in Euro-American culture, is marked by a concern with the generation and

Box 1.9: Postmodernity

Postmodernity is marked by massive Information and Communications Technology (ICTs), fragmented production processes, and global cash and information flows. There is the rise of the knowledge-elites, increased consumerism and an over-reliance on images and illusions. The local meets the global and the human is no longer the unified individual of modernity.

control of information. Features of a postmodern, globalizing cultural ethos are visible in the metropolises of Bangalore, Hyderabad, Gurgaon, and other such sites of India's ICT revolution.

The emphasis on illusion, brands and simulated reality obscures the exploitative conditions of labour that make the illusions possible. Philosophically, the contingent, the ambivalent and the transient become central to the history of ideas. There is a refusal to accept grand narratives of emancipation or explanation and a preference for the local and the 'small'. Postmodernity is closely linked with globalization, an increasing 'informatization' of the world with its internet technologies, which have serious effects on cultural forms in politics, arts and civil society (see P. Nayar 2004 for a study).

In 'Third World' nations there has been a radical rethinking on the ecological, social and cultural implications of Western—though by no means is the West or 'modernity' a monolithic, homogeneous entity—modernity and rampant globalization. Further, the movement against modernity has also been a movement to retrieve native, local and traditional forms of culture. Though negotiating with the pre-modern—which had its own forms of oppression, such as patriarchy, caste system and feudalism—has not been easy, numerous 'Third World' thinkers see indigenous traditions as essentially plural. Others propose minoritarian modernities and a provincialization of European modernity (Chakrabarty 2000; Pollock et al. 2000).

Globalization

Twentieth-century globalization is characterized by the expansion of trade, the development of transnational and global communication networks,

---

Box 1.10: The hyperreal

The hyperreal is used to describe the postmodern image-culture of the late 20th century. The sign does not refer to any external reality (or referent), it merely refers to other signs. Simulation is when the image becomes more real than reality: the hyperreal. This hyperreal is characterized by simulation: where real life is imitated by television, and television inspires real-life actions (reality TV and others). In the age of perfect reproduction and endless repetition of images, the distinction between the real and the illusory, between original and copy, between superficiality and depth has broken down.

---

the diminished role of the nation-state, the rise of transnational cultural, economic and political networks (such as the IMF, Greenpeace and Amnesty), and the increased circulation of Western consumer products and cultural artifacts.

Globalization has several aspects that come in for critical scrutiny in Cultural Studies.

Global culture

The most self-evident forms of cultural globalization are the products of Western media: television, pop/rock music and Hollywood icons, sartorial fashions and Pepsi/Coca-Cola. Global culture is increasingly *global consumer culture*. Cvetkovitch and Kellner argue:

> Global culture operated precisely through the multiplication of different products, services and spectacles targeted at specific audiences. Consumer and media industries are becoming more differentiated and are segmenting their customers and audiences into more categories. In many cases this involves the simulation of minor difference of fashion and style as significant, but it also involves a proliferation of more highly differentiated culture and society in terms of an ever-expanding variety and diversity of cultural artefacts, products and services. (1997: 19)

Globalization, however, cannot be seen as a one-way effect of Western culture on local ones. A commodification of ethnic products is essential to a global consumer culture.[4] Local products such as Indian cuisine and ethnic wear have now reached global markets. When the 'curry' is declared UK's 'national dish', we have a very globalized local product. African music and Italian pizza are now as much global as Coca-Cola (even granting that these do not quite match the market reach of American products). Further, the migration of software and communications workers into all parts of the world has altered the demographic, and therefore cultural, constitution of various countries in Europe. Indians in the USA, for instant, build their 'own' places of worship as well as social relations with 'other', different cultures. Indians returning from the USA to work in India constitute a doubly diasporic culture (Sen 2004: 6–7). In both cases the result is a globalized culture that has combined, modified and hybridized several cultures.

Box 1.11: Consumer culture and consumerism

Consumption is the relatively simple act of purchase and use of a product. Consumerism is a cultural expression of the act of consumption. When we purchase a can of Coke or branded jeans, we are not just purchasing commodities, we are also purchasing the cultural value attached to these objects. We are purchasing, wearing and adopting an entire value-system: American culture (say Levi's), youth culture (boys in jeans), and counter-culture (casual as opposed to formal/official). The commodity is thus a sign of something which is not *in itself* a commodity. The sign stands for status, class, political affiliation. Commodification is a process by which values, signs, even identities can be turned into commodities for sale.

Glocalization

Roland Robertson speaks of 'glocalization' as being at the heart of globalization. Robertson argues that goods are targeted on a global scale, but aimed at local markets (the term 'glocalization' is actually a Japanese marketing term!). Robertson defines glocalization thus: 'The creation and incorporation of locality, processes which themselves largely shape, in turn, the compression of the world as a whole' (1995: 40). What is important is that 'local' communities can also become communities of resistance to the imperialistic designs of the forces of globalization. Thus fora such as Mumbai Resistance (which held parallel sessions opposite the World Social Forum, Mumbai, January 2004) and the Seattle protest marches are indictments of consumer imperialism (Gilroy 2002).

Globalization can be resisted through recourse to a 'national imaginary'. The 'national' facilitates an oppositional discourse to the global. However, this does not mean that the national itself is homogenous. Rustom Bharucha's national imaginary, for instance, argues that 'the right to criticize the official agendas of the state is eminently possible within the seeming constraints of a national imaginary, *along with new articulations of cultural representation* relating to women, dalits, tribal communities, and other minorities' (2001: 32, emphasis added). This is, I believe, a possible solution to the 'imposing' structures of a globalized or even 'national' culture. By suggesting that 'new articulations' by/of women and Dalits must be worked into the national, Bharucha seeks to remedy the obvious defect where the national is itself hegemonic.

Resistance, alternatives and counterculture

Globalization has generated an inquiry for alternatives and produced its own counterculture. This is the case with cultural forms, research and epistemologies. Arjun Appadurai argues that there is an increasing disjuncture between the globalization of knowledge and the knowledge of globalization. Appadurai proposes a 'globalization from below' or 'grassroots globalization' of local, national and regional groups and non-governmental organizations. We need to pay attention to the vocabulary of grassroots globalization, to their modes of inquiry, and formulate new protocols of inquiry that have thus far been rejected as unacceptable by Western models (Appadurai 2000b: 17–18). This sketch of a new agenda of research in the social sciences that Appadurai draws for us is, I believe, a salutary call for Cultural Studies in general. It calls into question so-called 'established' forms of inquiry, the hierarchization of knowledge, the exclusionary principle on which 'research' has been institutionalized, and so on. The return to the vernacular, the parochial and the local is the attempt to 'de-gentrify' research and cultural criticism.

Rustom Bharucha favours the intracultural interventions and exchanges that occur between differences within a region. The intracultural resists the homogenizing methods of the multicultural state (2001: 11–12). The problem is that the regional/national/international cannot be treated on par with each other, or as 'translatable', since they are very different—in terms of both production and consumption—from each other.

Globalization's cyberculture of high-power business, increasing corporate control over daily lives, the division of the world into domains by corporations rather than nation-states has generated its own counterculture. John Perry Barlow's Electronic Frontier Foundation set up in 1990 is an example of a countercultural movement within cyberculture. Cyberfeminism and cyberfeminist cultural studies showcases the work of groups and activists such as DNA Sluts, Geek Girls or the VNS Matrix (Adam 2002; Flanagan and Booth 2002; Wolmark 1999). A countercultural movement, which adapts the very 'technologies' of capitalist, elite culture, is clearly evident in the 1990s.

Box 1.12: Counterculture

Countercultures express opposition to the dominant class/race/gender/ideology that imposes 'order'. That is, countercultures are basically cultures of dissent and protest. Countercultures may be in direct opposition to the dominant values, power structures, and the patterned exchanges that are entangled in those values, and may deal with the power structures through aggression, avoidance (retreat into cults) or acceptance. Some countercultures are built around the recreational use of specific drugs. The Beat generation of the 1950s used marijuana, as did the hippies in the 1960s. In the 1990s ecstasy (street name for 3.4-methylenedioxyme-thamphetamine, or MDMA) was linked to the rave subculture. Hiphop popularizes the use of cannabis.

Western developmental models are critiqued because of an increasing awareness that such post-Enlightenment notions of 'modernity' cannot easily 'apply' to nations such as India. Thus new conceptions of modernity lie at the heart of the process of postcolonial transformation. The modern is 'resisted' and used at the same time. Strategies and techniques can be used without a 'wholesale absorption into the culture of Western modernity' (Ashcroft 2001: 23).

The global cultural hybridization debate suggests that postcolonial societies do not accept globalization's transformative processes passively. Local cultures modify Western cultural forms and artifacts, producing a mixture of the traditional and the received. One can see globalization as a space for radical revisioning. It spreads ideas—such as that of equality or emancipation, the legacy of the maligned European Enlightenment—that help, enable and create agencies where none existed previously. Caste, class, gender oppression and exploitation can be studied, and fought, using new forms of discourse (feminism, postcolonial studies, queer theory) that transform the terms of the debate. Much of the Cultural Studies work in India and other 'Third World' countries reveals an intersection of Western models/theories/ideas with local cultural inquiry and modes. This is what makes Cultural Studies one of the most powerful, eclectic, adaptive and *transformative* approaches.

The nation-state and its discontents

Globalization has called into question the aims, form and future of the nation-state itself. Governments in the globalized world order increasingly serve purposes such as decision-making about external investments or the development of the local telematics infrastructure for global firms.

Box 1.13: Nation

The nation is a discourse, constructed out of a set of narratives that represent this community, space/geography and culture in a certain way: 'This *is* India'. It enables a people to see and project themselves in certain ways, since meaning (of, say, 'Indianness') is produced within discourse. A nation is narrated through five main modes: histories, literatures, the media, popular cultural forms, and images of landscapes, historical events, 'great' figures, experiences, triumphs and disasters, festivals and rituals; an emphasis on origin, continuity, tradition and timelessness; the 'invention' of a tradition that projects a set of practices and rituals as 'true' or 'authentic'; the use of a foundational myth (such as 'Bharatvarsha') which locates the origins of a nation/culture; and the frequent use of the idea of 'pure' or 'original' people to prove authenticity.

Jurgen Habermas's exploration of the 'postnational state' argues that the idea that societies are capable of democratic self-realization has until now been realized only in the context of the nation-state (2001: 61). In the present era, however, we need to start thinking of 'finding the appropriate forms for the democratic process to take *beyond* the nation-state' (p. 61, emphasis in original). Habermas argues that democratic procedure is defined by the general accessibility to the decision-making process. Thus a *functioning public sphere* may not be a substitute for conventional procedures of political representation, but they certainly free at least to a limited extent, democratic legitimacy from state-controlled procedures and interventions. Habermas suggests the institutional participation of non-governmental organizations in the decision-making process at national levels. World organizations can demand that member states carry out referendums on important issues. This may ensure a 'transnational will-formation'. Global powers may have to involve themselves in the institutionalized procedures of transnational will-formation. They have to willingly broaden their definitions of 'national interest' into a viewpoint of global governance, marking a change from 'international relations to a global domestic policy' (Habermas 2001: 110–12).

In the 'Third World', the task is to induce social mobilizations in order to create a national society, while simultaneously retaining a degree of autonomy and neutrality in society. To achieve this, the social and political elites of the country seek to create a supra-cultural entity through the discourse of nationalism—frequently coded as majority ethnicity. This meant that a nation-state like India has since political independence sought to assimilate ethnic minorities into a 'national' society through educational, cultural and social policies, even though these policies reflect the interests of the ethnic majority. It is this forced homogenization that has created a feeling of minoritization and marginalization (Sheth 1999: 25–29). What was effected, then, was a set of legal–political institutions of citizenship which articulated minority rights as the cultural rights of communities, in addition to the rights of individual members as citizens (ibid.: 34).

The discourse of nationalism and the jingoist reiteration of India as 'home', and the spontaneous celebrations of 'Indianness'—I write this to the background noise of whoops of joy and bursting firecrackers, celebrating the Indian cricket team's first series victory in the One-Day International Series against Pakistan, in Pakistan (2004)—are factors that enable this attempt to forge a unity.

Dipankar Gupta argues that secularization—which he distinguishes from the *ideology* of secularism—is a functional differentiation of the social order. It is a process which implies the development of institutions that are not bound by local customs and practices (1999: 42). One of the principal features of secularization is the creation of an objective social space and centralized forms of governance where mutual needs are negotiated. Gupta argues that minorities are seen as permanent entities by secularists (ibid.: 47). It is not just religion that makes a minority, but certain privileged and dominant ways of designating them as well. With every passing year the categories of minorities become more rigid. The process of minoritization targets those who are not official minorities. Secularism as an ideology estranges itself from the process of secularization, and becomes impervious to the actualities that secularization generates (capitalism, for instance).

Gupta suggests that we stop thinking in terms of stable minorities and majorities. Instead, we need to pay attention to the *process* of minoritization. Secularism has two variants: it sees the world as incapable of bigotry now that religion has been privatized, or it sees the world in terms of fixed expressions of bigotry (Gupta 1999: 50–51). New minorities emerge without warning, and communities are picked on for persecution by the majority: the South Indians of Bombay in the 1960s, the Sikhs after 1984, Tamizhs after 1991 (ibid.: 52–53). Gupta believes minority listings do not hit out at minoritizing sentiments: official minorities continue to be viewed by the majority as suspect members within the nation-state. Thus SCs (Scheduled Castes) and STs (Scheduled Tribes) in India—once described as 'minorities' by the Constituent Assembly—are no longer considered as such. This is so, Gupta argues, because the majority accepts the fact that they have no loyalties outside the Indian nation-state (ibid.: 56). However, Muslims and Christians continue to be treated as minorities because they have their holy sites outside the geopolitical borders of India. What we need, argues Gupta, is a greater protection of the identity as citizen rather than as minority or majority (ibid.). Gupta's argument is attractive because it addresses the issue of minoritization. However, in order to see citizenship as a protection and protecting device (the public sphere), we need to have a degree of homogeneity—literacy, political interest, capability—among the people. Such a homogenization cannot be achieved except through affirmative action (such as reservations) aimed at those who have had little role to play in the process of secularization. Gupta does not address the fact that the very process of secularization is determined, run and administered (like the public space it creates), unfortunately, by an *elite* citizenry (of certain classes and castes) with extraordinary privileges. Secularization as a process is unequal and uneven: it does not guarantee the same privileges or protection to every citizen. And it is here that the pedagogic, cultural, social, and, ultimately, political interventions in the public discourses become significant.

Homi Bhabha argues that a new public sphere is emerging 'in-between the state and the non-state, *in-between* individual rights and group needs ... an analytic and ethical borderland of "hybridization"' (2000: 4). The 'new minorities', argues Bhabha, do not fit into the liberal theories of rights because such theories tend to focus on 'national cultures'. Such interpretations either privilege a certain kind of cultural identity amenable to liberal norms, or demonize them as appropriate for liberal intervention. Bhabha writes:

> Individual and group, singularity and solidarity, need not be opposed or aligned against each other. They are part of the movement of transition or translation that emerges within and between minority milieux. For an international community of rights cannot be based on an abstract inherent 'value' of humanness: it requires a process of cultural translation that, each time, historically and poetically inquires into the conflictual namings of 'humanity'. (Bhabha 2000: 6)

With such views of the liberal ideology, contemporary critical thinking seeks new grounds for debates about identities, communities and cultures.

Box 1.14: Multiculturalism

The term denotes a society where several cultures co-exist, and is now used synonymously with 'pluralism'. The term's scope and usage expanded after the 1960s and 1970s' 'second wave' immigration into Europe and the USA, which triggered debates about the rights of ethnic minorities. Countries and agencies seeking to accommodate refugees, for instance, were faced with the task of understanding new ways of life, patterns of kinship and family, and moral values. Equality of opportunity, affirmative action, representation and other issues came to be foregrounded in the USA and Europe. Multiculturalism is frequently debated in the context of what is believed to be a 'national' culture. The limits to multiculturalism, it is argued, are the boundaries of what constitutes the 'core' of 'national' culture.

Duncan Ivison (2002) proposes a new paradigm of 'postcolonial liberalism'. Postcolonial liberalism is based on three main liberal values and ways of thinking: that individuals and peoples are fundamentally equal; that they are free; and that social and political arrangements should be such as to promote the well-being of individuals and groups *in the manner that they conceive of it* (ibid.: 5, emphasis added). Ivison proposes a normative thesis of 'complex mutual coexistence', since even when indigenous peoples conceive of themselves as peoples or nations, they tend to seek rights of self-government that fall short of statehood. We need to focus on the conditions of the struggles for both recognition and particular forms of distribution (Ivison 2002: 112–13). In an age where both the governmental (that is, regulatory) and democratic (that is, participatory and emancipatory) have been dispersed through globalization, modes of restriction and resistance cut across national borders. In such a situation there is both challenge and opportunity for indigenous peoples. The challenge includes contesting the legitimacy of the state (in India, state-sponsored violence against the tribals in Kerala in 2003 demands an interrogation of the legitimacy of the state) and normative concepts of justice, equality and freedom. Such principles and norms are mediated through concrete social contexts, and what we need to do is explore alternative forms of mediation that are less distorting and alienating for those subject to them.

An important challenge to the nation-state comes from ethnic and other minorities. Subaltern historiography in India, and in the 'First World' academia, for example (exemplified in the *Subaltern Studies* series), draws attention to the way the Indian nation has been constructed through a process of exclusion and marginalization—of the Dalitbahujan, of women and of the working classes—despite its claims to being socialist and democratic. (However, the irony of the *Subaltern Studies* project itself should not be missed out: written almost entirely in English— sections have been translated into Bangla and Hindi—with a heavy dose of *Western* poststructuralist theory, by scholars almost all of whom studied and now teach in the 'First World', the project also uses, effectively, non-subaltern contexts [like the Bengali *bhadralok*] documents and sources for its theorization. The resultant elitism of 'subaltern' studies— it's a moot point as to how much of the project's language/jargon is subaltern in any sense—cannot be ignored. Kancha Ilaiah's work (1996) emphasizes this exclusivity of Indian nationhood. Ilaiah argues that the exclusivity of the Indian nation-state—which he clearly defines as 'Hindu'—meant that throughout (Indian) history Dalitbahujan voices have been silenced, though their hands and bodies have been working. The Hindu (read Brahmin) culture of learning alienated upper-caste Hindus from the Dalitbahujan culture of work, and kept Dalits away from learning. Ilaiah suggests a programme where the Dalit histories must be based on their own epistemology, their own selfhood. The nation-state must therefore be interrogated for the ways in which it concentrates power and culture in the hands of a few. The women's, queer, Dalitbahujan and working-class movements/counter-narratives seek to recast the nation-state by revealing its elitist biases and exclusionary structures. Thus the retrieval of local, indigenous and thus-far marginalized narratives and alternative traditions (eg., Dangle 1992; Merchant 1999; Sukthankar 1999) moves towards a de-totalization of the grand narratives of India produced by mainstream, discriminatory historiographies.

A vision of social arrangements and structures built upon notions of local rights/beliefs and the freedom, opportunity, and means of fulfilling these are beginning to emerge in such critiques. The more egalitarian view of thinkers such as Ivison and Nandy seeks to underscore the illegitimacies that have informed even so-called liberal nation-states. The emphasis on local and alternative ways of conceptualizing identities, the nation, the individual and the community, social interaction, justice and 'emancipation' enables a whole new way of culture.

New social movements

Social movements have been integral to human history. The Luddites in 19th-century England, for instance, smashed machinery in factories. In a sense the Freedom movement in India was a social movement, as was the Chipko. Greenpeace is an important social movement in contemporary times. What is interesting and relevant to understanding the contours of contemporary public culture and civil society is the increasing political influence of such movements. Greenpeace, for instance, has a significant role to play in world politics. A social movement is a 'set of opinions and beliefs in a population which represents preferences for changing some elements of the social structure and/or reward distribution of a society' (McCarthy and Zald 2003: 172). It is a collective, organized and almost always non-institutionalized challenge to authorities and established social/cultural practices. Social movements therefore tread the blurred line between collective action and institutionalized action. They may be formal organizations—such as Greenpeace or the World Social Forum—that frequently develop a system of hierarchy and cultural/social practices.

Social movements demonstrate the process of social change. New social movements may therefore have a political agenda, but their primary focus and scene of impact is 'civil society' or the 'public sphere'. The

Box 1.15: Class

Class is essentially an economic group. Marxism sees class divisions as integral to societies, where the relations between classes are structured around power. This power depends upon the ownership of the factors of production. Class is a context, a condition, and a marker of the individual. That is, class gives an individual an identity. Class is also linked to *status* (in the English language, the term 'status' pre-dates 'class'). Questions of class for Cultural Studies take into account not just professions, but social attitudes, lifestyles and aspirations.

new social movements work closely with the media to influence opinions through information-dissemination about alternative ways of looking at social and cultural practices.

Social movements are about identity. The American Civil Rights Movement, the Women's movement, and the Gay and Lesbian movements have essentially been 'identity movements'. These movements assert radical racial, gender or sexual identities in order to build communities and challenge hegemonic cultural norms that have consistently refused certain identities. Identity movements are based on a shared characteristic such as ethnicity, gender or sexual preference. Reform movements in 19th-century India were also social movements seeking transformation of social and cultural practices. Dr Ambedkar's movement for the rights of 'untouchables' and the protests against globalization in late 20th-century India are also significant examples.

9/11

9/11 is a crucial date in human history. The collapse of the World Trade Center towers in New York, and the subsequent wars against Afghanistan and Iraq have changed not only the geopolitical scenario of the world/ earth, but also the contexts in which politics and politically edged critiques can be made.

The famous 'Huntington thesis', revived in the wake of 9/11, makes the dangers to Western culture and civilization very clear. Huntington suggests that after the Cold War the great conflicts will no longer be between nation-states or ideologies (capitalism versus socialism, liberalism versus communism), but between civilizations. He argues:

The balance of power is shifting: the West is declining in relative influence; Asian civilizations are expanding their economic, military, and political strength; Islam is exploding demographically with destabilizing consequences for Muslim countries and their neighbors; and non-Western countries generally are reaffirming the value of their own cultures. (1996: 20)

He goes on to add that while the rest of the world has benefited from Westernization and modernization, the West itself has declined. Huntington's central causal factors here are nativism and opposition. To add to the conflagration, American culture is also under siege *internally*. Huntington suggests that 'a common American culture' is being marginalized in favour of racial, ethnic and other cultural identities (ibid.: 305). What is urgently needed is the reclamation of American identity and culture in order to thwart the divisive forces of multiculturalism.

The row over Business Process Outsourcing (BPO) in 2004 must be read as a politically charged cultural issue that extends the Huntington arguments. The Presidential candidate John Kerry described outsourcing as 'unpatriotic'. This is supremely ironic. Freespeech.com, which devoted an entire section to 'Kerry Embarrassment Watch', notes:

HJ Heinz & Co, the family business of Kerry and his wife Teresa has spread its ketchup operations across the world. Of the 79 factories that the food processor owns, 57 are overseas. Heinz makes ketchup, pizza crust, baby cereal and other edibles in such countries as Poland, Venezuela, Botswana, Thailand, and most of all, China and India. (http://www.freespeech.com, 12 April 2004)

The website further notes that Kerry's campaign also received money from outsourcers such as Citigroup ($68, 000), Morgan Stanley ($38, 000) and Goldman Sachs ($50, 000).

America is thus fighting enemies within: ethnic groups who seek more rights, who support their 'home governments', and Americans who are unpatriotic enough to betray American interests in the cause of profits or multiculturalism. Such formulations pose a great danger to minority rights. The Patriot Act and the America Council of Trustees and Alumni (ACTA—founded by Lynne Cheney, wife of the Vice

President) make it clear that public discourse in America is moving away from its consciously multicultural format. Curtailing of civil liberties, privacy and freedom of speech, and racial profiling are consequences of such thinking. Cultural expressions from minority communities, museumization and festivals, ethnic artifacts, associations and funding of academic programmes may alter drastically (though there seems to be a conscious effort, at least in the USA and Britain, to show how Islam is *not* under attack: research fellowships and teaching positions in Islamic culture and civilization continue to be advertised in www.jobs.ac.uk, *The Times Higher Education Supplement*, and for the Fulbright by the United States cultural offices round the world [on American university-academic reactions to 9/11 and pedagogy, see Apple 2002; Palumbo-Liu 2002]).[5]

A parallel can be drawn from Britain, where the Centre for Public Policy Research (CPPR) notes, there has been 'widespread opposition to the government's proposal for more state-funded faith-based schools' since 9/11. At least 80 per cent of the people surveyed by *The Observer* opposed the policy. Fears are expressed about 'Osama bin Laden' academies in Britain (Centre for Public Policy Research 2002: 312, 316–17).

Fundamentalism

The 20th century has been marked by an increasing intolerance towards, and hatred of, difference. While the term 'fundamentalism' is most often used to refer to *religious fundamentalism*, it applies to any chauvinistic rejection of an alternate form of thinking or belief system. For Cultural Studies in the 20th century, dealing as it does with everyday life and modes of meaning generation, fundamentalism is an important context and location.

Steve Bruce identifies two varieties of fundamentalism: the individual and the communal. Islamic fundamentalism in the Middle East is a communal version, where a 'particular kind of religion is associated with big issues of economic development, geopolitical power and social evolution, and what is at stake is the relative power of communities'. American fundamentalism—especially that of conservative Protestants—is 'essentially a voluntary association of self-selecting individuals, competing to define the culture of a stable nation' (Bruce 2000: 9–10). The Islamic

---

Box 1.16: Fundamentalism

The term 'fundamentalism' comes into the popular lexicon with the 20th century, especially with the publication of the series of pamphlets called *The Fundamentals* (1910–15), and through a set of conferences of the World's Christian Fundamentals Association in 1919. Fundamentalism is a movement that responds to modernization by seeking a social obedience to the scripture(s) or tradition. Further, it seeks political power that can impose this 'renewed' tradition.

---

version is 'pre-modern', since the close relation between religion, ethnicity and nationalism seen in Islamic or Hindu cases were common in the pre-modern West, but are now rare there (Bruce 2000: 9–10). Fundamentalism can be defined as the defence of a way of life that was being rapidly superseded, and as being rooted in revivalism and pietism.

Fundamentalisms claim that some sources of ideas, usually a text classified and revered as 'scripture', are complete and beyond error. Thus Protestants believe that the Bible is the actual word of God and complete in its revelation. Islamic fundamentalists see the Qurān as God's word and the Hadith as the true record of the Prophet's sayings and actions. Hindu fundamentalism of 1990s India is also a communal one, since it seeks social cohesion and power based on a particular belief system (see Katju 2003). The Ram Rajya of Hindutva is based on the chief figure of the Ramayana. However, monotheistic religions such as Judaism, Christianity and Islam are much more amenable to fundamentalist 'versions' than Hinduism or Buddhism with their in-built variety and divergences. Thus fundamentalists believe that the original sources provide a perfect guide to living and society. Fundamentalism also claims the existence of some perfect social embodiment of the true religion in the past, and thus advocates a return to true religion in order to reclaim that golden age. Changes in the community and belief systems or values—due to modernization and its modes of inquiry—are perceived as threats to the continuity of the past. The goal, therefore, is an aggressive return to the past.

Bruce's interpretation of comparative fundamentalism relies on the older binary of modern West versus pre-modern (read 'primitive') non-West. The argument that a fundamentalism such as the Islamic one is 'pre-modern', as it *once* existed in the West, equates Islamic fundamentalism with early American/European primitivism. Bruce thus reinforces the very binaries that helped colonialism and imperialism in the name of evangelicalism and 'development'. This is, to me, a very dangerous trend.

In the Asian nations modernization has been traumatic for many social groups. In the Middle East there has been little scope for popular political participation—the monarchy rules firmly. Social institutions could not keep pace with the changes being wrought in Asian societies. The Nehruvian socialist model of modernization, Structural Adjustment Programmes with economic liberalization, the IT revolution, and now disinvestments (India had the peculiar distinction of having a minister for disinvestments!) have all produced changes in demographic patterns and changes in institutions such as the family. The injunctions on compulsory *purdah* for women by Islamic fundamentalists in Kashmir (and Afghanistan under the Taliban), the BJP–ABVP's objections to Western clothes on Indian women—a topic that comes up with reasonable frequency—are explained as the fundamentalists' need for control. In her reading of fundamentalism's gender issues, Karen McCarthy Brown argues that fundamentalism emerges from a sense of threat. It seeks arenas to control, and invariably turns to the woman—her clothes, sexuality, behaviour, rights—for this purpose (1994: 182). The debates over Roop Kanwar's Sati or women's clothes are inflected with this ideology of control over the female (on Sati, see Hawley 1994a; Nandy 1995b. For a collection of representative essays on Hindutva and gender, see Sarkar and Butalia 1995).

Ideological cohesion—such as Hindutva—is a property that emerges from the interaction of the belief system with the environment. Thus Hindu fundamentalism emerges when Hindus are asked to pay attention to their sense of identity. In a strategy for mass mobilization and 'Hinduisation' proposed by the 1989 Dharma Sansad, the Vishwa Hindu Parishad (VHP) recommends, as a method, 'hoist[ing] saffron flag atop houses of all Hindu families residing in urban rural and tribal areas of Bharat'. Following this, in a section titled 'Ways and Means for Hinduisation', it states:

Political leadership should be bestowed only on such persons, who are capable of determining the national policies on the basis of Hindu dharma, Sanskriti and Hindu values of life.

In future, society at large should be aware of such politicians who indulge in appeasement of minorities and accede to their anti-national demands at the cost of national interest, only aiming to fulfil their personal or party ends. (Qtd. in Katju 2003: 163–64)

External pressure from a source—in this case, Muslims—is presented as anti-Hindu to promote a common identity. Hindus then see themselves as sharing a common culture/belief system that is under threat from the 'outsider' (the 'anti-national' or foreigner is a Muslim, invariably).

Secularism

With secularization society and culture are removed from the domination of religious institutions and symbols T.N. Madan notes that in India secularism has been defined as equal respect for all religions (*sarva dharma samabhava*). In the Preamble to the Constitution secularism is defined, in Hindi, as *pantha nirpekshta* or neutrality of the state in relation to different religious communities. A related term is pluralism, which may connote (*i*) mutual exclusiveness or absolute difference—which suggests mutual exclusion but not conflict; (*ii*) a convergence of the fundamentals of different faiths; and (*iii*) that every religion requires the others, for no religion has a monopoly over the whole truth. Madan argues that the current use of pluralism as one of the two elements of secularism (the other is a non-discriminatory state) is not quite enough (1997: 31–33).

Madan notes that while the state was theoretically neutral towards all religions, this did not prevent it from providing special protection and treatment to minorities (he notes that the reservation policy of the Indian state does not quite fit with the idea of secularism; ibid.: 256). This, Madan suggests, has led to the majority–minority conundrum. Ashis Nandy, likewise, argues that religious communities in traditional societies had known how to live with each other by developing internal principles of tolerance, which ought to play a role in contemporary politics. Religious strife has escalated with Independence, and though it did occur in traditional India, it was far rarer (Nandy 1995c: 52–53). Nandy argues for freedom from the 'hegemonic language of secularism' because it is a language of the Westernized intellectuals and middle classes in India (ibid.: 30–31. For another critique of nationalism-as-ideology, see Nandy 1998a [1994]).

Western meanings of secularism suggest the relegation of religion to the private sphere. There is no space for it in the public sphere. In non-Western societies, however, secularism means equal respect for all religions. It implies that while public life may or may not be kept free of religion, it must have a space for a continuous dialogue between the religious and the secular, and between religious traditions. This secularism is *accommodative* of religion and difference (Nandy 1995c: 38–39). This accommodative meaning of secularism is what is being increasingly lost in India. This is so because there is a 'clearer fit' (as Nandy puts it) between the ideology of the modern Indian nation-state and the secularism that fears religion (ibid.: 40).

With an increasing secularization religion-as-faith is marginalized. Fanaticism proceeds from a sense of defeat on the part of the believers since there is no space for faith any more (ibid.: 46–47). When a nation makes a plea to a minority community to secularize or confine itself to secular politics, it is actually asking the community to dilute its faith so that it can be integrated into the nation-state (ibid.: 47). Secularism itself begins to be intolerant of faith. The modern nation-state asks its people to give up their faith in public, but cannot offer them protection against the sufferings inflicted by the nation-state itself. Secularism is part of a 'larger package' with development, mega-science and national security (ibid.: 48; also see Nandy 1999: 145–46).

Nandy suggests that the power elite in modern nation-states begin to see the state exclusively in terms of scientific principles—secular, amoral and dispassionate. Therefore, modernist elites fear the divisiveness of minorities and ethnic plurality. All forms of religion and faiths are seen as threats to nation-building. Secularism legitimizes this marginalization— even rejection—of religion and faith (Nandy 1995c: 59–61). Srirupa Roy, reading the celebrations of the 50th year of independence, concludes, like Nandy does, that Indian identity was increasingly captured in two signifiers. The first involved the expression of Indian identity in civic-republican terms (citizenship), and was obviously statist. The second signifier of the nation was cultural diversity, which also reproduced the state-centric logic (2001: 263; also see Khilnani 2004 [1997]).

As a viable option for the secularized and secularizing nation-state, Nandy proposes what he calls 'pre-modern' or 'non-modern' 'alternative traditions of cosmopolitanism' (1999: 160). He notes that even in ancient India urban centres catered to inter-community, inter-cultural and inter-continental exchanges. Cosmopolitan centres of learning were such sites of exchange: Varanasi catered to Hindu and Buddhist scholars, Ajmer attracted Islamic scholars. Nandy argues that such a tradition can be revived (1999: 160–61).

Nandy's critique of the nation-state does not account for the discriminatory and exploitative practices *within* religious traditions. Religions may be doctrinally pluralistic, but their practised form is far from egalitarian. Religion-as-faith can be as exploitative as anything else. Other than the state, there is no mechanism that can ensure justice to those oppressed by religion (Ilaiah's critique of Hinduism is central here). A viable alternative to secularized legislation and state practices to protect the interests of the oppressed is not clearly visible yet. Nandy, of course, has nothing to say about the affirmative actions taken by the state—and there have been such steps, the reservation policy being one, land rights to tribals being another—to improve the condition of those outside the state sector. While he admits that religious strife and ethnic conflicts have occurred in the past, he seems to suggest that they were aberrations. Communalism, for Nandy, is a product of modernization and secularism. This argument fails to account for the ways in which religious traditions have always warred with one another. Granted that the nation-state has been created with a Western (colonial) influence— however, Nandy's thesis does not see it as *inheriting* a history of strife (Akeel Bilgrami notes that 'all the basic elements in the construction of Brahmanism ... were in place well before the deliverances of modernity' [1995: 11]). Further, by locating religious strife *outside* the issues of class and the economy—we need to explore, for example, the literacy levels, living conditions, or per capita income of Muslim or 'lower-caste' communities and families, and compare them with Hindu families in the same geographical area, as a test case—Nandy is ignoring a very significant component of civil society. Part of the problem here may very well be unequal economic opportunities for these communities within (Hindu-dominated) India. To ask what seems a very naïve question, why did the Arab nations appeal to so many Muslim boys and young men in the 1970s and 1980s? Was it because India, despite its adherence to 'secular' principles and equality, did not provide them with adequate means? What purpose does religious or political freedom and equality serve when the nation-state does not ensure economic rights or welfare? To disjoin religious tradition from class interests and the economic contexts in which practitioners of such traditions live/battle is to wilfully misread the situation.

Box 1.17: Caste

The term 'caste' comes from the Portuguese *casta*, meaning 'pure breed'. The concept of *varna* is an approximate Indian equivalent to 'caste'. *Varna* refers to the four-fold division of society based on function. *Jati*, on the other hand, refers to endogamous groups that are more localized. The term 'caste' combines the two indigenous concepts. *Varnas* manifest themselves as endogamous communities that are localized or regional. *Jati* is thus the empirical manifestation of *varna*. The concept of both *varna* and *jati* are rooted in ideas of purity and pollution.

Caste informs systems of eating and marriage, social gatherings and communication. Based on notions of purity and pollution, caste undertakes the ritual ordering of such systems of everyday life: protecting the purity of the kitchen from a menstruating woman, the prohibition of marriage between *jatis*, and so on. Though concepts of purity and pollution are still current, these are appealed to only in the discussion of certain castes rather than as a general ideological principle (Sharma 2002: 37). It is important to note in contemporary (late 20th-century) India the notion of purity and pollution is only one of the ways in which caste identity is expressed. Since class is de-localized in urban India (most urban Indians work and study away from the places where their caste had its roots), it plays a more decisive role than caste in urban, middle-class social relations. People who do engage in social relations pay more attention to family and class identities today.

Akeel Bilgrami, in his response to Nandy, notes that the latter sees nationalism as being only exclusionary. Bilgrami, I think correctly, suggests that what is most salient about nationalism is its inclusivity. He argues that occasionally the state excludes regional interests in favour of a set of dominant economic interests at the centre. But—and this is significant—it attempts to keep these regions included in the ideal of the nation (1995: 9). Nandy does not see something positive that evolves with the nation-state, which is that the 'regulation'—however wicked it may seem—enabled a limited emancipation of women and the 'lower' castes. But for the mechanisms put in place by the modern state, the unequal relations that existed in a heavily Brahminical patriarchal society would have continued. It is here that the inclusivity of the nation-state has a major role to play (P. Chatterjee 1999 [1998]: 10–11. For a critique, see Kesavan 2001). This 'transformation' is, I believe, a search for social justice, and a revitalization of those processes that enable it. However, this process of transformation is not without its problems; indeed, in many cases this gets coded as homogenization and appropriation of all communities into an Indian nation-state. Kancha Ilaiah thus is sceptical of the appropriation and assimilation of the lower castes into a 'Hindu' nation-state. He therefore seeks a transformation from the Brahminical learning-based society to one built on the Dalit productive culture. In terms of a feminist agenda equivalent to Ilaiah's Dalitization, Rajeswari Sunder Rajan argues that the recent acknowledgement of women's *productive* capacities can provide the possibility of activating their rights and resisting community strictures (Sunder Rajan 2000).[6] A problem that escapes the attention of both Ilaiah and Sunder Rajan is that emphasising on productive culture for Dalits and women means that the onus is on a *productive* body. This implies that only healthy and youthful bodies that are economically productive will possess rights in the new envisioning of the nation-state. This kind of *ableism* means that the old, the infirm and the sick automatically become lesser citizens. If citizenship rights are based on an obligation to work, then those who do not work will not be full citizens.

Cultural Studies thus pays attention to strategies of discourse and representation as they reflect existing socio-economic conditions. Seeking out political agendas within cultural forms, Cultural Studies examines possibilities of dissent, resistance and emancipation. It thrives on oppositional readings and rigorous analysis.

Dissent, debate and the search for alternatives are central to a nation. For, a 'rigorous criticism of a nation's policies demonstrates a commitment to the nation itself. It says that one demands action on the principles that are supposedly part of the founding narratives of a nation and that are employed in the legitimation of its construction of particular kinds of politics…. No national narrative that excludes the rich history of dissent as a constitutive part of the nation can ever be considered legitimate' (Apple 2002: 306). Dissent indeed is integral to a process of social transformation. The emphasis on alternative traditions, dissenting voices, and difference is what makes Indian Cultural Studies fertile and politically useful. Their opposition to any form of 'authoritarian populism' (to borrow Stuart Hall's phrase, qtd. in ibid.: 305) means that identities, power, positions, however attractive they may seem at that moment, cannot be rigidly slotted, enforced or static. They must be negotiated constantly.

Difference and dissent must constitute a frame for reading culture. Cultural Studies thrives in and provides an atmosphere of constant vigilance, opposition and interrogation. Located at the tertiary levels of education and university departments—the classroom is *still* our battleground—Cultural Studies fosters constructive dissent and debate by paying attention to the politics of cultural forms and narratives. It remains suspicious of homogenizing, grand narratives of emancipation—feminism, Marxism—even as it promotes an emancipatory programme at the local and particular level. To this end, a Cultural Studies approach gives voice to the voiceless. At the university level—the one I am most familiar with—this entails providing more space for students from diverse backgrounds who have hitherto been disallowed from speaking. Its interdisciplinarity enables access to new ways of thinking and methods that upset the hierarchies established in disciplines. Its emphasis on the role of power relations in meaning-making interrogates hierarchies within the classroom and departments. Are students allowed to read 'freely', or is it proscribed reading only? Are they allowed to engage in dialogue with 'alternative' forms of thought, ideologies and approaches (I know at least one Department of English Chair who, addressing new research scholars officially, prohibited them from speaking to other faculty members without the permission of their allotted supervisor!) How best can their multiple marginalities of class, caste, gender and literacy be channelized into acts of reading? How can the many 'positions' in a classroom provide insights into the operations of the interpretive acts? These are not questions I hope to answer within the scope of the present book, however. I merely foreground these issues, alerting us to the questions involved, when reading genres in public culture.

Cultural Studies' emphasis on dissent, debate, egalitarianism and constant vigilance to socio-political oppressions and injustices enables a pedagogic practice that imbricates literature and culture with democracy, justice and emancipation. It can lead the way to what Jacques Derrida once termed 'the university without condition':

> The university without conditions is not situated necessarily or exclusively within the walls of what is today called the university. It is not necessarily, exclusively, exemplarily represented in the figure of the professor. It takes place, it seeks its place wherever this unconditionality can take shape. Everywhere that it, perhaps, gives one (itself) to think …. The university should thus also be the place in which nothing is beyond question, not even the current and determined figure of democracy, not even the traditional idea of critique, meaning theoretical critique, and not even the authority of the 'question' form, of thinking as 'questioning'. (2002: 202–37)

❏ NOTES

1. In Western academia the rise of Cultural Studies as a discipline is associated most commonly with the Birmingham Centre for Contemporary Cultural Studies and the work of Stuart Hall. Inspired by the work of Marxist historian E.P. Thompson, and the cultural criticism of Raymond Williams and Walter Ong, the Birmingham School offered a one-year interdisciplinary course on popular culture, 'U203' between 1982 and 1987 at the Open University. More than 5,000 students took the course until it was terminated in 1987. The course was directed by Tony Bennett and evaluated by Terry Eagleton, Raymond Williams, and others. On Theory and Cultural Studies, see McKee 2002 and Barcan 2002.

2. Ian Hunter (1994) notes the strong parallels and similarities between popular schools and working-class schools. Hunter notes that while the first was evidently 'conservative', the second made claims to radical education. However, what both achieved was a similar effect with regard to images of class, morality and society. Despite their avowedly different approaches, both served the same goal: the same politics of culture.

3. In a related argument about the civil society–public culture interface, Sandra Freitag suggests that agency in South Asian postcolonial societies can be 'traced both in the direct acts of consumption (and the resulting, personalized recombinations of acquired objects) and in the indirect acts of producers aiming to satisfy consumers' (2003: 389). Together, these acts constitute civil society that exists independent of the state. Thus Freitag sees acts of popular culture as interacting with and even challenging the actions of the nation-state. Freitag points out that the collective pursuit of values—as *rath yatra*s in public spaces or domestic pujas conducted collectively for small groups of housewives—leads to 'an expectation and demand that the state protect such values' (p. 390). Drawing upon a 'new' vocabulary and 'traditional' significations—a process Niranjana terms 'post-national-modern' (2002 [2000]: 145)—this creates a rhetorical space within civil society that enables individual agency to rework meanings for new situations and circumstances (such as globalization). For the role of civil society in the new network society, see Schuler and Day (2004). On transnational television, with a specific reference to Indian contexts, see Butcher (2003).

4. Anita Roddick, the founder of The Body Shop, captures in her autobiography the contours of the 'New British Empire' and a global consumer culture beautifully:

    > I wanted to be Christobel Columbus, going into little villages in Mexico or Guatemala or Nepal and seeing what they had to trade instead of going to those boring old trade fairs where everyone buys the same mediocre products year after year. (Qtd. in Brabazon 2001: 189)

5. I have analysed the Nietzschean rhetoric of 9/11 in 'Deleuze's Nietzsche: The Nomadic War Machine and the Martial Sublime' (forthcoming). For a brilliant account of the gendered rhetoric of evil post 9/11, see Mary Anne Franks (2003). For readings of American fundamentalism, the war against terror and socio-cultural, political and military effects of 9/11, see Der Derian (2002), Giroux (2004) and Philips (2003).

6. On gender, religion, secularism and the nation-state, see Kesavan 2001 (especially pp. 51–58), Nivedita Menon (1999 [1998]), Rajeswari Sunder Rajan (2000) and Srirupa Roy (2001), among others.

❑ FURTHER READING

Theories, practices, contexts

Barker, Chris. 2002 [2000]. *Cultural Studies: Theory and Practice*. London: Sage Publications.

Bhabha, Homi K. (ed.). 1995 [1990]. *Nation and Narration*. London and New York: Routledge.

Castells, Manuel. 1996. *The Rise of the Network Society*. Oxford: Blackwell.

———— 2000 [1998]. *End of Millennium: The Information Age: Economy, Society and Culture, Vol. II*. Oxford: Blackwell.

Fiske, John. 1991 [1989]. *Reading the Popular*. London and New York: Routledge.

Giddens, Anthony. 1990. *The Consequences of Modernity*. Cambridge: Polity.

Miles, Steven. 1998. *Consumerism as a Way of Life*. London: Sage Publications.

————. 2000. *Youth Lifestyles in a Changing World*. Buckingham: Open University Press.

Watson, C.W. 2002. *Multiculturalism*. New Delhi: Viva.

Screen Culture

CINEMA

Films are an integral component of leisure and relaxation. Entertainment is increasingly becoming the largest industry and spending area of human life. In the USA, entertainment ranks ahead of clothing and healthcare as a percentage of domestic spending: 5.4 per cent on entertainment, 5.2 per cent on healthcare and 5.2 per cent on clothes (Sayre and King 2003: 17).[1] Film culture is more than just the film (see box). It is a large system of printed, staged, spoken and visual representations. It is the merger of reel and real life as the film star steps out of the screen onto a stage, road or public meeting. Everything here is part of the entertainment industry.

Theories that have dealt with spectatorship, ideology, and issues of gender/sexuality have much relevance for Cultural Studies because they foreground the power relations at work in cultural representations. Thus feminist theories of film provide insights into the way cinematic representation informs and distorts unequal social relations between men and women. For Cultural Studies, any analysis must take into account the ways in which the dominated/dominating peoples/ ideologies are portrayed in film. Contemporary work in Cultural and Film Studies has increasingly turned to an analysis of the cultural and economic contexts of texts and audiences. Audience studies today take into account spectatorship and the historical conditions of film reception. The new frameworks of Cultural Studies move beyond mere interpretation of film narratives into areas of cultural consumption, meaning-dissemination apparatuses, and the media-technology interface. They move, therefore, from the production of screen representations to the consumption of these representations, locating both within the prevalent cultural politics.

Box 2.1: Film culture

The films: Spectacular canvas (70 mm), extraordinary characters, dramatic, artificial lighting and 'sets', glamour, predictable plot, lengthy (averaging three hours), song and dance routine.

Film culture: Advertisement posters, film magazines and their reviews, pre-release publicity, music released before the film's opening, stage shows, fan club, non-film work done by film stars (philanthropy, buck-shooting), awards ceremonies (widely televised).

This chapter provides a few points of entry into contemporary Cultural Studies of conventional (that is, popular) cinema, focusing on the ideologies, representational modes and discourses embedded in the genre.

❑ FILMS AS MASS CULTURE AND ENTERTAINMENT

The reinvention of film studies suggests that we need to focus on the 'massness' of cinema itself. Cinema 'makes available structures of visibility, modes of conduct, and practices of judgement, which together constitute a culture of public participation' (Donald and Hemelryk 2000: 114). Jane Gaines argues that we need to produce a theory *for* the masses, rather than about them. The popular film is a space where the 'forces of containment meet the forces that cannot be contained' (2000: 107). Ashis Nandy points to the 'self-assertion of the low-brow' that threatens to overwhelm the high culture of the middle classes (1995a: 198–99).

Entertainment is a key word in discussing films. The word 'entertainment' comes from the Latin 'inter' (among) and 'tenere' (hold). Entertainment is all about holding the attention of audiences. Modern entertainment in the Western world can be traced back to live performance and gaming, where audiences were both participants and spectators. In contemporary times, sports, travel and games are participatory forms of entertainment, while play or cinema-viewing are spectatorial forms of entertainment. Reality TV and interactive cinema have, since the last decades of the 20th century, been breaking down this distinction too.

The audience keeps wanting something different. Today's entertainment may not hold the same appeal tomorrow. As a result, companies vie with each other to provide more and more of different things to hold TRPs and audience attention. Thus film-makers seek exotic locales, previously 'untouched', for their settings. Settings, the music and songs, action sequences and comedy are integral to this 'cinema of attractions' (Vasudevan 2000: 131. On romances, setting and leisure practices, see Dwyer and Patel 2002).

One recalls that most song sequences in Hindi (and Telugu, and Tamil, and Kannada) films were once set in Mysore's Brindavan Gardens until film-makers began trying out foreign locations. These are attempts to offer the audience something new, so that the spectator is tempted to return to the movies. While studies such as Prasad's, Nandy's and Kazmi's explore the ideological roots (and shadows) of the Hindi film, they fail to treat the film as *primarily* entertainment. They fall into the same trap as literary critics—of various ideological persuasions and perversions—who treat texts as merely ideologemes. However, this approach can never fully explain the role of films or popular fiction *as* entertainment. The film may be a super genre (the feudal family romance, which for Madhava Prasad [1998] is such a super genre), but we go to watch it for its entertainment value first: the song, the dance, the spectacle. Satyajit Ray, on the subject of songs in Hindi cinema, wrote as far back as 1967: 'the craving for spectacle, for romance, for a funny turn or two, for singing and dancing ... has somehow to be met'. Ray adds: 'There is no denying that if you think in terms of tired untutored minds with undeveloped tastes needing an occasional escape through relaxation, you will have to admit that the best prescription is a well-mixed pot pourri of popular entertainment.' Ray's not-so-subtle comment on 'untutored minds' suggests an elitism that rejects forms of popular entertainment (Ray 1983 [1976]: 73). Somewhere, one needs to resurrect antiquated concepts such as 'aesthetic pleasure' to explain *this* appeal. In a recent essay Martin Jay gestures at this problem in contemporary critical thought. Jay writes: 'aesthetic experience ... cannot be entirely freed from a consideration of which objects and events may justifiably evoke it, or else it courts the charge that it produces a theodicy of beauty, which is no less problematic than its ethical counterpart' (2003: 19). What we need here, in addition to the careful attention to ideologies and politics of the Hindi film, is an *artistics* of the genre. I am suggesting that we expand the notion of aesthetics, explicating the concept of art with particular attention to beauty, to include the range of aesthesis in everyday life, science, politics and art (Mathews and McWhirter 2003: xvi). This includes looking at the needs of the audience, the aesthetic appeal of a scenic footage, the resonating music that in many cases precedes the film viewing, and so on: an *artistics*. The 'uses-and-gratifications' approach to mass entertainment is such an artistics that proposes that individuals use the media in order to satisfy their needs.

The 'commercial' or 'popular' Hindi film is really an extraordinary mass entertainment genre. Fareed Kazmi terms it 'conventional cinema', defining it as 'one which restates in an intense form value and attitudes already known' (1999: 56). Sheila Nayar argues, in an innovative reading of the genre, that many of the genre's conventions stem from 'the need-cum-desire on the part of film producers to appeal to oral habits of thought and expression' (2001: 122). To an extent, all commercial Hindi films are written by spectators themselves, since their acceptance or rejection of the films defines the success 'formula'. Over a period of some few decades, the 'formula' or ingredients became standardized and embedded in a 'cinema of expectation'. The Hindi film relies less on linearity than on shock value. Oral narratives are structured according to the convenience of the speaker; it thus stays uncertain and 'untidy'. It does not depend on mere linguistic structure—as writing does—but on episodic 'stitching together'. Excursions and tangents, repetitions and 'breaks', digressions and multiple plots, and retrieval (flash back) are all integral to the Hindi film, just as they are to the oral story-telling convention. Nayar notes that the movement between present-past-present is typical of the Hindi film because the viewer does not expect a strict linear narrative, but rather the digressive structure of oral story-telling (ibid.: 130–31. Sudhir Kakar argues that the Hindi film is a 'collective fantasy' with roots in the fairy tales; qtd. in Valicha 1988: 34–35).

Hyperbole and exaggeration, both integral to the Hindi film's dialogues (note, especially, the nationalist rhetoric in films, or Dharmendra's bloodcurdling threats in the action films of the 1970s and 1980s), derive from the 'copia', amplification and volubility of oral cultures. Oaths and swearing, for Nayar, represent such an emotive component derived from oral story-telling traditions. The trust in the spoken word is validated through such ceremonial verbal gestures of dialogue. Debates between protagonists are structured in a way so as to inscribe them into the audience's memory. (Here one can add, as a postscript to Nayar, the monologue/public speech valorizing virtue, justice, the mother, the nation, or revenge by the hero at the climactic moment just before he kills the villain.) Repetition of dialogues, clichés and formulaic phrases are essential to oral processes of thought.

Thus princesses become 'beautiful princesses' and suitors become 'love-sick suitors'. Terms like '*dil deewaana*', images of the corrupt politician, the crooked businessman, and the golden-hearted vagabond are staple fare in Hindi films. The stereotype that we see 'unfolding' on screen works to restore stability in an unstable society. That is, images of the chivalrous Rajput or the romantic Bengali are not present there for entertainment alone: they reflect the tensions inherent within a society where such notions of chivalry and romanticism are being eroded and/or interrogated. Rather than restore stability and opinion, they gesture at the uneasy structure on which such attitudes and opinions rest. The stereotype is not a sign of confidence or stability for the consumer to take away from the cinema screen/story, it is a symbol of the need to *re-discover* stability in a fast-changing age. In a consumerist, globalized society where the middle class finds itself increasingly the victim/purveyor of desirable signs and brands, the stereotype presents unchanging values. It is not, therefore, a sign of stability, but rather one of anxiety and fear. The very quaintness of the stereotype is what renders it attractive to a postmodern world of flux and quick redundancy. Thus the Hindi film's valorization of the family, the patriarch, the 'home' is to be read as a nostalgic assertion of a sign system that is increasingly unavailable to many metropolitan Indians of the 1990s. It is surely of some significance that with increasing divorce rates, and separated families, the nostalgia for the 'family' recurs in public life as Sangh *Parivar* and the Sahara India *Parivar*?

Films with violent themes have been very successful in India, and Nayar suggests that this might have something to do with an oral tradition whose own context was of physical hardship and labour. However, it is rarely plain violence. A glorification of socially prescribed good relations is a standard theme that runs alongside the theme of violence. Praise poems about mothers, sisters/brothers, the family, friends are common in Bollywood films. Such archetypes of Mother or Villain, which are rooted in the oral tradition for Nayar, populate Bollywood films. The reason, Nayar suggests following Ashis Nandy's formulation, is because the Hindi film spectator already possesses a certain familiarity with the story which s/he is about to see unfolding on the screen. Key themes and situations are constant in all Hindi films. This is not because of an absence of ideas but because the Hindi film, as in oral tradition, must repeat known materials. Walter Ong has argued that 'oral societies must invest great energy in saying over and over again what has been learned arduously over the ages' (qtd. in S.J. Nayar 2001: 138). This means that there is no real scope for originality, and the genre must 'reshuffle' the old and the already existent in order to accommodate the novel. The conformist mentality that Nayar discerns in the endlessly repeated myths is, for her, the direct consequence of the 'oral mindset' (S.J. Nayar 2001: 139). The Hindi film also demands very little thought on the part of the spectator. There is no need, according to Nayar, for the spectator's self-analysis or intellectual deliberation. Distanced abstraction is not part of an oral tradition. Self-analysis, which Hollywood films seek, requires an isolation of the self, and this the Hindi film does not expect of its audience. Nayar suggests that such an abstraction 'is a divorce from the world' (ibid.: 144).

Fareed Kazmi argues that violence is integral to the Hindi film. He notes that unlike Hollywood films with their guns, the emphasis here is on hand-to-hand fights. Comparing it with the gladiatorial battles of ancient Rome, Kazmi suggests that it privileges the physical over the mental, the primitive over the cultured (1999: 80–81). Kazmi's point is interesting but problematic, as he works this binary against the binary of Bollywood versus Hollywood. This reinstates the opposition between the 'cultured', technologized West and the barbaric, in-a-state-of-nature East. However, there is considerable difference in violence *in* genres. The violence in thrillers such as *Kucch to Hai* (2003) is very different from the average 'action' film. 'The emotional terrain of the slasher film,' writes Carol Clover, 'is pre-technological.' The preferred weapons of the killer in films predicated on stealth are knives, hammers, axes, ice picks, hypodermic needles, red-hot pokers, pitch-forks, and the like (Clover 2000 [1987]: 139. For a general account of screen-violence, see Prince 2000). Moreover, the violence in the stalker film has a heightened effect because, frequently, we are shown things through the killer's eyes, as in *Darr* (1993) or *Kaal* (2005). The use of montage-slow motion and graphic mutilation is integral to such violence: the repeated slashes and screams, the chase, the dead-end where the victim turns to face her/his death, and so on. Both Nayar and Kazmi argue that conventional cinema often aestheticizes violence. The arousal of emotions like fear occurs as part of the pleasure-inducing experience. Do spectators who enjoy (or at least tolerate) gory violence and mutilated bodies in action films respond similarly to a documentary on surgery (with incisions, blood)?

Changing camera positions, controlled lighting, music and special effects in action films create 'significant aesthetic pleasure and emotional distance' for viewers (Prince 2000: 28–29). This enables them to insulate themselves from the depicted violence, something the dryness of a documentary on surgical procedure does not enable them to do. Hence we are more willing to watch a violent film than a documentary about surgery or war victims. The audience is aware of the genre conventions here—an awareness which is to do with the pool of common knowledge in a culture—and responds differently to different representational modes. In the case of the cinema the viewer takes a certain pleasure in the depiction of violence—however abhorrent it may be—since it is staged and *not* real. In the latter case there is no such aesthetic pleasure, but only the stark reality of blood, gore and death (it might be interesting to study responses to hospital thrillers such as *Coma*, 1978, or *Anatomy*, 2000). There is also, in the Hindi film, the long drawn-out speech of the dying man/woman, the extraction of promises, the safe-custody theme (*Meri ma/bahen/baap/bachche ka khayal rakhna, unka is duniya mein koi nahin hain*—'Please take care of my mother/sister/ father/children, they have nobody [to care for them] in this world [once I am gone]), and even a background song. The scene, with the dying man/woman in the centre, emphasizes the tragedy. The blood spattered body, the harsh breaths, the stammered/whispered speech, and the camera cuts to the people around this 'body' underlines the pathos. This melodramatization of the death scene somehow effects a change in the preceding violence. The audience is forced to view sentimental scenes as an aftershock, which negates the graphic violence that led to the scene.[2] We are numbed by the violence, aroused by the 'fight for justice' call, and finally driven to sentiment by the speeches and songs. It reinforces a sense of mortality (like Rajesh Khanna's famous laugh at the end of *Anand* [1970], Shah Rukh Khan's cheery bluster at the end of *Kal Ho Naa Ho* [2003], or John Abraham's defiant speech at the conclusion of *Dhoom* [2004]). While Hollywood victims of violence die *quickly* and (mostly) silently (Samuel L. Jackson is swallowed up in a three-second span in *Deep Blue Sea* [1999], while he is in the *middle* of making a speech), Hindi film heroes/heroines crawl, speak, sing and in general *draw out* life.

The Hindi film thrives on the belief that nationalist allegiance—in this case to the State—must be achieved *through* the traditional apparatuses of authority (parental, religious figures). Thus, even the critique of the corrupt politician or the incompetent policeman will occur from *within* the community of the State: which itself remains above all evil, and incorruptible. Mother India therefore must be protected against all these internal apparatuses, but no film ever asks whether 'Mother India' itself should be interrogated (Sumita Chakravarty, qtd. in S.J. Nayar 2001: 144).[3]

Hindi films often suggest recourse to the judiciary and legal measures of complaint-redress. This is not to suggest the sacredness of the State. Rather, it suggests to the consumer/spectator that the State, or rather a system of laws, enshrined in the constitution and exemplified in the judiciary, does acknowledge her/his right, indeed duty, to be an agent. It suggests that with adequate legal procedures, even against the extra-legal, justice can be restored. The belief is not, as Nayar seems to propose, in the State, but in a set of principles that created the State, which have been subverted by corruption (note Gayatri Joshi's spirited speech in *Swades*). The faith expressed is in the laws of the land, while making, I think, a clear distinction between the laws and the State's executive 'bodies' (the minister, or the MLA, who stands for the State in the film). The law is good, its executioners (!) bad. The film usually adds dollops of moralizing subtexts even as it valorizes the individual's right to rebel. Thus individuals taking the law into their own hands (armed hands, of course—let us not forget that, despite so much postcolonial obsession with the subaltern's oppressed state, in military terms even the subaltern is *armed*) are common Hindi film material. It becomes less of a community than an isolated individual situation. Nayar seems to ignore such successful films. The film seems to suggest a moral law that comes above the State's laws. The Hindi film therefore suggests a 'double movement': acceptance of the dominant ideology and social structures, and resistance to the same. Thus on the one hand these films project moral laws as being above the laws of the State, but they also suggest that citizens should acquiesce to State laws.

True, the films rarely question the efficacy of the State. But then, they do not question the efficacy of the family either. *Dhoom* (2004) is an unusual film because it focuses entirely on youth with no extended families. So there are no melodramatic family scenes. The metropolitan youth culture that *Dhoom* showcases depicts self-contained youth, who move only within their own circle with no sense of community.

What the Hindi film tries to do is propose ways of being agents within a system that has been subverted from its original 'good' form. It does not seek to erase the spectator's thought processes, but rather to provide a scheme whereby the processes, already severely affected by the continual hardship of the average Indian, can be channelized. It definitely moralizes about these processes, but also persuades us that we need not be passive recipients. Fareed Kazmi argues that the conventional Hindi film interpellates and involves the audience by making the protagonist a member of the oppressed classes. The fortunes of the hero are linked to the fortunes of the society. The hero may be of the common, oppressed class, but he is an extraordinary individual. Kazmi suggests that the cult of the movie star and the aura around him all present an extraordinariness. Such a theme engenders hope and a belief in individual opportunity and individual action as the only guarantees of success (1999: 170–202). There is no democratic overthrow of the corrupt minister, for instance. He is generally killed in order to cleanse the system. The hero—who usually performs the killing—leads the rebellion. Kazmi believes that this individual rebellion is an attempt to thwart the revolutionary potential of society.

Conventional Hindi films, while portraying the hero as an extraordinary individual, also suggest an interesting shift: from a mass revolution (like the independence struggle) to an individual one. The films do not contain the subversive potential, they channelize/cathect it into *one* individual. The Hindi film does not seek a revolution *except* at an individual level. Society is changed from within not by a mass democratic or military movement, but by an *individual's* actions. Notice how Hindi films never show a *military* take-over of the Indian State: its commitment to a democratic Indian State formation is absolute. And hence the military/ violent purging of corruption is individual rather than communal/ social. It proposes change in the system and the functionaries of the State, but rarely recommends an overthrow of the State or a shift to another form of government, or a military coup.

❏ FILM AND CULTURAL IDENTITY

The film has a great deal of significance for debates about cultural identity. Hollywood seeks to capture an American cultural identity against that of an Other (see Chow 1998 and Chowdhry 2000 on 'empire cinema'). Thus Hollywood's (masculinist) image of the European 'civilizing' missions, drawing on earlier colonial narratives of exploration, is cast in images of penetration into non-Occident lands.[4]

Numerous writers have stressed the Hindi film's connection with Indian traditions (for a critique, see Kazmi 1999: 61–65). Modernity's potential schisms and fractures are subsumed under the coherence of tradition and national identity, and this process of subsumption is clearly ideological (Prasad 1998: 7–8). Existing oppressions and inequalities (caste, class, gender and economic) in the Indian nation are glossed over and India-as-nation celebrated (see Niranjana 1994 on *Roja*, for an exemplary reading of this theme; also Dirks 2001 and Roy 2003).

Prasad argues that the feudal family romance in popular cinema is linked to the nature of power—held by a coalition of a pre-capitalist social base and a bourgeoisie—in postcolonial India. The social is reconstituted around the figure of the citizen, and represents not so much a tension between tradition and modernity as that between two ideologies of modernity itself: the conditions of capitalist development in the periphery and the 'ideal' features of the primary capitalist states (Prasad 1998: 55). Thus the feudal family romance resists the 'invention of the private'—which is a characteristic of the modern state (ibid.: 71). As a result, the representation of 'private' sexuality in Hindi films is radically different from Hollywood's. The kiss is only now beginning to appear on the screen (*Khwaish*, 2003, publicized its 17 kisses; the film flopped). Eroticism and sexual desires were for a long time confined to the heterosexual couple dancing in the rain, with close-ups of flowers or birds moving towards each other. Asha Kasbekar notes that most (supposedly sensual or erotic) song sequences are presented as fantasies or dreams (1996: 372). Madhava Prasad draws attention to the paradox that while the representation of sexuality circulates *in* public spaces, it is definitely not *of* the public. Kissing, as Prasad's reading suggests, cannot be presented on screen because it threatens the integrity of 'Indian' culture and community sentiments (Prasad 1998: 92–93, 97–100; see also Vasudevan 2001).

I suggest that eroticism is not contained within the main diegetic space, but is *highlighted* through the song sequence. The song suggests a passionate intimate moment, which deserves its own space, *separate* from the larger themes/story of the film. The above critics do not quite explain the predominance of the displaced symbolisms that stand in for the kiss or courtship. How does the representation of two flowers/birds in intimate contact affect the reading of the hero-heroine's (invisible, off-the-scene) kiss? I suggest that the metaphor of flowers or birds functions not so much as concealment as titillating *revelation*. They are displacements that enhance the value of what is not seen (literally the *ob-scene*, what is not staged, is not in the 'scene'), or partially seen and therefore *imagined*. The paradox is that while voyeurism requires a 'view', the Hindi film develops its strategy of displaced voyeurism, of providing, literally, the stuff that dreams/fantasies are made of. It is the occasion when the audience is invited to move beyond the screen into the private spaces of intimacy.

This may be a prohibition of the private, but it is also the encoding of the private into a set of *public symbols*. This kind of coding is also visible in another common feature of the Hindi film. The heroine who (in the 1990s, at least) wears skirts and/or jeans as a regular costume is suddenly transformed with her engagement or during 'meet-the-parents' (on clothing and the movies, see Bruzzi 1997). From skirts she shifts to salwars and saris. (Patricia Uberoi [2001] notes that 'a romantic commitment marks the end of youthful playfulness, and the beginning of restraint and seriousness'. Tejaswini Niranjana, reading Maniratnam's

Geetanjali, notes that the new Indian woman is simultaneously modern and feminine: 2002 [2000].) The coding is fascinating here: while the heroine's initial sex appeal (for the hero and the audience) is coded into her 'flamboyant' clothes, she will not meet his parents in them. More modestly attired, she suggests a tradition that is (literally) a strong fabric. After her legitimation—or formal engagement—she emerges in traditional Indian attire, eschewing Western clothes. It seems to suggest that (*i*) she may wear such clothes before her 'legitimization', but (*ii*) once her 'ownership' has been established she should not exhibit so much of her body to *other* men. That is, the sartorial switch is a switch in the rights of viewership: only the husband (and not even the fiancé) can gaze upon her body. The body retires into the private realm, away from public 'view'.

Film music and songs

Central to any film's success in the Indian context are its music and songs. The music is released months before the film arrives in theatres. In addition, previews of song sequences are telecast in numerous programmes on television. Thus, in a sense, the songs constitute a film-in-advance. I look at one genre in particular—the patriotic film song in Hindi films. My reason for the choice is the fact that these songs have an independent circulation outside the film. On 26 January (Republic Day, when the Indian constitution came into effect), 15 August (Independence Day) and 2 October (birthday of Mahatma Gandhi), these songs are played at street corners and at any location where the Indian tricolour has been hoisted. They thus constitute an important public cultural artifact. In addition, they are played over All India Radio and Doordarshan—State-owned facilities—and other channels celebrating India's national festivals. During the Kargil conflict such songs made a big comeback. These songs foreground particular versions of culture.

In the decades after Independence such songs as *Saare jahan se achcha, Hindustan hamara* (This country of ours/Hindustan, is the finest in the world) (from *Bhai Bahen*, 1949) eulogized the freedom struggle. The songs were characterized by fulsome praise for the struggle and the courage and determination of the national leaders, and embodied a sense of mission for the future (now firmly in Indian hands). Hence Pradeep's *Dedi hamein azaadi bina khadag bina dhal, sabarmati ke sant tune kar diya kamaal* (You delivered us into freedom, sans arms/O saint of the Sabarmati [river in Gujarat, near which Gandhi lived], you have worked miracles) (*Jagruti,*

1954). There was a renewed appreciation of India's natural beauty, wealth and traditions. Nothing was impossible for the Indian, since the (mother) earth was herself (Mehboob's *Mother India*, released in 1957) waiting to yield its bounty: *Mere desh ki dharti sona ugle, ugle heere moti* (The land of my country/yields gold and pearls) (*Upkar*, 1967). Or in Rajinder Krishan's famous lyric from *Sikander-e-Azam* (1965): *Jahan daal daal par sone ki chidiya karti hai basera, woh bharat desh hai mera* (My country: where golden birds nest on every tree branch). Everyone was happy with past achievements, and looked forward to better successes. Alongside Nehru's injunction that India was not to be shackled to its past but must seek a new outlook, Prem Dhawan penned this: *Chhodo kal ki baatein, kal ki baat purani, naye daur mein likhenge, milkar nayi kahani* (Forget the yesterdays, let's script a new story together, today) (*Hum Hindustani*, 1960). Nehruvian socialism—the informing ideology of the age—with its emphasis on collective effort is clearly echoed in these lyrics. It continued the nationalist age's emphasis on community. The idea extended the theme of a collective struggle, this time for 'national development'. A pan-Indian nationalism that ignored all local resistance movements during the freedom struggle—and protest movements afterwards—was extended into the lyrics: the only faces shown were those of figures like Gandhi, Tilak, Bhagat Singh and Subhash Chandra Bose. These pre-Independence faces paradoxically became the canonical faces of a *new* India. The suggestion of continuity is very clear in this invention of tradition.

Part of this invention suggested a unified, homogenized India. As critics have pointed out, the Hindi film projected an image of a single, cohesive unit of India, where individual (regional, local, linguistic) identities were subsumed into a 'national' identity. The songs demonstrate this inclusive paradigm. In the famous 'dulhan chali' song from *Purab Aur Paschim* (1970), the lyrics declare: *Ho koi bhi pranth ke vasi, ho koi bhi bhasha-bhashi, subse pehle hain bharath vaasi* (No matter where we live, or what language we speak, we are primarily Indians). This 'national spirit' devolved upon the children of India. It was suggested in numerous songs that children and youth were invested with the task of building India. Shakeel Badayuni's lyrics instruct:

Insaaf ki dagar pe, bachchon dikhao chalke
Yeh desh hai tumhara, neta tumhi ho kalke. (*Gunga Jumna*, 1961)

(Walk along the just paths, children
After all, this is your country, and you are the leaders of tomorrow.)

The children are figured as the songsters, or as attentive listeners to these songs. Thus in *Jagruti's* famous sequence the children are instructed:

Aao bachchon tumhe dikhayen jhalke Hindustan ki
Is maati se tilak karo, yeh dharti hai balidan ki

(Let me show you a few glimpses of India even as you bless yourself with this earth/land of sacrifices.)

In *Son of India* (1962) the boy sings: *Nanha munna raahi hoon, desh ka sipahi hoon* (I may be a small traveller, even so I am my nation's soldier), with the song's entire emphasis being on a future condition and ambition (*Aage hi aage badhaoonga kadam,* 'I shall always march forward'). Transforming the child into a soldier was a stroke of disputable genius. On the one hand it suggested that the defence of India was everybody's business—even a child's. It also conveyed a sense of purpose, where the child grows up hoping to fulfil ambitions on India's behalf. Finally, it renders a certain masculine militarism for the male child. The child, aware of this role, has 'manfully' transformed himself into India's soldier. This interesting conflation of the innocent Indian boy with the brave and mature Indian soldier is crucial. This is a *male* heir to India's leadership (which was ironically reversed when Indira Gandhi came to power and the Congress slogan became: 'Indira is India and India is Indira').

This heir is to be brought up on a diet of revolutionary rhetoric, militarism, and a certain vision of India's past. Sahir wrote: *Yeh desh hai veer jawaanon ka* (This is the nation of brave soldiers) for *Naya Daur* (1957). Shakeel Badayuni wrote *Apni azadi ko hum ... sar kata sakte hain lekin sar jhuka sakte nahin* (We cannot forgo our freedom, we are willing to die rather than bow our heads) (*Leader,* 1964). However, this was not a simple, linear transition from the historical freedom struggle to modern India. With development came other tensions and ambivalences. In the period of heavy industrialization, the lyrics sought to retain a particular view of India. One of the ways in which a sense of India was highlighted was by paying attention to its topography and natural beauty. Nationalism requires a territory, and this is what is clearly evident in the songs.

Neeraj's *Yeh kaun chitrakar hain* (Who is the artist?) in *Boond Jo Ban Gaye Moti* (1967) was a particularly fine lyric, poeticizing the Indian countryside. Interestingly, the lyric is visualized as a song sung by a teacher (played by Jeetendra) and his students, in a re-working of the *guru-shishya* tradition (also seen in *Jagruti's Aao bachchon* and other songs). Indeevar, in an unusual deviation from his routine, spiritualized and feminized India's landscape with the sensationally successful *Hai preet jahan ki reet sada* (*Purab Aur Paschim*, 1970). In a film that worked the East/West binary to death, the visual accompaniment to the song was crucial: a Westernized Indian woman. The lyrics go:

Itni mamta nadiyon ko bhi jahan maata kehke bulate hain
Itna aadar insaan to kya, pathar bhi puje jaate hain

(The [Indian] kind of affection—we even address rivers as 'mother'
The [Indian] kind of respect—we even worship stones.)

As any viewer will recall, many of these songs present a scene where the hero pays homage to Indian *earth* (Manoj 'Mr Bharat' Kumar used to be particularly fond of this action). Thus *Lagaan's Sun mitwa* with its *Tujhko kya dar hai re ... yeh dharti apni hain, apna ambar hain re* (Listen, my companion, do not be afraid: this land, the skies and the horizons are all ours) is a continuation of this obsession with the earth. Songs also depict and praise India's rivers, fertile land and culture. The Ganga, Cauvery and Yamuna figure prominently here. The Brahmaputra, much larger in flow, does not figure in such songs because a lot of it flows outside Indian territory. Nationalism has to be firmly inscribed within India's politico-geographical boundaries.

In addition to India's topography, these songs also promote a certain understanding of India's history. Glorifying its historical figures—from *rishi*s to scientists to monarchs—and highlighting its particular social values, the songs sought to present a great culture (which was, of course, a Brahminical, Hindi one). Thus in *Jis Desh Mein Ganga Behtee Hain* (1960) the song went:

Mahman jo hamara hota hai, woh jaan se pyara hota hain.

(Any guest of ours is dearer than our own life.)

In *Hai preet jahan ki reet sada* from *Purab aur Paschim*, Indeevar wrote about the Indian 'discovery' of zero and the glories of India's ancient past. Indian festivals are celebrated in numerous songs, most of which are 'picturized' on such celebrations. And then of course there is the Indian woman, idealized and worshipped: *Jahan Ram abhi tak hai nar mein, naari mein abhi tak Seeta hain* (Where the Lord Ram still lives

within the man, and Seeta in the woman)—so sang Mahendra Kapoor in
Purab aur Paschim. Or look at India-as-bride in the well-known *Dulhan
chali* (The bride departs) song (*Purab aur Paschim*), where the new
bride's relations (in this case the husband's family) are exhorted: *ho na
padosi ki neeyat khoti, ghar waalon zara isko sambhalo, yeh to hai badi
bholi* (o family members, guard this innocent bride, lest she fall prey to
the neighbour's guiles) suggesting that the neighbours are lascivious and
may well desire the new bride. The woman becomes the repository of
tradition, morality, family values, and even national virtue.

India is thus feminized in many such songs. She is the bride, the mother
(as in the classic *Mother India,* 1957), or the beloved. She is the object of
desire and affection, while also being the embodiment of the great tradition: *Ai mere pyaare watan, ai mere bichchde chaman, tujhe pe dil kurban,
tu hi meri aarzoo, tu hi meri aabroo, tu hi meri jaan* (My beloved mother-
land, my garden that I have been displaced from/I dedicate my heart to
you, for you are my desire, my prestige and my very soul) (Prem Dhawan's
famous lyrics for *Kabuliwala,* 1961). She is the great provider-mother:
Yahaan apna paraya koi nahin, hain sabpe ma upkar tera (Here there is no
difference between stranger and family, your [mother earth's] blessings
shower equally on all) (the lyrics from *Mere desh ki dharti* in *Upkar*), or
even a mother–father team in *Dharti meri maata, pita aasman* (This land
is my mother, and the sky, the father) in *Geet Gata Chal* (1975). As late as
Pardes (1997) we have *Yeh duniya, ek dulhan, dulhan ke maathe ki bindiya,
yeh mera India* (This world is a bride, and India is its 'bindi' [the mark
Indian women wear on their foreheads]).

Closely aligned with such a feminization of India is the masculine
patriot. As noted above, even the boy is soldiering on in India's cause.
Extending the notion of all Indians as a large family (very large, going
by the census), we have the male/protector of son-father-husband-brother
to the daughter-mother-wife-sister. The patronym is 'father of the nation',
while the jawans are all *bhai* (brother). Thus the equation is made: it is the
duty of the male to safeguard the virtue of the woman/India. The woman
is charged with the duty of caring for the family. She is charged, literally and
figuratively, with reproducing, nourishing and bringing up the nation.[5]

❑ FILM AUDIENCES

A film, one of the most public of activities, has many audiences.
Audiences are heterogeneous, anomic, multiple, even conflictual, and

respond to films in heterogeneous ways. Fans that go as a team to watch 'their' star's film constitute an adulatory/adoring audience *within* the larger mass audience.

The audience is increasingly seen as a market segment. A market audience is conceived of as a commodity: numbers that generate revenues, and spectators whose attention-giving or withholding governs content. Media studies focuses on the role the audience plays in the circulation and popularity of certain images, genres, forms of entertainment, and so on. Thus impact studies are integral to the study of audiences who are seen not as mere consumers of messages sent down from media towers, but active participants in the coding of social, political and ideological meaning. We thus need to look at the extra-filmic events and contexts that accompany, supplement and affect the 'consumption' of films and film stars. Thus stage-shows, fan clubs and film magazines are integral to film culture. We cannot restrict the analysis of films to mere textual exegesis, since an audience consumes not simply the film, but information about the film/star from the extra-filmic context too. As an example, one need only look at the large number of Bollywood films about the non-resident Indian—a genre that was kick-started by *Dilwale Dulhaniya Le Jayenge* (1995). While the film's own narrative contributes to its huge success abroad (this was followed by *Pardes, Kabhi Khushi Kabhi Ghum* [2001], down to *Kal Ho Na Ho. Hum Aapke Hain Kaun ... !* [1994] ran for nine weeks in the New York and New Jersey markets. On an average, 90–100 titles are released annually by the Hindi film industry on the international market. Between 1998 and 1999, four Hindi films entered the UK top 20 on release—*Dil Se*, 1998; *Kuch Kuch Hota Hai*, 1998; *Biwi No. 1*, 1999; and *Hum Dil De Chuke Sanam*, 1999), one needs to situate these films in the extra-filmic space of the Indian diaspora in the UK, USA or Arabian nations, which sponsor massive stage shows featuring these stars. Such events suggest that the filmic narrative spills over into the non-filmic space, and affects audience-response and consumption significantly. Thus, for example, it is believed that the décor in Mira Nair's *Monsoon Wedding* has been imitated by non-resident Indians in the UK and USA (Gopalan 2001: 364). Social concerns about the impact of films on audiences have been to do with the popularity of the medium among the potentially 'subversive' working classes. Thus censorship became a common phenomenon from 1910 in most Western countries. It was accompanied by public debates about audiences, especially the consequence of films on adolescent and child audiences. A research tradition where the medium of the film was treated primarily as a social problem was established around this time. The cause-effect concept of the relation between the medium and the audience dominated debates, and borrowed from psychological theories of the time. Closely linked to this was the rise of theories of the mass, increasingly viewed as a characteristic social form. Demographic shifts of people from traditional, rural origins to cities, this line of debate went, were responsible for the creation of a vulnerable mass of people ready to be influenced by film. Cinema was thus a social problem because the audience—the masses—was a social problem.

A curious phenomenon in India—based on similar concerns about the impact of films—was the censorship of foreign films. Madhava Prasad has demonstrated how the prohibition on the depiction of intimacy in Hindi films was related to a certain 'nationalist politics of culture'. Hindi and English/Hollywood films were judged differently. Foreign films were judged differently because (it was argued in the *Report of the Enquiry Committee on Film Censorship*, 1969) 'foreign films cater[ed] to a higher stratum of society' (qtd. in Prasad 1998: 88). This evaluation of a film's content was based not only on their affective power, but also on the nature of the audiences. By arguing that Hollywood films in India—with their scenes of nudity or intercourse—had a different ('higher') audience, the *Report* was arguing for the multiple kinds of audiences of films. It is also, I believe, necessary to look at the kinds of audiences that are envisaged by authorities. Film certification is a crucial area where such debates are foregrounded. Thus Star TV's films on the Star Movies channel announce before the film the category of film: 'Suitable for children above the age of 15 only' or 'PG' (parental guidance), and so on. Such a certification *presupposes* a certain kind of audience, and the possible impact of the film on those members. It would be interesting to see how, in addition to the censorship board, film-makers, in the process of finalizing their film, themselves envisage their audiences.

Bindiya Goswami, former actress and now the wife of J.P. Dutta, declared: 'How can anybody not like *LOC* [directed by Dutta]? Anyone who says that *LOC Kargil* is not a good film, is a desh-drohi [traitor]' (*Deccan Chronicle*, 'Cinema Cinema', 22 January 2004). Note the way in which the audience is being constructed: a taste/liking for a particular film is linked to nationalist sentiments. One cannot criticize the film even on aesthetic grounds because that would be unpatriotic! In post-Kargil India, one cannot do anything other than praise the stream of 'patriotic films' from the Duttas and the Deols.

Hindi cinema as a mass cultural medium has always had a close link with the project of constructing a certain view of India itself. Such a nation-building, based on certain views of 'Indian' culture and 'modernity', worked on a certain idea of the citizen itself: as middle-class, upper-caste, Hindu and male (Tharu and Niranjana 1996). In recent years there have been many films made on colonial and postcolonial themes: *1942: A Love Story* (1993), *Gandhi: Making of the Mahatma* (1996), two films on Bhagat Singh, and films on Sardar Patel, Babasaheb Ambedkar, Subhas Chandra Bose (Benegal's 2005 film was, for some inexplicable reason, subtitled 'The Forgotten Hero'), among others. Other 'blockbusters' include *Border*, *Roja*, *Mission Kashmir* (2000), *Maachis* (1996), *Bombay*, *Dil Se* and *Lagaan* (2001). Some of these have dealt with issues of identity, religious and ethnic conflict, terrorism, and so on. While emphasizing the family as sacred space, much middle-class cinema conceptualized the nation-as-family (Prasad 1998: 161–87; Schultheis 2004). With the late 1980s and 1990s things began to look slightly different. With numerous secessionist movements and demands for local identities all over India, the idea of a homogeneous 'modernity' itself began to alter. Tribal and women's rights, and caste-based identities as criteria for affirmative action (reservations) redefined India. Studies of the Hindi film and its audiences in the last decades of the 20th century account for this shift in the very idea of India. To begin with, we can look at the 'technology' of spectatorship.

Seeing and spectatorship

Christian Metz (1982 [1975]) proposed that cinema spectatorship involves three central processes: identification, voyeurism and fetishism. Laura Mulvey's early work on the spectatorship of cinema (1975) suggests a sexualizing code in film viewing. Mulvey argued that scopophilia, a desire to look, is central to film viewing. A spectator's pleasure depends on the effective manipulation of certain codes, such as the woman's body, on the screen. Scopophilia renders certain objects desirable, which are eroticized for the pleasure of the male viewer. The very circumstances of viewing—the dark cinema hall/room, the bright screen—make the screen a window that opens into another, desirable world. The viewer is separated from the story, yet is able to watch it as it unfolds. The masculine gaze sets up women as desirable and desired objects.[6]

Geeta Kapur, Ashish Rajadhyaksha and others have argued that in Indian popular culture—theatre, art, cinema—the aesthetic of *frontality* is crucial. The frontality of the performer in relationship with/to the spectator, for Anuradha Kapur, is a relationship of 'erotic complicity' and a contract (qtd. in Prasad 1998: 19). Building on the theory of spectatorship and the 'gaze'—articulated in different contexts and with different 'technologies' by Mulvey, Kapur and others—Prasad argues that the aesthetics of frontality and its active intersection with realist conventions in Hindi cinema must be seen in 'the light of the individual subject's position within different political orders and the corresponding constraints and protocols of spectatorship' (ibid.: 20–21). Prasad's is an important insight into the working of cinematic meanings. Meaning is produced in the realist mode by the spectator, who is an active collaborator in the production process. It is simply not enough to look at the technologies of cinema; the specific locations of the viewer and the technologies of seeing have also to be taken into account. This is where film studies needs to work closely with audience studies and film reception studies.

Box 2.2: Audience types

- Audience as a *group* or public: such as news viewers/listeners.
- Audience as a *gratification set*: where people with particular interests or tastes seek out media to satisfy their need, such as rock concerts, or those who read *Stardust* or *Cine Blitz* for gossip/information (with a very thin line separating the two) about their favourite stars.
- *Media audience*: this includes TV/film viewers, magazine readers, and such. Ratings are determined by these audiences, who determine market value. (Adapted from Sayre and King 2003: 52)

The theory of *darshan* (which Diana Eck [1986] discussed in her reading of Hindu iconic theological images) is useful in understanding the spectator's role in the Hindi film. The priest is the mediator, bringing the devotee to the divinity's attention. The devotee stands mute in the presence of the image. *Darshan* is not a look of verification, but 'one that demonstrates its faith by seeing the divinity where only its image exists' (Prasad 1998: 75). This differs from the scopophilic 'gaze' in two ways. The *darshan* embodies a relation where the object invites itself to be seen, and thus confers a privileged status on the spectator. The object is a spectacle to be seen. In the feudal family romance, the hero belongs to the class of the 'chosen'. Then, the object of the darshanic gaze is available only to symbolic identification. In symbolic identification, the viewer identifies with the hero on screen at the precise moment where the hero is inimitable (Prasad 1998: 76). The star in Hindi films frequently appears in tableau scenes that seem to invite *darshan*, and hierarchizes the look, providing the star with associations with the traditional granters of *darshan*, especially kings and gods (Dwyer and Patel 2002: 33).

Combining the darshanic with voyeurism, the female figure is, crucially, available for erotic viewing only in the space of songs and dances. Song and dance is a form of spectacle that is staged, explicitly drawing the viewer's attention to the female form (Prasad 1998: 76–77, 93). Woodman Taylor (2003), working with a more sophisticated concept of visuality, detects two primary modes of the gaze. The *darshan* has a specifically religious connotation, where the devotee receives the *darshan* given by the god on display. *Nazar* is mainly to do with the theme of love. This gazing sequence, writes Taylor, is suggestive of a romantic devotion, usually beginning with the feet and moving up (closely paralleling the *darshan* of a deity). Thus *nazar* partakes of a *tradition* of *darshan* (ibid.: 310).

In the Hindi film the song-and-dance routine is almost always romantic/erotic and embodies, literally, the scopophilic regime of the viewing of the actress's body. We need to distinguish between the kinds of eroticism projected and offered to the audience. A voyeuristic engagement with the female form often has two models: one involving the heroine of the main story, and another that is a 'cabaret' or an 'item' number involving the vamp in the villain's den. In the case of the first, the cinematic technique transforms the heroine's body into an exotic/erotic space, with the camera lingering over her body, while she cavorts around the hero. Here the woman's body is offered up primarily to the gaze of the hero and only incidentally to the (male) audience. The hero's *nazar* is a gaze that is singular—in both senses of the term—but to which the male audience is secretly privy. We need to distinguish the vamp's dance from that of the heroine's, since it makes for a very different construction of the gaze. The vamp-dancer's body is a true spectacle: offered less to a particular individual hero than to the larger male audience in the club, as well as 'outside' in the cinema hall. The gyrating vamp constitutes this second type of song-and-dance. Personified by Helen and others from the 1970s, this form of song-and-dance invites the spectator—and the entire audience—to stare at the female form. The entire sequence is *staged* (the club-room setting, as opposed to the 'natural' setting for the first form of song-and-dance involving the hero-heroine), literally *asking* for the male to gaze at the female form (what Ravi Vasudevan terms 'disco-sensuality' [2001: 202]). The dancer's garish, often 'revealing' clothes, the club-room atmosphere, the music, the smoking-and-drinking men whose (bloodshot) eyes linger lasciviously over the dancer's body are clearly contrasted with the more erotic/less spectacular 'natural' setting of parks, the softer and more lilting music (rarely disco or rock-and-roll), and the 'intense' hero-heroine looks. The club dance suggests a spectacular community eroticism, whereas the hero-heroine form suggests an intimate one. In certain cases the cavorting couple is surrounded by 'adjunct' dancers, who run around them in a celebratory dance movement. The appeal and eroticism of these adjunct dancers are never independent of the couple's: they provide the outwork to the purportedly intimate moment—thereby neutralizing the group's voyeurism of the latter. (And of course there is the ultimate male fantasy of many-women-one-man in numerous song sequences.)

Contemporary song-and-dance sequences make an interesting change: the heroine herself dances in a club scene. Here the 'traditional' role of the heroine—dancing for the hero alone—is altered. This 'subversion' is explained/defended/justified—thus retaining the heroine's symbolic 'purity' coded as monogamy—variously: she is drunk (the most recent example is of Preity Zinta in *Kal Ho Naa Ho*); has been betrayed (by the hero); is diverting the villain's attention (thus contributing her mite to the hero's heroics); has been dared or forced. Zeenat Aman redefined this role when, in Feroze Khan's *Qurbani* (1980), she played a club singer. The '*Aap jaise koi*' numbers were significant shifts in the image because the hero falls in love with a woman who wore 'revealing' clothes and danced to the gaze of many men. Even here, the act was defended by making the heroine stare only at Feroze Khan (and later, Vinod Khanna), thus singling out (monogamously) *one* man for her attention and favours while having to do this 'act' for her livelihood. Such sequences thus invite a different reading of the darshanic-voyeuristic (male) gaze.

Fans and fan clubs

The theatrical and the performative are a part of everyday life. The audience is both participant and spectator. We play separate roles all the time, and our social activities create illusions that are difficult to sustain outside that activity. Thus activists who support political causes, consumers who shop, patrons who support the arts, students who study, voyeurs who view porn, worshippers who pray, fans who adore are all playing roles, and constitute audiences that perform.

Fan clubs are a special form of the audience that performs. They constitute a class of consumers engaged in an interpretive activity that is *social*. These are consumers who also produce texts and their own art. Fans adopt a distinctive mode of reception. Fandom is characterized by a conscious selection of a specific programme, viewed faithfully and repeatedly (in the theatre, and then subsequently on hired VCRs/DVDs). Fan interpretations must be seen in institutional rather than personal terms. Fan club meetings, newsletters, fanzines are readings of shared texts, and suggest a different set of reading protocols. Fandom constitutes a particular art world. Henry Jenkins (1999 [1992]) suggests that fan conventions play a crucial role in the distribution of knowledge about media productions, and provide a platform where stars can meet their fans and audiences. The usual garlanding of cut-outs, celebratory processions on movie release days, and the publicity these invoke contribute to the market value of a star or a film. Fandom constitutes an alternative social community, where fans share a common identity and constitute a form of solidarity in an increasingly fragmented society. This community is not defined in traditional terms—though caste and gender do play crucial roles here (fan processions in India are mostly constituted of men).

Fans and fan clubs write poems, sing songs (from the films of 'their' star), compose paeans, and generate meanings. Fan texts such as songs or music, termed 'filking', extend pre-existing media texts. We thus have fan clubs whose members style their clothes or hair after their preferred film star, extending in a sense, perhaps parodically, the cinematic text. Fans are involved in an emotional and psychological relation with the star(s), which extends beyond the screen or show. Such parasocial relations involve a degree of commitment between the viewer/fan and the object of her/his adoration. It is thus both an interpretation of an existing text and the creation of a new one in a new context.

S.V. Srinivas (1997) in his formidably astute analysis of fan clubs in Andhra Pradesh teases out various factors in the construction of such parasocial relations. Srinivas suggests, using Nancy Fraser's (1994) idea of 'subaltern counterpublics' (defined as emerging in response to exclusions within dominant publics, and which expand discursive space and widen discursive contestation), that fan activity is a curious 'imbrication' (his term) of publicity with a *nonpublic* discourse of devotion to the star (Srinivas 1997: 25). Srinivas writes: 'the conditions under which fans constitute themselves as fans is the ability or opportunity to form a public. And this public articulates a discourse of *rights* in the language of devotion, admiration and commitment' (ibid.: 48, emphasis in original). This public-within-the-public, for Srinivas, is based on a spectacularization of their activities. Excesses and the 'spectacular act of devotion' enables fans, members of a subordinate class/caste, to gain access to those spaces which do not acknowledge their presence (ibid.: 53). He suggests that the fans' address to the star is a displaced address to themselves, which creates a 'double inversion'. The star appears on the screen because of the presence of the fans, fans address the star and in the process themselves: note the fact that every activity of the fan club is photographed and sent to the star (ibid.: 46). Srinivas is alert to the composition of these fan clubs and their subaltern demographics ('lower' caste/class). However, he fails to see how the spectacularization of their activity in fact reproduces a discourse that on the one hand may enable a greater degree of visibility, but on the other *condemns them to an imitative role*. Srinivas argues that fan activity is the creation, by subalterns, of a counterpublic within an elite, exclusivist culture. However, to suggest that their devotion, admiration and address to the star re-casts their role within the elite public sphere is to miss the irony of their performance. It cannot be denied that such headline-seizing activity (processions, garlanding, distribution of sweets at film releases and, increasingly, charity work in the name of the star, etc.; ibid.: 44) does create a certain space. However, since much of fan activity relies on the star's own image/success/role, it suggests a derivative discourse (though derivative discourses have their subversive, emancipatory potential). The irony is that fan activity reinforces the star's iconic status (as Srinivas points out, they are usually from the upper caste, and wealthy; for his later work on the subject, see Srinivas 2002 [2000]; also see Dickey 2001: 212), while reinforcing the fans' role/status as mimics and second-order audiences rather than constructors of identities: their identities are defined *as fans of a particular star, outside of this they have no identity.*

Transforming the ordinary

One of the features of mass entertainment is that it renders ordinary and mundane life unusual. One of the ways in which this is achieved is by focusing on exceptional individuals or situations in otherwise ordinary contexts. Thus a Bruce Willis chasing the killer through the crowded mall, or (a frequent spectacle in Hindi films), a car chase through the bazaar, upsetting vendor's carts and stalls, becomes an exceptional event in an otherwise boring everyday. Content analysis in US mass entertainment media over the past 40 years has demonstrated that Blacks are almost always depicted as perpetrators of crime more often than is the case in 'real time' (Sayre and King 2003: 121; on race and the science fiction film, see Kakoudaki 2002). One of the reasons for Amitabh Bachchan's phenomenal success is the use of what Madhava Prasad has called the 'aesthetic of mobilization' (1998: Chapter 6). His films, argues Prasad, 'constructed the mobilized (and mobilizing) subaltern hero as an agent of national reconciliation and social reform' (ibid.: 141). The theme of 'the revenge of the orphan' or the 'mobilization of the dispossessed' means that the 'proletarian hero' is also a representative of the State where, despite being extra-legal, he remains morally in the right (ibid.: 143–44). Ashis Nandy, on the Hindi film hero after *Zanjeer* (1973), argues that the protagonist starts as a personality that is 'soft', but is forced by circumstances into becoming a tough, hard-hearted violent man operating on the margins of law (Nandy 2001: 157–58; also see Dwyer and Patel 2002; Lutgendorf 2003; Mazumdar 2002). Prasad points to a critical theme in the 'construction' of star identities and audience reception—the star's moral uprightness frequently makes him a 'system victim': wronged by the law, by society, and even by his own family. The fact that he is outside the law does not make him 'bad': he has been forced into this role. The audience, attuned to the various injustices, petty corruption, and several legal/bureaucratic hassles that entrammel and wrong them, see themselves reflected in the hero's situation. They mobilize behind his (star) personality: a messiah (indeed that is what the Hindi film hero is: a messiah, perhaps without the messianism). Subsequent roles develop this same persona of the star, and he increasingly *becomes* the role he plays. As Prasad points out, the extra-cinematic authority of the star as mobilizer was clearly visible in the rise of Tamizh superstar and Tamil Nadu's eventual Chief Minister, MGR (Prasad 1998: 158).

Do media images affect and influence behaviour? Cultural theories suggest that the nature of violence, especially images of perpetrators and victims, do have actual societal influences on the power, roles and status of certain groups. Homophobia, racism and sexism are affected by and in turn inform the further imaging and stereotyping of already marginalized categories such as homosexuals or women. Thus it is interesting that the controversy over the Shah Rukh Khan starrer, *Kal Ho Naa Ho*, is about the depiction of gays (the scenes where 'Kantaben' interrupts what she perceives to be intimate moments between Saif and Shah Rukh, for instance). In an earlier film, Mani Ratnam's *Dil Se*, when Shah Rukh is about to get engaged to Preity Zinta and obviously reluctant to say 'yes' (he is in love with Manisha Koirala), Zinta's query is: *Tum aadmi to theek ho na ... ?* ('You are all right as a man, aren't you?'). The implication being that if he is not 'theek', i.e., interested in *pretty* women/heterosexual relations, then he must be gay, and gays cannot, by definition, be 'theek'. This is the heterosexual imaginary of mass entertainment. Finally, a recent interview of Rajesh Khera (who plays a gay character in the enormously popular serial *Jassi Jaise Koi Nahin*) illustrates the link between popular perceptions of certain classes/groups of people and media representations of them. Khera, asked by the interviewer: 'Can you identify gays from a distance?', responds:

> Very easily. Not because I am playing one. It's actually a simple process. They invariably stand with their torso jutting ahead. They are pansy in their movements. Their voice is not deep. (Entertainment and TV Guide, *Deccan Chronicle*, 14 February 2004: 9)

Note the image of the effeminate gay that Khera is projecting, while smoothly dissociating himself from any such affiliation—'Not because I am playing one.' Carefully leaving out his own orientation, he emphasizes the gay *role*, which grants him the authority to speak of gays in real life.

Why do audiences watch violence on screen? Violence as a means of 'getting even'—as the tons of Hindi films about vengeance and justice demonstrate—is appreciated and even justified ('He deserved it'). It appeals to our sense of justice, even when the protagonist takes the law into her/his own hands. Legally such individualized and individuating violence is unacceptable. The Hindi film audience, accustomed to images *and* realities about courtrooms, juridical delays, inquiry commissions and the frequent subversion of justice due to missing witnesses, or witnesses who turn hostile (the Godhra and Best Bakery cases are the most recent examples), find the independent jury/executioner role enacted by the victim of injustice a justifiable and attractive fantasy.

It is evident from the above discussion that audience response must be read at *both* the ideological and the emotional (affective) level. While theories of representation and ideological criticism pay attention to the rhetorics of cinema and the political and social agenda that such a representation seeks to distort, reinforce or mask, it is impossible to see cinema-viewing as a purely ideological situation. Cinema-watching involves emotional involvement of a very intimate kind. Just as political criticism of the novel tends to eschew the *emotional* appeal or psychological pleasure of a melodrama or a comedy in favour of issues of race, class or gender, film studies of the purely ideological kind runs the risk of ignoring an important aspect of film viewing: emotional affect. Spectator emotion does govern the form and content of mainstream film production, whether it is Hollywood or Bollywood. Yet spectator emotion is difficult to describe or analyse.

Carl Plantinga (1997) ties spectator emotion not only to private feelings, but also to cognition—inference, appraisal, judgements and hypotheses (p. 378). He begins by suggesting that rather than posting universal ideological effects for film forms and styles, we must relate film form to narrative representations and to the kinds of cognitions and emotions such forms encourage (ibid.: 379). As examples, I would suggest films that clearly situate the Indo-Pak relationship as their subject/site. The genre of Pak-bashing films (*Sarfarosh*, 1999; *Border*, 1997; *Gadar*, 2001; *The Hero*, 2003; *LOC Kargil*) uses the form and style of a war movie and evokes a strong emotional response from the audience for its virulent Pak-bashing. In the case of 'patriotic films' such as *1942: A Love Story* or *Lagaan*, we are constantly *made aware* of the racist nature of colonialism. Cognition here involves inferences, hypotheses and evaluative judgements. The content of the film drives the emotion, and the Indian audience, used to news reports of terrorism in Kashmir and with memories of earlier instances of Pakistan's 'treachery', reacts both viscerally and through evaluation to a similar scene/story unravelling on the screen. *Gadar* is an especially remarkable film, where the hero, Sunny Deol, is able to frighten off Pakistani soldiers by simply screaming at them, thereby suggesting that the Indian army needs only to recruit high-decibel soldiers!

Watching a fiction film (as opposed to a documentary or edutainment film) is to participate in a ritual. When we assent to the narrative of a film, writes Carl Plantinga, we become 'absorbed' or 'immersed'. We thus also accept an emotional role. This dual role of the spectator is akin to the actor who may experience emotions similar to those of the characters he plays (Plantinga 1997: 379–80). We experience a 'double consciousness' (Flanagan 2002): we are conscious of watching illusions, but also revel in them as 'real'. In mainstream films, allegiances with and antipathy towards characters orient us, and we react emotionally as a result. Yash Chopra's latest *Veer-Zaara* (2004) works at the level of emotion. In one scene, Kiron Kher has come to plead with Shah Rukh Khan that he allow her daughter, Priety Zinta, to marry the person the family has chosen. Khan, though desperately in love with Zinta, magnanimously agrees, stating that all mothers, even in India, are like her (Kher). The appeal to motherhood as universal—and transcending the barriers of nation, us/them—cleverly elides the audience's awareness that we are watching a Hindu/Indian boy and a Muslim/Pakistani woman. This is the allegiance based on moral explanations/awareness that the film extracts.

We need to explore the reification of spectatorship itself. How does a Muslim spectator react to veiled—and sometimes not-so-veiled—comments about the Muslim community's loyalty to India? How does the community-as-spectator react when they watch a film like *Lagaan*, which projects Hindu India as 'the' India? Here it is the Hindu temple that concentrates the village, when Muslims and Hindus alike gather to pray for help during a crisis. A common, community prayer has to be performed only in a *temple*, is it?

We rarely watch films indiscriminately. We decide what films to watch for the kind of emotional experience they offer. Even though we are circumscribed by social norms and conventions, we choose from a range of emotions available at the cinema. Thus, routinely (and falsely) associating sentimentality with family dramas or the 'woman's film', and violence with war films, we pick and choose what to watch (Plantinga 1997: 382–83). We cannot characterize spectator emotions as 'good' or 'bad', and any emotion can be used for rhetorical and ideological purposes. A film that evokes hate or jealousy, such as war films that demonize the Other or the 'enemy', elicits sentimentality (for the martyrdom of 'our' heroes) but has a political purpose/agenda.

Ashish Rajadhyaksha suggests, in a particularly innovative reading, that Indian cinema's story-telling can be treated as a mode of creating a narrative community through a 'narrative contract'. Components of story-telling are contracted to the instruments of negotiating political and social positions. The narrative contract in cinema is defined thus:

In maintaining the concept of the category of the 'individual'— here the individual viewer for whom the film has supposedly been made—as a necessary fiction, the narrative structure has to enact, and in various ways further aid, the transformation of that category, and the rights it underpins, into something like the bestowing of citizenship rights to what [Partha] Chatterjee calls 'political society'. (2002 [2000]: 277)

Rajadhyaksha argues that realist cinema enables the audiences to recognize and 'slot into' the narrative contract. The narrative's 'baseline address'—the address to all those looking unidirectionally at the screen—induces the viewers to see the camera-projector gaze as theirs alone. This is intrinsic to the moving image (ibid.: 280–81). He argues that the cinema recognizes the citizen-viewer, and makes sure the viewer is aware of this recognition. Actual people are named as possessors of democratic rights by the state, and the cinema identifies the actual viewers as such 'actual' people (ibid.: 283).

Rajadhyaksha's reading pays attention to discursive strategies, institutional structures, acts of viewership, the negotiations between viewer and 'structures'/apparatuses, and the creation of a social contract, and is perhaps the most useful analysis of audience-participation in film.

❏ FILMS, GENDER AND SEXUALITY

Media studies in the later decades of the 20th century has benefited from feminist approaches that have explored (and exposed) the male dominance among media professionals and the masculine discourse in media texts. Critics such van Zoonen argue that there is a close link between the masculine discourse in the media and the male-dominated/oriented material, economic and social factors of this discourse's production (van Zoonen 1996 [1994]: 7).

Distortion is integral to stereotyping, pornography and ideology in media representations of women, working classes, ethnic or racial minorities, or homosexuals. More women work in the media than are reflected by the content in these media. That is, though the demographics of work have changed, the attitudes towards women have not. Films do not, mostly, represent or capture this changing demographics of gender, but rather distort them, and suggest a patriarchal ideology.

In the preceding sections we have seen how theories of spectatorship invariably treat the viewer as male. In Laura Mulvey's view (1975), the scopophilic drive informs all cinematic representation. Mulvey's argument is that looking is defined as a male activity, and being looked at belongs to 'natural' female passivity. Women function as erotic objects for male protagonists with whom the male viewer can identify. That is, the male viewer looks through the eyes of the male protagonist (on screen) at the woman-as-object. It is therefore a *simultaneous* process of identification and objectification. Cinema, however, is more than just a fantasy world: it is rooted in actual social conditions and relations. In order to study spectatorship we need to look at actual material conditions, the role of cultural capital, the language of the film, its distribution. Finally, we need to ask how the gendering of spectatorship occurs. Cultural Studies, dealing with consumption of images and representations, reifies spectatorship. How do female spectators respond to particular kinds of films? Or, in the case of India, a Dalit female, or lesbian spectator? Can the process of identification and objectification be reversed in order to focus on the woman spectator's pleasure (erotic or otherwise)?

Mary Ann Doane (1992) argues that one of the preconditions for voyeurism—which, as we have seen in Metz (1982), is integral to film viewing—is a physical and psychological distance between the viewer and the object of the look. The viewer's ability to create this distance is based on the different childhood experiences of boys and girls. Boys, quickly realizing the 'lack' (of the penis) in their mothers, dissociate themselves from the mother. Girls, on the other hand, identify with the mother because of the recognition of sameness. Girls thus find it difficult to dissociate themselves from the female object—even the one on the screen. They suffer a 'masculinization' when they identify themselves with the female object on screen. In a film like *Dhoom*, for instance, there is an explicit connection made between technology and masculinity, and the woman is excluded as anything other than a sex object for the song sequences.

Women looking at women, for Doane and others, encodes a homosexual desire. Since girls never dissociate themselves from their mothers, they carry a latent homosexual desire that co-exists with heterosexual relationships. Thus, the female spectator looking at women (heterosexual female stars in films, or explicitly lesbian women images in films such as *Fire*),[7] is involved in what van Zoonen calls a 'double desire': an active homosexual one which is rooted in the bond with her mother, and a passive heterosexual one that proceeds from her identification with the woman as object of the male gaze. As an example of this 'double desire', van Zoonen points out that heterosexually-constructed stars like

Greta Garbo and Bette Davis have also featured in the lesbian subculture as objects of desire (1996 [1994]: 93–94; on race, sexuality and aesthetics, see Hammonds 1994 and Hobson 2003).

But what about women looking at men on screen? Since the cinema and other visual spectacles are predicated on the idea of the male viewer and the female viewee, a female gaze upon the male body is unacceptable. It is, therefore, interesting that Hindi film stars such as Sunjay Dutt, Sunny Deol, Salman Khan and, more recently, John Abraham, are constantly showing large sections of their hyper-masculine torso. Philip Lutgendorf sees the cultivation and display of the 'buff' torso as contemporaneous with the rise of both consumerism and politically-energized middle classes. The male body, he suggests, has become another good for men to acquire (Lutgendorf 2003: 98). Rachel Dwyer notes that Salman Khan is usually clothed in American sportswear or gym-wear. She suggests that 'the male at the end of the 20th century … is groomed, maintained, exercised and dressed in the clothes of consumer society. An object of his own narcissistic gaze he also invites the gaze of the audience on his body in a way traditionally associated with women' (Dwyer and Patel 2002: 83–84). It seems as though it is only the iron-pumped, hard and muscled male body that can be 'revealed'. It has to, above all, *never* appear soft or feminine (or even hairy, except for the occasional Anil Kapoor chest, or in an earlier era, Vinod Mehra, who never quite qualified as a macho-hero despite his appearance with his shirt unbuttoned to reveal a hairy chest). The male body that loses its clothes is frequently the object of derision in scenes that are meant to be farces and are not to be taken as *erotic* (the dropping of trousers—consciously or unconsciously—by Shakti Kapoor, for instance, or Govinda). When the male body is defined as strong and muscled, the exhibition of such a body carries with it some peculiar complications: these become the potential objects of female as well as male homosexual desire.

Claudia Springer, reading cyborg films (exemplified by the *Terminator* series), argues that the erotic appeal of muscled cyborgs lies in the 'promise of power they embody' (1999: 47). Violence in cyborg images substitutes for sexual release. Springer suggests that films and images that caress a naked male body may trigger (unacceptable) homoerotic responses in a male audience. She argues that cyberpunk and techno-thrillers defend masculinity against femininity by transforming the body into something only minimally human. Technological props are used to 'shore up' masculinity. Thus, the irony is that the masculine subject can be preserved precisely by disintegrating its coherence as a male body—with its prostheses of electronic systems. Masculinity is defended as masculine only with its appendages and transformation. Springer argues that by escaping identification with the male *body*, masculinity in cyborg imagery suggests an *essential masculinity that is beyond the merely corporeal* (1999: 48). All-female audiences would, of course, reduce this risk. Such an audience, however, cannot be easily ensured in large movie-houses. But what about a spectatorship for scenes of women's desire? The desiring woman is not a common feature of the Hindi film at least. Films such as *Fire* (or the aggressive sexuality of Bipasha Basu in *Jism*, 2003, or Mallika Sherawat in *Murder*, 2004) that depict the woman's desire are rare because in the Indian context a woman does not *present* her desires. Bipasha Basu's experience at the hands (literally) of 'fans' in various towns in India is partly to do with the fact that she represents a *desiring* woman, and not just a desirable one. Thus the woman on screen is not the subject of a *female* spectator's desire. The female spectator is offered pleasure through an identification with the female star (Kasbekar 2001: 305). Kasbekar argues that the female gaze is 'solicited by the kaleidoscopic changes of extravagant sets, sumptuous costumes, fashionable jewellery, imaginative hairstyles, and daring make-up' (ibid.). Nowhere does Kasbekar, in her otherwise astute analysis, refer to the female spectator with lesbian preferences. The argument here suggests that the female gaze is '(s)topped' by/with metonymic displays of sartorial extravagance. Such an argument is dangerous in that it assumes—like all of India does—that the female spectator is always heterosexual. This is the heterosexual imaginary of Indian mass entertainment. It is the stereotype that effaces the gay except as a figure of ridicule, and enforces a heteronormativity on viewers of cinema and television.

It would also be interesting to look at representations of third genders and cross-dressing in popular cinema. Heroes and heroines in Hindi cinema, for example, have donned costumes of the opposite sex for comedies (Amitabh immortalized this in *Lawaaris*, 1981). Cross-dressing is usually intended as comic relief. Yet, there is also something else at work here. Let me situate cross-dressing in the context of the *routine* costumed heroes/heroines: the leather-jacketed macho man, the delicate lover boy, the dandified urban man, the 'correct' middle-class man, the traditional sari-clad heroine, the colourful village belle, the fashionable 'society lady' ... the range is enormous. Each stereotype has its own peculiar dress code. In fact identity—whether rural/urban, educated/illiterate, hero/villain (where the villain wears brightly coloured clothes, smokes a pipe, and is surrounded by men in tight T-shirts with horizontal stripes—difficult to believe people can look at themselves in the mirror and not want to change costumes—or vamps), wife/college girl—is *coded* as costumes. I have already noted how the college girl shifts costumes from fashionable Western clothes to saris or salwars *after* she is formally engaged to be married. The seductress invariably wears Western clothes. Rachel Dwyer, reading *Stardust*, notes that 'the actress is heavily made-up, wearing a particular type of western costume which is more high street than high fashion.... The actresses rarely wear Indian clothes for these shots' (Dwyer and Pinney 2001: 270). In a subsequent analysis Dwyer notes that the wife wears saris and the mistress or girlfriend wears Western clothes. Even the kinds of saris worn are symbols and social markers. Thus a woman who is not a mother wears a type of sari that is deemed unacceptable for a mother, most often a transparent chiffon one (Dwyer and Patel 2002: 87–88). With such great emphasis on costumes, it is surprising that studies of the popular Hindi film do not look at the problematic area of cross-dressing. What happens when characters do not wear clothes deemed appropriate to their gender? What does it mean when action-heroes such as Aamir Khan (*Baazi*), Amitabh (*Lawaaris*), Anil Kapoor (*Jhoot Bole Kauaa Kaate*), Govinda (*Aunty No. 1*) and Kamal Haasan (*Chachi 420*) 'perform' as women? Or when a superstar such as Shah Rukh Khan does an 'item number' (*Kaal*, 2005)?

In the Hindi film, cross-dressing is used to desexualize the transvestite, and erases the potential subversiveness of the act by rendering it comic. Thus, when a Rishi Kapoor or Salman Khan insinuates himself into a women-only ceremony (such as the Sangeet before the wedding day), it is in effect a subversion of a feminized space. It suggests a male colonization and intrusion into a space barred to them. Rishi Kapoor, barely concealed underneath a dupatta, is sent away with a glare and a gesture when he thus intrudes in the 1989 hit *Chandni*. It is thus a political reconfiguration of the feminized space that the cross-dressing male achieves. While it reveals a male power/domination code in society, it also represents, I believe, a certain *cultural anxiety*. What takes place behind the doors with all those women? Why are men excluded from such events? (Like childbirth. In India men are not allowed in yet.) The male, anxious at this exclusion from a social space, strives to penetrate it. Like the conquest of the woman's body itself—and most of such scenes are to do with *wedding* rituals—the male inscribes himself onto feminized spaces. *Chandni*, appearing at a time of economic liberalization and a changing gender demographic of the workplace, reinforces this anxiety. As the woman seeks to move into spaces hitherto definitely male (such as the office), the man's anxiety moves him into a *woman's* space. (The theme of gendered spaces can be read alongside 'real life' attempts by numerous successive governments and political parties to thwart the Women's Reservation Bill, which would ensure a greater women's presence in Parliament: a clearly male-dominated space.) A woman cross-dresser is warrior-like, seeking revenge, fighting like a man, and never sexual. A woman as cross-dresser is not meant to be erotic. And therefore female cross-dressers in Hindi films invariably return to their 'true' (ultra)feminine form.

Cross-dressing disrupts the relationship between the body and social appearance. It emphasizes the fact that gender identity is cultural. What the Hindi film does is point out this constructedness of gender identity— but does not re-negotiate it. The masculine body 'shines through' despite— or maybe because of—the cross-dressing. The audience is made doubly aware of the male in female clothes. Watching an actor on screen can never be an isolated experience: we have watched him or her before, we are aware of the roles played prior to this one, we have listened to the music, we have seen the publicity stills/postures (on advertising's integral role in film production and consumption in India, see Patel in Dwyer and Patel 2002). Like folk tales, we never see a film for the first time; we have *already* seen it. Thus watching a macho man dressed as a woman reinforces the gender roles. A common theme in such sequences in Hindi films is that of the male dressing up as a female in order to seduce the villain or someone else. The villain is fooled into believing that he is wooing a woman. When the hero dons the woman's costume, he dons the *role* which women are traditionally 'given': the seductress or the care-giver (for example, *Chachi 420*, a remake of the Robin Williams starrer, *Mrs Doubtfire*). Thus the cross-dresser, under the guise of a comic situation, is actually doing two things: (*i*) penetrating (literally) a feminized space, and (*ii*) reinforcing the stereotype of women and the woman's role. Cross-dressing overdetermines the 'real' gender beneath the apparently subversive clothes. The male can access any space because he is male. And the female's role as care-giver or seductress can be mimicked by the male at any point with minimum effort. In both cases it is the overdetermination of the male's domination. In the case of *Mrs Doubtfire*, for instance, the hero dressed as a matron actually defends his sexual empire. When the estranged wife appears even remotely interested in another man, 'he' tries very hard to scuttle a potential rival. In the classic role of the male 'protector', the hero defends his woman and children from another male. The sexual jealousy coded as care is a male stereotype that emerges (literally) from beneath the pancake make-up. The male/hero is in control despite the female costume. When Kamal Hasan fights and pummels villains as a woman, he (like the audience) is unconsciously recreating the myth of the male protector.

Studies such as those of Marjorie Garber (1993) and Kim Michasiw (1994) see cross-dressing as a potentially subversive subcultural practice. Garber argues that we tend to treat the transvestite as man or woman in another clothing. Rarely do we see the transvestite *as* transvestite, as a third category that defies the male/female binary. It thus 'confounds' culture itself. In India, when the hero is role-playing as a woman for comic effect, cross-dressing is almost always drag, that is, *theatrical* cross-dressing. Consciously—and obviously—cross-dressed as a woman, the hero delivers the comic relief. It thus takes the political edge off the moment, the event. It nullifies the possibility of a cross-dresser ever achieving *any* cultural value, except as a comedian. When it also reinforces stereotypes and the male domination of space, drag and cross-dressing clearly favour the status quo. Thus when Amitabh pretends to be a woman in the '*mere angane mein*' sequence—surely one of the most famous drag scenes in Hindi cinema—he fragments the woman's identity into material parts of a household: a ladder, a mattress, light bulb (here coded as '*bijli*', electricity), a child, eye-liner (*kajal*). The woman is split into various 'parts', all of which are to do with her *physical* appearance: tall, short, fair, dark, stout. Nowhere is there a reference to any other attribute of the woman. This excessive fragmentation into material household parts and physical features reinforces the cultural emphasis on a woman's *appearance* and her *utility* to the house.

Song sequences in Hindi films have frequently appropriated the female body for the male's voyeuristic pleasure, as discussed earlier. Madan Gopal Singh (1983), reading the famous *Mehbooba, Mehbooba* number in *Sholay*, argues that the female dancer's body is fragmented in such sequences and generates viewing pleasure (qtd. in Gopalan 2001: 369). However, as Lalitha Gopalan points out, Singh does not acknowledge the fact that these sequences interrupt the narrative sequence, and distract the spectator. It thus breaks the codes of realism that such a psychoanalytic theory of voyeurism relies on. What is significant is that even the most superficial sequences carry an 'ideological charge', which heightens our viewing pleasure (ibid.: 369).

In Hindi cinema moments of crisis invariably revolve around the women—from the heroine's tortured dance (Hema Malini in *Sholay*) to the sister's rape or failed marriage (too many to be mentioned). Indeed, the sister's main function—after tying the *rakhee*—is to arrange for herself to be inconveniently kidnapped by the villain. The hero's task is to rescue the women. Lending itself to gender-sensitive readings, such themes suggest that the '*izzat*' of the Indian family rests in its women. Perhaps harking back to the (in)famous ordeal-by-fire of Sita and Rama's continued anxiety about her chastity, the hero runs, fights and risks death to save his mother/wife/sister/fiancée from villainous hands (the films invariably present a scene where the villain extends a paw/hand to lasciviously caress the woman, emphasizing the corporeal threat she is in). The virtue of the woman becomes the virtue of the nation itself, and hence the emphasis on 'protecting women' in these films (for a related reading of the mother/land, matricide and postcolonial interpretations in films, see Niranjana's 1994 reading of *Roja* and Madhava Prasad's work demonstrate the close ties between patriarchy, nationalist ideologies and gendered representations in Hindi films, and Margaroni 2003 on Jane Campion's 1993 film, *The Piano*).

The thriller genre invariably shows the woman as under threat from the killer. Films such as *Gupt* and *Kuch to Hai* present what Carol Clover has termed the 'final girl' theme. The Final Girl is the survivor. She is the one who discovers the (mutilated) bodies of her friends. She is the one who registers the true horror of the killings. She screams and runs from the killer—just that one crucial inch ahead of the killer/knife. The victims know that they are going to die seconds before the event. However, the Final Girl possesses this knowledge for long hours (when she is hiding in the house, away from the killer, but aware that he is closing in). She is also the one who would (*i*) either fight back and kill the killer; or (*ii*) be rescued (Clover 2000 [1987]: 143).

❏ FILM STARS

Richard Dyer (2000) suggests that the star phenomenon consists of everything that is publicly available about the stars. This includes interviews (at least a part of Mallika Sherawat's popularity can be attributed to her 'dare-me-if-you-can-I-don't-care' interviews; for a sample, see the one available online at http://www.rediff.com/movies/2003/mar/29mallika.htm), postures, websites and web-pages, public appearances, studio hand-outs, biographies, and other such material. A star's image is made up of what people write about her/him, the way this image is used in other contexts (advertisements, novels, pop songs). Thus star images are always multimedia. Stars are produced by media industries, and film-making corporations are only one element of this set-up.

The audience is part of this star-making enterprise. They select from the plethora of media images, and the complexity of the images themselves, meanings and feelings that work for them. In addition to this, the audience image of the star is recursive: it works back to the media producers of the star's image. Dyer is emphatic about the fact that the audience is not 'wholly controlled by Hollywood and the media' (2000 [1986]: 606). Thus images of film stars working with AIDS victims, in some incredibly convoluted fashion, work their way into audience appraisals of their film roles too.

Stars are made for profit, and they constitute an important component of the way in which films are sold. The 'presence' of a star in the film ensures saleability and audiences. In contemporary times, producers and directors also acquire star power. This is illustrated by the fact that film previews advertise directors/producers as the makers of an earlier, hugely successful/popular film. Thus stars become commodities. Dyer argues that they are both the labour and the thing that labour produces. He discerns two stages here:

(i)   The person is a body, a set of skills that have to be worked up into a star image. This includes make-up, dialogue delivery and speech patterns, dancing techniques, clothing, and others.

(ii) Part of this manufacture of the star image is achieved in the films. But by now a star image is a given, something that can be used with further labour (scripting, editing, managing, filming) to produce another commodity—the film. (ibid.: 607)

The star image thus consists of what we refer to as her or his 'image' made up of screen roles and stage-managed public appearances, as well as of the images of the manufacture of that image and of the real person who is the site or occasion of it. Stars, argues Dyer, articulate what it is to be a human being in contemporary society. They express the particular notion we hold of the person or individual. The individual is a way of thinking and feeling that sees oneself and others as a coherent and discrete entity. Each person, in this view, is seen to 'make' her or his own life. The idea that there exists a separable, coherent quality located 'inside' in consciousness (called, variously, 'self', 'soul' or 'the subject') is counterposed to the idea of a society that is 'out there'. Stars, states Dyer, articulate such ideas of personhood. The fact that the star is not simply a screen personality but a flesh-and-blood person expresses the notion of the individual. The audience begins to see the individual *beneath* the screen roles. That is, no matter what roles they 'play', they are ultimately always 'themselves'. Thus the reality of the star's private self is what we seek.

What is significant is the degree to which the star is located in some private core. Dyer argues that many stars appear to be their private lives even in public. But they are also in the *business* of being *in* the public sphere constantly (2000: 614). The private/public and individual/society dichotomies are embodied by stars in various ways. The emphasis is usually on the private self: stars are really themselves in private or perhaps in public (ibid.: 615). On a collective scale fan clubs are embodiments of the star-audience relationship. In South India fan club culture began in the 1960s for stars such as M.G. Ramachandran, N.T. Rama Rao and Akkineni Nageshwara Rao. This was part of a process were the star was idolized. Fan clubs render the star-audience relation in a different dimension. Thus the Telugu superstar Chiranjeevi stated in a recent interview: 'My relationship with my fans is more on a personal level. I have a strong bonding with them, and it *goes beyond the relationship that exists between a star and fan*' (Metroplus, *The Hindu*, 19 February 2003: 1, emphasis added). While most Indian fan clubs exist to publicize and perform public adorations of their chosen star, there have been significant departures from this norm. Fan clubs have had other social roles in the 1990s. Chiranjeevi's fan associations, for instance, have organized and run blood banks, and numerous charitable trusts.

Sara Dickey notes that the information that circulates about stars is very substantial, and constitutes a 'parallel text', one that audiences read in tandem with the films themselves (2001: 220). Fans' descriptions of the stars are engaged in a curiously intertextual relationship with the films and such parallel texts. Their descriptions of stars suggest the qualities they find attractive in the film heroes. All primary features of these descriptions share a connection with the attributes and/or desires of the urban poor: the star's triumph over poverty, their status as guru or elder brother, etc. (ibid.: 220–21). She further suggests that fan clubs 'construct an alternative cultural capital that is parallel to that produced by the dominant cultural systems' (ibid.: 213–14). Like S.V. Srinivas, Dickey sees fan activity as a parallel discourse that lends fans a certain agency and distinction. Admittedly, such a construction does take place (as evidenced by fan-club activity). There is also a limited amount of distinction and political visibility to be had from such activity. However, both Srinivas and Dickey disengage fan activity from the crafted and organized actions of stars and their publicists. Planted information, carefully circulated gossip, public performances, and the like use fan clubs to their advantage. There is a great degree of mediation and orchestration of fan-club activity, and there have also been instances of fan clubs indulging in unruly behaviour. Also, the publicist and the star's managers surely cultivate fan-club activities to suit the star's current image and needs. To argue for the fan clubs' activities as embodying a clear agency is to ignore the fact that like the films themselves, even fan-club activity—especially the high-profile ones, since the low-profile ones lack political visibility anyway—is staged, mediated and (maybe) bankrolled by the star. The process of mediation may be obscure and far too tenuous, but it is logical to believe that such mediation exists.

❏ NOTES

1. In the UK the earnings of *Trainspotting*, Jamiroquai and the Spice Girls, *Tomb Raider* (video game), *Teletubbies* and *Mr. Bean* (television programmes) and *Miss Saigon* (musical) have created a trade surplus greater than the British steel industry. The major Hollywood studios, all but one owned by the nine mega-conglomerates (Fox/Paramount, BVI/Touchstone, Sony, Paramount/Dreamworks, MGM/United Artists, 20th Century Fox, Buena Vista/Touchstone, Sony/Tristar, Warner), make more than half their money outside the USA. Statistics reveal that the top movies in Brazil, Japan, Russia and South Africa are all American or American/UK films: Brazil, *Titanic*; Japan, *Titanic*; Russia, *Titanic*; South Africa, *Tomorrow Never Dies* (Sayre and King 2003: 29).

2. Melodrama is characterized in Hindi films by the exaggeration of plot and characters straining for effect, and the domination of emotion over other considerations. Melodrama foregrounds language, making all feelings exterior, with characters verbalizing their feelings and creating discourses on their emotions (see Dwyer and Patel 2002: 28–29).

3. Makarand Paranjape comments on *Lagaan*: 'For the subaltern point of view to be really represented, the film would have to be made *of* the subalterns, *by* the subalterns, *for* the subalterns themselves. But if they could make such a high-budgeted film, would they be subalterns at all?' (2004: 96–105). Paranjape argues, rightly, I think, that the category of the subaltern is *unstable*, that any value ascribed to it is *transitive* and historically specific, resisting attempts at any easy *translation*. A provisional legitimacy—a necessary essentialism—as Paranjape argues, must be accorded the nation-state where the subaltern might find some representation/voice.

4. Well before 9/11, Hollywood films had portrayed non-Westerners negatively. Recent films such as *The Mummy* extended themes from the earlier *King Solomon's Mines* and *Romancing the Stone* by providing stereotypes of Africans, Egypt and the Western hero/ine. Many contemporary films foreground issues of cultural and national identity in the face of terrorism. Tom Clancy's *Debt of Honor*, released after the failed 1993 bombings of the World Trade Center, has strong parallels with 9/11: the antagonist flies an airplane into the Capitol building and other targets. Microsoft, all set to launch *Flight Simulator 2002*—believed to be so realistic that student pilots use it for training—eliminated the WTC from its skyline in the video game. Activision postponed release of *Spider-Man 2—Enter: Electro* just a day before schedule because the game has villains battling the superhero atop skyscrapers that resemble the WTC. The release of Arnold Schwarzenegger's *Collateral Damage* was famously postponed after the attacks. Finally, Hollywood representatives met Karl Rove, senior advisor to President George W. Bush, after the attacks, and endorsed the government's request to make film and television projects that promoted American values.

5. For a feminist appropriation of the wife-mother image iconized in Kali, see Dalmiya 2000.

6. For a recent argument, via Mulvey, of the female body's unself-consciousness while nude in mixed company in public space—a situation which radically redefines scopophilia, body consciousness and objectification—see Barcan 2001. Barcan argues that nudism 'diminishes the power differential in looking ... through negations of "ordinary" modes of looking and the constructions of new modes of looking' (ibid.: 307–8).

7. Mary John and Tejaswini Niranjana (1999) point out that gay and lesbian rights groups in India have received almost no support from the women's movement or other democratic organizations. Thus, in order to understand the controversy over films such as *Fire*, we need to be aware of the political, linguistic and religious contexts in which such films are received and interpreted.

❏ FURTHER READING

Gledhill, Christine and Linda Williams (eds). 2000. *Reinventing Film Studies*. London: Arnold.

Hill, John and Pamela Church Gibson (eds). 2000. *Film Studies: Critical Approaches*. Oxford: Oxford University Press.

Kazmi, Fareed. 1999. *The Politics of India's Conventional Cinema*. New Delhi: Sage Publications.

Prasad, M. Madhava. 1998. *Ideology of the Hindi Film: A Historical Construction*. Delhi: Oxford University Press.

Vasudevan, Ravi S. (ed.). 2002 [2000]. *Making Meaning in Indian Cinema*. Delhi: Oxford University Press.

3

Panel Culture
THE
COMIC BOOK

A guy can't jump around in his underwear and make a spectacle of himself without the ladies acting like he's some kind of guy running around in his underwear making a spectacle of himself.

(Spider-man # 14, 2001)

When I designed this suit, why the heck didn't I design it with pockets? Anything I gotta carry, I gotta carry it in a web-pouch. The F[antastic] F[our] have pockets in their uniforms. Reed Richards' alone are huge .... But that's because he has to carry trans-dimensional megadoodads and whirlydoos in them .... Or maybe he's just happy to see Sue .... 'Course if I had pockets, stuff would fall out of them every time I did this [wall- crawling]. Okay, so maybe I could have pockets with zippers, maybe Velcro ....

(Spider-man # 1, 2001)

The comic book has been, before (and even after) the advent of cable television and the Internet, arguably the most popular form of entertainment for children. It remains one of the most popular and wide-reaching forms of mass communication, and the comic strip has even been described as a 'folk movement' (White and Abel 1963: 1). Superheroes such as Batman and Superman, Indian mythologicals from *Amar Chitra Katha* (*ACK*), masked crime fighters of African jungles such as The Phantom, noble savages such as Tarzan, magicians such as

---

This chapter is dedicated to my Venu-maman, who bought me my first comic book, an *Amar Chitra Katha*, all those years ago, and set me on the track to reading.

Mandrake, crime-fighting organizations such as the Justice League of America (JLA), intrepid warriors against the empire such as Asterix and Obelix, adventurous lives such as Tintin's ... the list is varied. The dialogue balloon, the onomatopoeic descriptions, the vibrant colours (which occasionally rubbed off onto the fingers), the exotic food, the locales ... comics introduced my generation to several aspects of life—especially Western life. If Beetle Bailey provided us with glimpses of military life, Archie introduced us to American/Western school/college life and youth culture (on par with what Enid Blyton's work achieved for Britain/Europe vis-à-vis India), and Blondie (the 'irrelevant male', Berger 1973: 103) to American corporate culture. In the 1990s Scott Adams' Dilbert provided us insights into the techno-financial cubicle culture of capitalism. Hagar the Horrible and the Flintstones provided a glimpse into ancient and medieval Europe. The superhero comic book—Batman, Superman, JLA—showed us how (American) justice and good triumphed over an assortment of monsters (with various technological, supernatural, preternatural abilities and prosthesis: Doc Ock [Doctor Octopus] in *Spider-man* is positively attractive in comparison with some other villains) seeking to destroy the human (American?) way of life.

The comic book is an integral component of public visual culture because it is one of those artifacts used as both entertainment and educational mechanisms for children by schools, teachers and parents. As Thomas Inge points out (1979), comics must be seen as a form of communication because they can be made to serve various purposes, including propaganda and social causes, and for raising social awareness. For instance, *Spider-man* comics in the late 1960s and 1970s dealt with problems of urban American culture—drugs, pollution, racism, organized crime. Like other forms of public culture—cinema, architecture, television, the museum—the comic book is inscribed into a politics. A recent article in the *Times of India* (5 July 2004) argues that ACK acts as 'an ambassador for Indian culture' abroad (http://www.timesofindia.indiatimes.com). The *Superman* comic book was shipped in hundreds of thousands to American soldiers around the world to raise their morale in the middle of fighting—an ironic event, since Superman himself did not go to war, Kent having failed his pre-induction physical! (Savage 1990: 11). One war-time advertisement for recruitment into the US army used Captain America. The advertisement read:

Captain America wants you to join more than 10,000 red-blooded young Americans in a gallant crusade against the spies and

traitors who attempt treason against our nation .... Be a sentinel of
liberty! .... And wear the badge that proves you are loyal believers
in Americanism. (qtd. in Horn 1976: 27)

It is surely no coincidence that in 1941, the year America entered World
War II, the world's first superheroine, Wonder Woman—'beautiful as
Aphrodite, wise as Athena, stronger than Hercules, and swifter than
Mercury'—also made her appearance in *All Star Comics*. Stan Lee's Spider-
man—now enjoying a fresh burst of popularity with the movie versions—
who first appeared in Marvel Comics' *Amazing Fantasy* # 15 (August 1962.
Marvel Enterprises, Inc., which 'owns' Spider-man, is one of the world's
largest character-based entertainment companies: it has control over
4,700 characters), foiled the Chameleon's attempt to hand over American
documents/secrets to communists in the 1963 Cold War numbers. The
salaryman comics in Japan—known as *sarariman manga*—associate the
salaryman's life with secure employment, predictable salary rises, rank,
and a sense of purpose derived from a commitment to a work ethic and
an organization (Skinner 1979). Of the nearly 100 Donald Duck
magazines (from the Disney stable), very nearly half (47 per cent) showed
the heroes confronting beings from other continents and races (Dorfman
and Mattelart 1991 [1984]: 43; in *Batman* # 6, 2002, the villainous cult of
killers is located in Calcutta). These examples—and they could be multiplied *ad infinitum*—suggest that the genre functions in the public sphere as
a conduit of transmission of the cultural, the political and the ideological.

Box 3.1: The 'seduction of the innocent'

There has also been a regular critique of the 'bad' influence of comics on children, with Frank Wertham's 1953 classic, *The Seduction of the Innocent*, being
the most famous. Dr Wertham was senior psychiatrist for the Department of
Hospitals in New York City from 1932 to 1952, directed the mental hygiene
clinics at Bellevue Hospital and Queens Hospital Center, and was in charge of
the General Sessions Psychiatrist Clinic. Dr Wertham's critique was organized
around the following issues: comics encourage illiteracy, delinquency and
practical jokes, and glorify violence; make children believe that there was pleasure in pain; and stimulate children sexually well before they are ready for it.
Children learn to 'transpose' sadism into their own lives when they see the link-
age between sex and violence in comics. They may even instil homosexual
tendencies. *The Seduction of the Innocent* has remained the most sustained
attack on the comic book. Also see Legman 1963, especially pp. 27–56.

Comics, evidently, are a serious business. The genre (along with genres such as graffiti and bumper stickers) has now attained a great deal of academic respectability—though not in India—with numerous studies on the ideology, cultural politics and narrative modes of comic strips.

In this chapter I look at two of the most popular genres in comic books in India: the superhero comic book and the *Amar Chitra Katha* (*ACK*).

❏ READING COMICS

The comic strip and the comic book

The comic strip, an antecedent of the comic book, owes much to the tradition of caricature and cartooning. It is a supreme example of graphic art in a narrative format. They are called 'comics'—even when they are not humourous (example: Art Spiegelman's cult work, *Maus*, 1973, was a comic book that detailed Spiegelman's parents' and family's life in Nazi concentration camps)—because the early strips in England and America were of a humorous nature (and called the 'funnies'). Political cartoons date back to medieval art in Europe. Anant Pai, the founder of *ACK*, argues that only speech balloons in comic strips are alien to India, and points to graphic art such as the Ajanta frescoes and folk culture traditions of narrative sequence as antecedents to comics (qtd. in Sircar 2000: 35). Mario Saraceni suggests that there are connections between comics and the communication systems of early civilizations such as Egypt's, which used a combination of images and hieroglyphics (2003: 1). According to Maurice Horn, it was Leonardo da Vinci who sought to provide a new language, mixing the written word and supplementing it with visual expletives (1976: 9).

The first regular comic strip appeared in 1884, and featured the first comics hero, Ally Sloper. In 1890 *Comic Cuts*, the world's first regularly appearing comic, appeared. American comics historians believe that The Yellow Kid, which appeared in *New York World* from 1895 and dealt with urban America through humour and fantasy, was the first comics character. Krazy Kat appeared in 1913. Through the 1920s the family comic strip was the most common genre with Moon Mullins, Little Orphan Annie, and others (what Arthur Asa Berger terms 'the innocents', 1973: 19). In 1929 the adventure strip became a distinct and dominant genre when Richard Calkins and Phil Nowlan introduced Buck Rogers. By 1930 publishers had begun to collect newspaper comic strips into books, and the 'comic book' was born. The first comic book which had its own material (rather than reprints from newspaper strips) was New Fun Comics, which appeared in 1935. The genre grew, and figures such as Dick Tracy, Terry and the Pirates (by the widely popular Milton Caniff, and the first comic ever to be reprinted in the Congressional Record), Mandrake, The Phantom (the first costumed hero) and Flash Gordon entered the public imaginary.

Box 3.2: Comic characters—A history

Flash Gordon	1909	Batman	1939
Krazy Kat	1913	Captain America	1941
Tarzan	1928	Beetle Bailey	1950
Buck Rogers	1929	Spider-man	1962
Popeye	1929	Amar Chitra Katha	1967
Blondie	1930	Hagar the Horrible	1973
Mickey Mouse	1930		

(For a detailed history, see Horn 1976: 9–46.)

The comic book hero/plot often drew inspiration from a variety of sources. *Flash Gordon*, *Prince Valiant* and the *Fantastic Four* drew on the heroic tradition of Arthurian legends, Samson, and others. Dick Tracy's hideous villains show remarkable affinities with the villains from the European Gothic tradition (the landscapes in *Fantastic Four* are almost always Gothic). Dick Tracy himself was modelled after Arthur Conan Doyle's immortal Sherlock Holmes. Superman was based on Philip Wylie's novel, *Gladiator*. Batman, as the 'biography' *Batman: The Complete History* (Les Daniels and Chipp Kidd, 1999) reveals, was inspired by *The Shadow*. Bob Kane, creator of Batman, stated in an 1990 interview that the idea for the bat wings came from a set of drawings by Leonardo da Vinci for a flying machine, and from those by Douglas Fairbanks, Sr. in *The Mark of Zorro* (available at http://www.npr.org). Then there is *The League of*

Extraordinary Gentlemen, a league made up of heroes from English and European literary classics. Charles Schulz, inspired by animal fables, created *Peanuts* in 1950. In 1930 Chic Young created a sandwich-munching Dagwood Bumstead in *Blondie*—described by Marshall McLuhan as 'a supernumerary tooth with weak hams and a cuckold hair-do', whose 'attempts to eke out some sort of existence in the bathroom or the sofa (face to the wall) are always promptly challenged' (qtd. in Berger 1973: 102–3)—which went on to become the most popular comic strip in the world (Inge 1990: 10). Robert Harvey, surveying the scene in 1994, argued that *Peanuts* (now defunct), *Blondie* and *Beetle Bailey* (the popular satire on the military) were the three most popular strips in the world (1994: 202).

There are various genres in comic strips/books. A genre such as adventure comics includes a wide range within it: domestic drama, war and crime stories, SF, horror, Westerns, detective fiction, fantasy, satire, slapstick, humour, adventures in exotic places, and so on.

The language of comics

Thomas Inge, one of the world's leading commentators on comics, defines the comic strip as:

> An open-ended dramatic narrative about a recurring set of characters told in a series of drawings, often with dialogue in balloons and a narrative text, and published serially in newspapers. (1979: 631)

They are closer to drama because they rely on dramatic conventions of character, dialogue, scene and gesture (ibid.: 637). This is still the most comprehensive definition of the comic strip, of which the comic book is an offshoot. Increasingly associated with graphic art, and modulated into animations and cartoons on screen, television and now the Internet, the comic form's main function is story-telling. In fact, Inge argues, the comic strip in Europe actually lured readers *away* from pulp magazines and dime novels (ibid.). Satire has traditionally been the main focus of comics. The genre draws upon the tradition of caricature and comic exaggeration (Inge 1990: 12), and is thus often referred to as the 'funnies'.

The comic book is one of those unusual genres that combines visual and verbal forms of communication. The pictures and the text complement each other, and the genre requires that the reader read them together in order to make sense. It has two primary features—the deployment of both words and pictures to tell the tale, and texts organized into sequential units, graphically separated from each other. The comic strip consists of three components: (*i*) a narrative told through a sequence of pictures arranged in *panels*; (*ii*) a continuing (that is, the same set of characters in every issue/number of the strip) cast of characters; and (*iii*) text or dialogue included within the picture (in the balloon). In a good comic strip the sense of words is dependent on the visual material and vice versa.[1] To be effective, the reader's attention must be focused on whatever element in that panel contributes most to the telling of the story. The panel is the window through which one sees the events: the window frames the events (Abbott 1986: 156). This may be the dialogue or the picture, which may deliver the image of an action, and is what Robert Harvey terms the 'graphic center of narrative focus', where the graphic centre emphasizes the visual nature of the medium, and narrative focus the story-telling element (Harvey 1979: 650).

The panel is the fundamental, smallest functional unit of comic art. The borders of the panel define the frame through which one sees the scene—not unlike a window onto another world. The drawings in the panel, therefore, closely resemble two-dimensional art forms, but unlike

---

Box 3.3: White ... At the heart of darkness

The Phantom ('Mr Walker', when he goes to town) and Tarzan ('Lord Greystoke') are two white men who speak the language of animals, natives, the seasons and violence. The Phantom, created by Lee Falk, is a costumed hero fighting crime. He rears dinosaurs and dolphins, and maintains peace in primitive Africa when he is not with his wife Diana and bringing up Kit and Heloise (his two blonde, clearly Aryan children). Tarzan, a character created by Edgar Rice Burroughs in his fiction, has English parentage. His parents were abandoned and subsequently killed in Africa. Tarzan, 'the lord of the jungle', grows up with apes, can talk to animals, and bursts into jungle songs and primitive 'curses' at the slightest opportunity.

The most determinedly colonial of comic books, the white warriors triumph over nature, savages and their own personal traumas. They represent the triumph of white civilization, ingenuity and courage over the ignorant 'dark continent', and reinforce traditional colonial stereotypes. Racist, patriarchal and anthropocentric—with some token gestures at animal/nature preservation—*The Phantom* and *Tarzan of the Apes* remain the raciest, and most vividly entertaining comic books of all time. Indeed, in lending libraries, these comic books circulate faster than the eye can see.

other such art, also carry written text. This means that the reader/viewer of the comic strip perceives the pictorial portion of the panel in conjunction with the written matter. Even if the pictorial space exceeds text space in size—as it often does—the text influences the reader's perception of the visual. The reader's attention must be focused on three aspects of the language of comics: the narration, the dialogue and the sound effect.

Narration is usually placed in squared-off areas at the top or bottom of the panel (Abbott 1986: 156). Dialogue is placed in 'balloons', with a tail to the balloon pointing to the speaker. Thoughts are placed in billowing balloons. Narration and dialogue are extra-visual (ibid.). The text influences the perception of the panel image. Sound itself is in text form with larger or smaller fonts,

RAT-A-TAT-TAT   for rifle/gunfire,

eeek!   for a hysterical reaction, or

Ouch!   to indicate pain,

but the 'text' of sound is not always placed in balloons. What is important is that there is no one way of reading a panel. The reader's eyes move right-to-left and top-to-bottom, and freely over the pictures. This is the order of perception (ibid.: 159). However, the text often determines the amount of time spent on the picture in each panel. This is the order of duration (ibid.: 162).

Each panel usually establishes a time duration for the picture depicted. A panel represents a single instant, or a scene that may be spread over a few moments (a dialogue between people), a journey, etc. The movement across panels is usually a movement through time, space and the story (see Figure).

There might be variations, with reversals in battle, some self-reflexive commentary, a discourse on justice by the hero, flash-back, and so on. But the general scheme is the same, where a movement across panels usually means a movement through time and events. The logic of a comic strip: the strips acknowledge no stable physical laws, and characters are welcome to do impossible things without explanation. Anything is permissible if it advances the story (Barker 1989: 77–82).

Each panel is separated from the other by a space called the 'gutter'. The gutter contains all the elements missing from the panels. The

| Panel 1:
Moment 1—Event 1
Old woman being
robbed | Panel 2:
Moment 2—Event 2
Batman hears/sees
woman in pain/upset,
criminals running away | Panel 3:
Moment 3—Event 3
Batman chases
criminals |

| Panel 4:
Moment 4—Event 4
Batman beats up criminals. Lots of 'ouches' and
sounds of beating, with some comments from
hero | Panel 5:
Moment 5—Event 5
Batman restores bag
to old woman |

Figure 3.1: Narrative schema for a comic book tale

actual width of the gutter is not so important, but there must be some division between the panels. The caption contains the linguistic elements. This caption may be at the bottom, top or left side of the panel, and is never inside it. The caption is often the narrator's voice, and may be used to provide background information, move the story along, or describe a set of events/actions not pictured in the panel. Pictures in comics are more symbolic. They are highly stylized and are used as a special vocabulary—expressions, events, situations, mental states, and so on. They are recognizable symbols, and this is what makes the comic book/strip a public cultural form—since the images and symbols are repeated.

Panels are linked to one another by the elements they have in common. These can be common characters, objects, buildings or background. Panels usually have two forms of information—*given* information, which is basically repeated information, and *new* information (Saraceni 2003: 38). The reader perceives the series of panels as unified text. This is the coherence of the comic strip. Coherence is achieved through (*i*) recognizing elements belonging to the same semantic field; and (*ii*) the capacity for inference, which enables a reader of the comic book to make sense of incomplete information (ibid.: 45–46). For instance, if panel one sets up a semantic field of a school scene, all subsequent events will be interpreted by the reader as located in the school, even without being told this in every panel. Teachers, students, building, books, tables and chairs will all be a part of this semantic field called 'school'. In reading comics, the reader needs to infer a lot about missing information, thus filling the gutter *between* panels with the missing information that has been inferred from the available ones.

❑ MONSTERS AND MARVELS: THE SUPERHERO COMIC BOOK

Perhaps the most popular genre in the comic book is the superhero comic book. Comic books of this type are characterized as 'adventure strips', because the storyline often involves a 'heroic-adversity' theme (Sayre and King 2003: 150). In fact, superheroes such as Superman, Batman and Spider-man—and we need to add characters of films such as *The Matrix* (1999) and *Unbreakable* (2000) to the list—are so pervasive as 20th-century cultural icons that Richard Reynolds even calls the genre a 'modern mythology' (1994: 9). A myth embodies a universal value. In the case of the superhero, the myth is of the triumph of good (it is perhaps the preponderance of myths in comics that leads Arthur Asa Berger [1973] to propose that the 'tendency to value illusion over fact seems to … be an essential aspect of American character' [p. 67]).

There have been superheroes in myths across the world. Hercules is a well-known superhero in Western mythology. Set impossible tasks, Hercules triumphs in all of them to emerge as something other than man—superman. Joseph Campbell best describes the hero:

> A hero ventures forth from the world of common day into a region of supernatural wonder: fabulous forces are there encountered and a decisive victory is won: the hero comes back from this mysterious adventure with the power to bestow boons on his fellow man. (1949: 30)

These powers may come from wizards/gods, or from scientific disasters/ developments (the radioactive spider that bites Peter Parker, the Cosmic Rays that bestow on the Fantastic Four their powers, and so on).

Superman represents:

> the 20th century archetype of mankind at its finest. He is courage and humanity, steadfastness and decency, responsibility and ethic. He is our universal longing for perfection, for wisdom and power used in the service of the human race. (Dooley and Engle, qtd. in Davenport 1998, http://www.othervoices.org/1.2/cdavenport/steel.html)

These superheroes have one purpose and one purpose alone: to defend society from drug-pushers, criminals, spies, deranged scientists seeking world domination, maladjusted personalities, and the enemy from across the border. They seek to protect society and mankind.

The superhero comic book, I shall argue, is an exercise in teratology (the science of monsters). The monster is also—etymologically speaking the term comes from 'monstrare', meaning 'to show' or 'reveal'—about revelation, portents and omens. What the monster reveals in the superhero comic book is an imminent future—of chaos, lawlessness, a different social order. What the superhero fights is a villain who is almost always a mutant monster, a freak, or one who has developed extraordinary powers which s/he uses to overrun society. In most cases the villains in the superhero comic books, with their bizarre physiognomies, anatomies and physiologies, resemble a case recorded in the encyclopaedia of medical anomalies. What exactly does the monster stand for? Monsters, as Timothy Beal defines it, are in the world but not of it. They are 'threatening figures of anomaly within the well-established and accepted order of things ... they represent the outside that has gotten inside' (2002: 4). Monsters 'threaten our sense of at-homeness ... one's sense of security, stability, well-being, health and meaning ... they are figures of chaos and disorientation within order and orientation' (ibid.: 5). They reveal nature's dark side. In the case of the superhero comic book, the monster is invariably someone who was once recognizably human, a mutant or freak who has become one through some horrible error in an experiment. That is, the monster is one of us, and yet different. The villain in the superhero comic book is thus the other within the same, thereby revealing our deepest concerns and fears.

The emphasis on mutants and deformities—both physical and mental— is a particularly interesting feature of superhero comic books. Mutants are versions of freaks who were exhibited in fairs and exhibitions—often called 'Freak Shows'—to entertain the public (see Fiedler 1978). The supervillains are almost always deformed, with hideous appendages and even more hideous physiognomies. This is especially so when they are named after 'funny' expressions: such as Batman's The Joker or Spider-Girl's Funny-Face. Indeed, as Leslie Fiedler has argued in his path-breaking work, there is a curious imbrication of the ridiculous with the terrifyingly monstrous in freaks and mutants (ibid.: 19). It is important to note here that the physical perfection of the superhero—with the exception of some superheroes, like Ben Grimm (The Thing), from the Fantastic Four—is contrasted with the physical ugliness of the villain. In a kind of meta-commentary on the beauty of virtue and the ugliness of evil, the superhero comic book presents the villain as a freak (again, there are exceptions, the most prominent being Lex Luthor, Clark Kent/Superman's arch enemy). Note the ugliness of the monsters in *Silver Surfer*, for instance: bad teeth, horned, asymmetric faces, contorted bodies. Even Mephisto, the Prince of Evil—the chief villain—is a freakish monster, and does not look like any prince (dressed as he is in a sartorial nightmare of loin cloth, cape and boots)! Freaks in literature are often creatures that defy classification. They occupy the border between man and anima, man and machine. In Gothic literature, as Geoffrey Harpham (1982), Kelly Hurley (1996) and others have demonstrated, whatever defies categorization is consigned to the realm of the monstrous. More importantly, the monstrous and the freakish represent what is unacceptable to society—in terms of looks, behaviour, philosophy, etc.

I am suggesting here that one of the central 'spectacles' in the superhero comic book is the villain's *form*. The superhero remains unchanged. S/he is recognizable as a superhero precisely because of this consistency of looks. So there is no surprise from that quarter. In the case of the villain, there is more scope and flexibility. Comic book creators and artists go to town designing villains as a result. In a perceptive reading of freakery, Rosemary Garland Thomson suggests that 'the extraordinary body is fundamental to the narratives by which we make sense of ourselves and our world' (1996: 1). A freak, argues Thomson, represents 'generalized embodied deviance' (ibid.: 10), and is somebody we view with both attraction and revulsion. In almost all superhero comic books the villain is deranged or malformed as a result of some experiment or mutation. He is mythic and mysterious for this reason. The monstrous arms or legs, or the brilliance, is a mixture of fiction, fact and fantasy, where the villain fulfils our worst nightmares (of science producing mutants), and appeals to our greatest fantasy—men with superior talents and strengths. (Grant Morrison's *Animal Man* [DC Comics, 1988–90], is a superhero who can take on the powers of any nearby animal. In *Teen Titans*, Impulse is described as a 'one-man animal kingdom' because he can take on the shape of any animal [# 02, 2004: 6]. As another parallel we have the Animagi of the Harry Potter books.) Such mutant villains— or even heroes—are hybrid forms. They thus challenge the conventional boundaries between human and animal and between reality and illusion, and are rendered more mysterious as a result.

In the superhero comic book the villains' revolting appendages and physiognomy are closely aligned with his or her mental deviance and moral turpitude. The villains represent, Leslie Fiedler argues, the 'absolute other', alien and hostile (1978: 17–18, 23). The villain is destroyed not only because he is evil: he is destroyed *as a freak.* Superhero comic books conduct a ritual murder of the freak as absolute Other, in line with the custom—practiced from ancient times in almost all Western cultures (ibid.: 21)—of destroying malformed children. The super-endowed villain must die because he somehow usurps the place of the mythic superhero. No one other than the superhero can be allowed to possess such talents. As the usurper of the privilege of being a superhero— and the Biblical Lucifer-the-fallen-*angel* may not be a bad analogy—the supervillain must be punished. When the villain is destroyed the reader rejoices because, as Fiedler puts it, 'we rejoice at the defeat of those who have illegitimately assumed the mythic guise of Hercules' (ibid.: 125).

The superhero comic book expends a considerable amount of energy on villains because there might be an inherent appeal of such monstrosities for children, and children are the main purveyors of comic books. Fiedler has argued that in childhood, reading texts such as *Alice's Adventures in Wonderland* or *Gulliver's Travels*, we are confused about the definitions of 'normal' and 'freaks'. This confusion is basically to do with issues of scale, as we read about Giants and Dwarfs, Fat Men and Fat Ladies (ibid.: 27–28). During the period of growth accompanied by an increasing awareness of the body's changes, the child—or adolescent—is alternately upset and fascinated by her/his own body's proportions and scale in relation to others (adults, babies, the other gender). That is, the superhero comic book's monstrous, ugly, villains appeal to a certain disquiet with proportions, shapes and oddities that children and adolescents go through. What the young reader of the superhero comic book faces is a visual representation of her/his own chaotic ideas of size, function, aesthetic appeal (feminine, masculine). The monstrous villain is created with an eye to this audience, for, as Fiedler has argued, ugliness also has a certain erotic appeal (ibid.: 137–53). The superhero or superheroine's physical perfection (see below) is contrasted with the villain's deformity and ugliness. The beauty and the beast myth is reworked when the well-endowed superhero/ine meets the deformed, malformed, or hyper-formed villain in a battle which is as much about good and evil as it is about the aesthetics of corporeal appeal.

But the superhero is *also* a freak—he disturbs the boundary between animal/bird and man in Batman, Superman and Spider-man. Whether they are naturally 'freaks' or the unexpected by-products of accidents, superheroes are not very different from their Others—the supervillains—because they too are endowed with super-qualities and features that 'normal' humans do not possess. The distinguishing feature is that these qualities are used for 'good' rather than 'evil' by superheroes. Unlike the villains, they possess a soul (and, in the case of Spider-man, indulge in some serious soul-searching), and dedicate their qualities to the greater good of the community. Geoff Klock goes so far as to suggest that 'every major member of the villain's gallery [in Frank Miller's revisionary Batman tale] operates as a kind of reflection of some aspect of Batman's personality or role so that an understanding of one of the villains always sheds light on Batman himself' (2002: 35). Such superheroes, I argue, sublimate not only the collective cultural anxiety about superheroes, but also the fear of freaks by transforming them into *servants* of the social order. Like the genie, who is actually more powerful than Alladin, but is likeable because he is Alladin's *slave*, when he could very well be master. The monster, as I have argued above, is a freak who was once one of us. He is the other within the same. We demonize the monster as a threat to 'our' order and the order of God. What the superhero does is restore the order of God and man by destroying the monster. The chaos the monster unleashes—as s/he seeks to alter the social set-up—must be stopped, and this is what the superhero does.

The superhero is one because he extends the powers normally available to all human beings. He is faster, more intelligent, stronger. He has better powers of observation, faster *responses*, and a more logical mind. That is, the natural faculties present in all of us are *heightened*—what Eco terms the 'extreme realization of natural endowments' (1979: 107; see also Savage 1990: 6)—in the superhero through scientific devices, mutation, or divine intervention. Superman can fly at the speed of light, lift entire planets, increase temperatures through thousands of degrees—yet lives as an ordinary, timid, short-sighted Clark Kent. That is, Superman resides as one of us, despite being 'superman'. He is 'inconsumable' (Eco 1979: 111), and is accepted only because his activities take place in our human and everyday world (ibid.). This is precisely what makes Superman or other superheroes a 'modern mythology': he is what each one of us wants to become some day *in this world, in our time*.

The problem is that, by definition, there is nothing that Superman cannot do. Hence, in terms of stories, the superhero presents a problem: what can the story do that is new? Eco points out that 'there is nothing left to do except put Superman to the test of several obstacles which are intriguing' (ibid.). This involves bizarre situations, machines, and newer and newer villains. For the superhero to be recognizable, he must be unchanging. That is, he cannot be really different from the first image of him that we, as consumers of the myth, possess. In this the superhero fits into the mould of the mythological quite easily. Superman, for instance, symbolizes the unchanging theme of the battle between good and evil. He is the messianic figure who saves the world (and Lois Lane). The superhero is a symbol of selflessness in a selfish and egoistic (and often stupid) world (as Jean-Paul Gabilliet [1994] argues about *The Silver Surfer*). He is, in short, an emblem, an archetype of the romance narrative of medieval and early modern Europe. He cannot die, and must remain unchanging for all time. The superhero comic book must break historical and temporal frames to keep the myth going.

The key features of the superhero include:

(*i*)   The hero is marked out from society. He often reaches maturity without having a relationship with his parents.

(*ii*) At least some of the superheroes will be like earthbound gods in their level of powers. Other superheroes of lesser powers will consort easily with these earthbound deities.

(*iii*) The hero's devotion to justice overrides even his devotion to the law.

(*iv*) The extraordinary nature of the superhero will be contrasted with the ordinariness of his surroundings.

(*v*)   Likewise, the extraordinary nature of the hero will be contrasted with the mundane nature of his alter-ego. Certain taboos will govern the actions of these alter-egos.

(*vi*) Although ultimately above the law, superheroes can be capable of considerable patriotism and moral loyalty to the state, though not necessarily to the letter of its laws.

(*vii*) The stories are mythical and use science and magic indiscriminately to create a sense of wonder. (Reynolds 1994: 16)

This is an extraordinarily prescient list of superhero features. Superman comes from another planet, and is brought up by the Kent family in the USA. Batman seeks to avenge crime because he has witnessed his parents' death at the hands of petty criminals. Spider-man's Uncle Ben is killed (his parents make their appearance in *Amazing Spider-man # 365*, and his clone appears in *Amazing Spider-man # 149*). Or, take even a minor superheroine like Donnay Troy, or Troia (first appearing as Wonder Girl in 1965), member of the group Titans. Here is the description of her 'known relatives':

Dorothy Hinckley (mother, deceased), Carl and Fay Stacy (stepparents), Jerry and Cindy Evans (stepbrother and stepsister), Terry Long (ex-husband, deceased), Robert (son, deceased). (http://www. hyperborea.org/flash/donna.html)

It seems almost mandatory for superheroes and heroines to lack a family. Comics invariably create what Maurice Horn calls a 'mythical ontogeny' for superheroes like Superman, just so that a notional family, lineage and relationships exist (1976: 60).

Supermen, endowed with super strength, are also freaks. In this case, they could easily pass off as 'normal' human beings by concealing their extraordinary strengths and talents. What the superhero comic book does is transform an ability into a *performance*. Superman's strength or Spider-man's 'spider sense' are *extensions* to unimaginable limits of human abilities (as noted above). However, such talents cannot be kept private. The superhero comic book showcases these talents by making them public spectacles—of crime fighting, saving the world, or messianism.

There are certain features of the superhero—by which I also mean the costumed hero (Batman, for example)—that readily invite ideological criticism. The superhero nips into a telephone booth, or round a corner, to change out of his everyday clothes into the superhero costume. But what of the costumed super*heroines* such as Spider-girl, Supergirl or Wonder Woman? In very simple terms, the comic book's conventions cannot show a woman *changing*. This renders the 'transformation' of the woman into a costumed heroine a problem. Richard Reynolds suggests that this transformation can be read only as an incomplete striptease, since such women are also—however 'super' they may be—objects of the male scopophilic gaze (1994: 37). However, this reading of the transformation of the hero/heroine identifies the gaze as exclusively heterosexual, as Christian Pyle in his 1994 review of Reynolds' work points out (http://jefferson.village.virginia.edu/pmc/text-only/issue.994/review-6.994). What of the superhero's transformation as the object of the homoerotic gaze?

Batman, when first created by Bob Kane, was a serious, often gloomy character. When Robin, with all his wisecracks (and jazzy outfit, in sharp contrast to Batman's sombre apparel), appeared on the scene in the 1940s, the tone of the books changed. By the early 1950s Batman was no longer a fly-by-night character—he walked about with the general populace and even attended ceremonies and public functions. Batman is different from other superheroes because he has no superpowers, and his mortality makes the disguise a necessity. He is the result of hard physical labour and a brilliant mind. In 1986 Frank Miller re-created the Batman magic—complete with the brooding vigilantism—with his graphic novel *The Dark Knight Returns* (also, Special # 10, 2004). It proved to be so popular that it inspired the 1989 Tim Burton movie. Batman is also different because he cannot fly, and he does not possess superhuman 'qualities' such as radioactive venom. In fact, in the 'Knightfall', 'Knightquest', and 'KnightsEnd' episodes (1993–94), Batman's back was broken and the disabled hero required a replacement for more than a year—thus making him a very different kind of superhero.

Spider-man/Peter Parker is a unique superhero. He is humane and has the same kind of problems as everyone else. As a college student he has difficulties with girls, peers, studies and social life. After he grows up and gets a job, he finds it difficult to manage on his income. The young audiences find him appealing because he is always being abused and shouted at by his boss, James Jameson. He cannot afford to miss classes. In short, as a common human being Peter Parker suffers the same restrictions and anxieties as anyone else. As Spider-man he is free, though not from anxieties. Further, many of Spider-man's battles are won because of his ingenuity and strength—spraying villains such as Electro with a hose (# 9, 1964) is a particularly fine example of his presence of mind—and not because of superhuman advantages. Another feature of the Spider-man comic book is that the super-villains degenerate as a result of scientific accidents, which is quite appropriate since Spider-man himself is the result of a scientific mishap.

The ideology of the superhero comic book

Comics and superheroes are embedded in ideological contexts and historical moments. In this section I shall quickly sketch the kinds of interpretations possible for the superhero comic book.

The superhero, in Reynolds' words, is informed by an 'ideological myth':

[T]hat the normal and everyday enshrines positive values that must be defended through heroic action—and defended over and over again almost without respite against an endless battery of menaces determined to remake the world …. The normal is valuable and is constantly under attack, which means that almost by definition the superhero is battling on behalf of the status quo. Into this heroic matrix one can insert representatives of any race or creed imaginable, but in order to be functioning superheroes they will need to conform to the ideological rules of the game. The superhero has a mission to preserve society, not to re-invent it. (1994: 77)

The key word is, of course, 'preserve': where the supervillain seeks to change society and the social order—mainly to suit his needs and whims—the superhero defends the order. Umberto Eco, in a perceptive reading of the superman myth, notes that Superman is almost never at war with corrupt politicians or a fascist (American) government. Instead, he is at war with an evil that constantly seeks to take over private property. The superhero is thus full of civic consciousness for Eco (1979: 123). As any reader of superhero comic books will recall, villains are constantly trying to steal secret formulae, wallets, nuclear weapons, inventions or valuables. Justice involves thwarting these attempts, and such a theme is closely aligned with the capitalist society's deification of private property. In terms of plot the pattern is well-established:

(i)   A community is threatened by some bizarre criminal/weapon.
(ii) The community's police/military/government cannot deal with the menace.
(iii) Superman (or Spider-man or the Incredible Hulk) takes on the task.
(iv) He wins and ensures that the status quo is retained despite the temporary interruption.

This is the 'American monomyth' (Robert Jewett and John Shelton Lawrence, qtd. in Lang and Trimble 1988). Each comic book in, say, the Batman series, may be cast in this same mould. Each tale is an interruption in the life of Gotham city. It is this everyday life that Batman seeks to protect and preserve.

When Captain America was launched in 1941 (three years after Superman appeared on the scene), he was dressed in a red, white and blue striped costume, making the American flag his preferred choice. It was the story of poor Steve Rogers making it good in a version of the American dream. Steve Rogers becomes a he-man with 'new power, new vigor, new vitality' (1941, reprinted in 1969 as *The Hero that Was—The*

Origin of Captain America, Living Legend of World War II). Captain
America was, as Andrew and Virginia MacDonald (1976) point out,
America's answer to Hitler's pure race. (In a contemporary retelling,
Grant Morrison et al.'s *The Invisibles*, a DC Comics production which hit
the stands from 1996, is about a group of rebels that fights fascism.) Later,
he fights the VietCong, and this is where he begins to question his motives
as a superhero. In the 1970s Captain America joins the administration.
Comic books such as Buck Rogers or Captain America basically seek an
Americanization of the globe, constantly touting the American way of life as
being the only one worth defending. Such a comic, suggests Berger, is 'a study
of man one step removed from robotism and totalitarianism' (1973: 1).

Superman is an alien. He comes to earth and grows up to become a
saviour of the human race—with whom he has no real biological or
genetic relationship. Superman's only real relationship with the human
race is through the surrogate family that takes care of him. Superman,
therefore, fulfils a debt of gratitude to 'his' people. He extends the notion
of 'family' beyond the Kents to include the entire human race—surely a
remarkable humanist theme. William Savage, Jr., argues that Superman
'embraced American ideals and Judeo-Christian values—a kind of spectacular immigrant', who came from another planet to participate in the
'American dream' (1990: 5. Berger argues, in a similar vein, that Dick
Tracy represents America's evangelical Protestant tradition where people
work to vanquish evil [1973: 122–23]). Savage does not push this ideologically loaded point to its logical extreme. Superman represents the
assimilationist rhetoric of America towards its immigrants: to be in
America is to adopt American values. Superman comic books send out a
message to immigrants: assimilate. Superman's agenda, as even a child
would know, is to fight for 'truth, justice and the American way'.
Superman, created during the most traumatic years of American history,
the post-Depression 1930s, became the embodiment of American values,
despite being from the other end of the planetary system. His fairness,
selflessness, respect for the law, and tenderness—he brings down kittens
trapped in trees when not saving the world—rendered him the most
popular comic book superhero for a long time. Batman, likewise,
represents basic American beliefs—the belief in the pietist-perfectionist
individual who makes it his duty to right all wrongs (ibid.: 166).
The success of the superhero is the success of American belief systems,
superior technology, and, most of all, superior moral values. The triumph
of the superhero is, in fact, the triumph of freedom and American
democracy itself.

Box 3.4: By Toutatis!

The funniest criticism of empire comes not from elite postcolonial theorists, but from the comic book. *Asterix*, created by René Goscinny and Albert Uderzo in 1959, with the 'indomitable Gauls'—one short (Asterix), one 'not fat, just well covered' (Obelix), a terrible singer, a druid, pirates (including some Latin-quoting ones), and assorted villagers—transforms the great Roman empire into a joke and Julius Caesar (who came, saw, but cannot believe what he sees) into a buffoon. The tiny village holds out against the mighty Roman army, beats up Roman soldiers with astonishing regularity, and dares Caesar himself. Anti-colonial resistance was never so much fun as when Obelix proceeds to decimate entire legions of Roman soldiers while dreaming of boar.

Full of puns, extreme violence, Shakespeare—reminding canon-hating academics that 'elite' Shakespeare catered to the *masses*, and continues serves the purpose of present-day non-elite, *mass cultural* forms— extraordinarily farcical situations and parodies, *Asterix* is a comment on modes of anticolonial resistance. There is little valorization, however, of even 'indigenous' cultures. The Romans are pompous, stupid and cowardly. The Gauls, led by a chief with the mental toughness of a slab of butter, are brave and also (often) silly. There are also acerbic comments on other European cultures (Belgian, Swiss, British). Innovative word-games, some seriously funny names (Getafix, General Electric, Cumulonimbus), and mind-boggling situations (Obelix obliterating the nose of the Sphinx [*Asterix and Cleopatra*], or General Metric's war strategies, called 'the metric system' [*Asterix and the Goths*]) mark *Asterix*.

Translated into about 30 languages worldwide, the indomitable Gauls remain hot favourites when it comes to casual reading with a serious political message. The message, of course, is inscribed on the menhir over there.

It was in the context of rethinking race relations that DC Comics launched an African American superhero, Steel. His parents (civil rights activists, interestingly) were killed. Eventually he resigns a government job (making guns), witnesses Superman's death, and realizes that the Metropolis needs a new superhero (though Superman's legacy is already available: with the last son of Krypton, Metropolis Kid [Superboy], and Cyborg). Curiously, Steel never calls himself Superman.

In one episode, *The Man of Steel* # 22, Johnson's legacy is traced to John Henry, the 19th-century African American steel-driver who beat a machine pounding steel into the ground. Thus, unlike Superman, Steel has a human ancestor, and a working-class one at that. He also lacks

Superman's extraordinary (superhuman) powers. Christian Davenport (1998) argues that DC Comics wanted a Black Superman, but not one that could 'upstage' him. Steel creates an armour for himself. For Davenport this is a crucial move by DC Comics:

(*i*)   it emphasizes the fact that he was a normal man, who through his own ingenuity created something that could address his problems;

(*ii*)   it drew upon Johnson's background as an engineer and inventor, highlighting the character's intelligence; and,

(*iii*)   it stressed the fact that he armed/shielded himself in order to do battle with forces that were in need of redress. (ibid., http://www.othervoices.org/1.2)

Davenport argues that a black Superman was never quite a Superman because 'the former [Superman] was naturally a superhero and secondly a man, the latter [Steel] was naturally a man and secondly a superhero' (http://www.othervoices.org/1.2/cdavenport/steel.html). Further, unlike Superman who has taken the entire planet as his domain, Steel remains parochial and ghettoized, fighting crime in his area: 'my job is on the streets. To make them stop the madness that's destroying so many lives' (# 5). Thus a white Superman does not have geographical limitations, while the African American superhero circumscribes himself.

In the new millennium's multiculturalist ideology we also have General Nicholas Fury, a black man who is in charge of world security as head of S.H.I.E.L.D in *The Ultimates*. However, all the team members he controls are white. Fury might be in charge of world security, but the Ultimates still require somebody more significant. S.H.I.E.L.D digs up Captain America, the true-blooded white American hero, from under the Arctic Ocean into which he had fallen on his last assignment (# 1, 2003). Captain America is of course perfectly preserved as a result of having fallen into ice (# 03, 2003). Why does S.H.I.E.L.D require the retrieval and revival of a white superhero now, in the context of terrorism from the non-white, non-Christian world? It is a question worth pondering over.

In an innovative and context-sensitive reading, Slavatore Mondello (1976) notes that in the 1962–67 (Cold War) period, Spider-man fought communist plots. In the early 1970s he fought drug-pushers, pollution, racism and organized crime. Mondello argues that Spider-man represents an American hero imbued with American liberal values. However, it is also curious that the creators of Spider-man never thought to show him joining a protest march or a church. There are no debates about God or Being, though Spider-man is the only superhero who constantly satirizes his own conditions. Donald Palumbo argues that Spider-man, unlike other superheroes, is an existential character. The situations in which Spider-man finds himself are all absurd. Spider-man is himself a social outcast, and his life as superhero ruins his friendships and his love life. He is also afraid that he is going insane, and has a deep-seated sense of guilt (Palumbo 1983: 67–82). These comments could apply to other superheroes as well, and in some cases to the supervillain. For instance, in *Silver Surfer*, Galactus, the planet-devouring 'amoral' 'demigod' (as he is described), is 'lonely' and often meditates on his lot:

> There is purpose to everything in creation. Even to my own existence, though much still is shrouded in mystery …. But this I truly know, only by devouring the life energy of a planet can Galactus survive … I know not the right of it. I know not the wrong. It is that it is. It is the way of Galactus …. (*Silver Surfer* # 7, 2002)

This is a truly existential meditation on being, doing and morals, and humanizes even the supervillain. Captain America's last thoughts before dying are about the family he could have had with Gail Richards (*The Ultimates* # 1, 2003).

When Frank Miller recreated Batman in *Batman: The Dark Knight Returns*, he gave the superhero another dimension. Bruce Wayne is now 50, and returns to fighting crime with great reluctance. He also has terrible nightmares and is an insecure, paranoid, brooding man. Miller's new Batman is a metropolitan millionaire who is unsure of his life, mind and destiny. Batman's rival, The Joker, also wakes up from a 10-year coma when he hears Batman's name. In Grant Morrison's *Arkham Asylum: A Serious House on A Serious Earth* (1989), the situation is even more complex. All of Batman's famous adversaries are now on Prozac and in an asylum—which they proceed to take over. They seek to bring Batman into the asylum, because they are convinced that he is mad too. The Joker makes disparaging remarks about Batman's weird costumes (campy, definitely), his preference for masquerade and bondage, and hinting darkly about his sexuality—referring to him as 'Darling' throughout the tale. The tale suggests that Batman may be a superhero, but he is also treading that thin line between sanity and madness. Superheroes are not immune to depression or mania. This is partly to do with the kind of lives they lead.

Abstinence and poor social relationships characterize most superheroes' lives. Spider-man is unusual since he *reflects* on these matters. The superhero comic in fact underlines the emptiness of urban existence, the ephemerality of relationships, and the transient nature of glory. Surely there is something curious about the fact that the superhero is constantly pursued as a *villain* by legal and civic authorities and is misunderstood by the common populace, even though he 'does good'? The misunderstanding-theme in *Spider-man* or *Batman* is interesting because the superhero treads the fine line between law-enforcer and law-breaker. He is outside the bounds of law because he is not *empowered* to do what he does. The vigilante's notion and ideas of justice skirt the edge of law enforcement. Batman, Spider-man and Superman do not seek to *kill* villains—they beat them to within an inch of their lives and then hand them over to the law enforcement authorities. In # 25 (2004) Batman and Tarzan appear together in Gotham. When attacked by thieves, Tarzan proceeds to overpower them and is all set to kill them. Batman stops him with: 'Greystoke, I won't allow murder … not in my city' (n.p.). This is a significant move for many reasons. First, the mode of address: Tarzan is not 'Tarzan' but Greystoke, the Englishman. He is no longer lord of the jungle, but another 'normal' citizen in Gotham city. Second, the law of the jungle—kill or be killed, as countless Tarzan tales show—does not apply to the metropolis. Batman prevents Tarzan from killing the villains because in Gotham the law (or the State) takes charge of such violence. Finally, it is Batman's law that operates here in Gotham. The 'my city' suggests a sense of possession. In Gotham Batman is the vigilante, not Tarzan. Batman is marking territorial rights here, and reinforces the jungle-primitive/city-modern dichotomy through the figure of the law. In the city, 'civilized' citizens such as Batman rule according to the provisions of the law.

The superhero vigilante represents a symbolic escape-route for law enforcers: it is only by stepping out of the bounds of the law that the law can be upheld. Where the police, the judiciary and the State cannot bring criminals to justice, the superhero steps in to do so by extra-legal means and violence. Violence is in fact integral to the superhero comic book, and, as Geoff Klock points out, there is a blatant disregard for civil rights and a flirtation with fascism in *Batman* and other superhero books (2002: 41).

Superheroes exist apart from society because, as Thomas Inge points out, their vision of what life should be is at variance with that of the city dweller (1990: 142). Their job is to cleanse society, not to join it. This is the reason why Batman retreats into his home, and Superman does not marry (though Clark Kent asks Lois Lane out on a date in the inaugural issue, *Action Comics* # 1, 1938). Superheroes are almost by definition a breed apart, and they cannot breed. There is a parallel here. In William Shakespeare's *The Tempest*, Prospero accuses the 'monster' Caliban of trying to violate his daughter, Miranda. Caliban's response goes thus:

O ho, O ho! would't had been done!
Thou didst prevent me; I had peopled else
This isle with Calibans. (Act I, Scene II)

Mary Shelley's *Frankenstein* (1818) dealt with the theme of a monster seeking a mate. The monster—now well-versed in human rights theories, liberal humanism and the poetry of John Milton—pleads with his creator to make him a mate. Victor Frankenstein refuses, because he is afraid that the race of monsters that the two might produce will eventually overrun humanity and the earth. Theoretically, there is no reason why Superman or Spider-man should not breed. The superhero comic book, I suggest, conceals an anxiety that such superhumans, if allowed to reproduce, may very well take over the earth. Created during contexts of war, geopolitical tensions and sour international relations, the superhero is the equivalent and potential progenitor of a super-race. And a super-race might spell doom for the human one.

The fact that every superhero takes to the skies is an interesting detail that bears examination. The opposition of heaven and earth in these comics—Superman flying, Spider-man and Batman descending from beyond the rooftops of the city—are metaphors for the good/evil dichotomy. The messiah descends (read 'swoops') from above like an angel or God. Earth is full of evil villains who seek to engage the superhero on the ground. But the superhero invariably takes to the air.

The science-fictional element of these comics—webs, grapples and hooks, powers of flight—is an extension of the theological-mystical theme of angels and Gods descending to rescue humans. The superhero is both a creature of heaven and a mortal. There is the element of the magical, the fantastic and the miraculous in all superhero books. Some superheroes are, of course, direct descendants/creations of gods or magical creatures: Wonder Woman was created by a goddess and Captain Marvel was granted powers by a wizard, Shazam. In *Silver Surfer*, Galactus, who is a 'demigod', uses the phraseology of prophets: 'So speaks Galactus'. This ambiguity, I suggest, is what renders the superhero attractive:

he is both one of us and yet divine, a mortal plagued by self-doubts and a messiah sent to save mankind.

Superheroes are liminal figures: they cross borders, occupy different positions, and are determinedly ageographical. Paradoxically, it is this ambiguous status that alienates the superhero from the rest of society. The superhero must always be 'outside' the pale without family, close friends or a club. The liminality is the source of his strength as well as of his existential crisis. The superhero's chastity and sexual abstinence make him wholly Other. His morality and ethical choices—selflessness and suffering (through fights and battles)—enable society to survive, but also make it impossible for him to integrate. Ideologically, this reinforces the ghettoization of the elite: the elite superhero who saves the humanity to which he cannot really belong as a superhero. Flying and taking to the rooftops symbolize freedom and a break from the everyday lives of other humans. It is only by soaring above the city—like an eye-in-the-sky sur-veillance device—that the superhero can guard the city. In a sense, the messiah must be separated from those he guards.

There is clearly a machismo cult that the superhero comic book engenders. The bulging muscles, the 'rational' mind, the control over

---

Box 3.5: Cartoon gospel

Jack Chick produces a special brand of cartoons and comic strips which may be called 'cartoon gospel'. These are *tracts* that seek to popularize the Gospel. The 24-page illustrated booklets are very popular, and sell all over the Western world. The comic hero in Chick's works is usually a crusading Christian. The villain, in this case, is often the Devil himself. The *Crusaders* series stars two tough Christians who are not averse to smuggling Bibles into 'closed' commu-nities as a method of fighting the Devil. The language is full of allusions to the Bible ('footnoted' in a text box at the bottom of the panel), Christian proverbs and prayers. In one 1982 tract, *Back from the Dead?* (http://www.chick.com/reading/tracts/0029/0029_01.asp), the hero dies, goes to hell, and comes back to life. He is recounting his experience to the preacher: 'It was dark down there. I was in some kind of room. I couldn't believe it ... all around me were these hideous, ugly, smelly things in all kinds of shapes, laughing at me, hurting me .... They were like some kind of demons .... Then all at once they opened a big door .... Beyond that door was an ocean ... an ocean of fire, flames everywhere, and I heard screams ...'(p. 14). The preacher suggests that the need to warn people of hell—which the hero has seen—is urgent. Here is

what the preacher says: 'Satan is trying to take as many into hell as he can ....
He's got kids into punk rock believing that hell will be party time. But they
will never see their friends, only darkness and everlasting punishment' (p. 17).
Then, at the foot of one panel, the text book carries this message: 'No church,
saints, Buddha, Mary, Confucius, Allah, no religion, can save you from the
lake of fire. ONLY JESUS CAN!' (p. 19). The tract concludes with the hero saying to himself—and to the audience—'Now I'm saved. My name is in the
Book of Grace ....' A text box at the foot of this panel asks: 'Is your name in
it? If not, here's what you must do ...' (p. 22).

The cartoon gospel is also explicit in its agenda to reject any other
form of faith or theology. For instance, a tract called *The Deceived* (1990)
is a frontal attack on Islam (http://www.chick.com/reading/tracts/0096/
0096_01.asp). Here the story of Islam is read as the story of how Satan
hatched a conspiracy to take over the world. Two men are discussing
the Islamic and Christian faiths. The Prophet Muhammad is portrayed
as a stooge of 'Vatican spies' whose 'military machine' was funded
by two popes in exchange for Jerusalem (p. 15). The Kaaba at Mecca is
described as having 360 idols behind each of which was a 'powerful
demon causing no end of problems' (p. 11). The tract ends with a simple
imperative:

> You must choose ...
> Jesus Christ Or The Deceivers
> If you choose Jesus Christ, you'll reign with him
> in heaven. If you pick the 'Queen of Heaven' or Allah
> ... you'll spend eternity in the lake of fire. (p. 22)

Within the cartoon gospel is the adventure tradition too. *The Crusaders* is
a series from Jack Chick (launched in 1974). Vol. 1, 'Operation Bucharest',
stars two Crusaders—Timothy Emerson Clark and the black James Carter—
whose job is to deliver the Bible (in the form of a microfilm) into communist Bucharest. In Vol. 10, 'Spellbound?', the entire rock music industry is
castigated as unholy—witches file into the recording studio to perform
demonic ceremonies. In Vol. 11, Clark and Carter redeem a backslider—
Gary, who has lost his faith—by revealing to Gary the history of the Bible,
and the many conspiracies to destroy the Holy Book. It concludes with
Gary's reconversion. In the last Crusader issue ('The Prophet', Vol. 17,
1988), Muhammad the Prophet is depicted carrying a sword and flag. A parallel to the cartoon gospel would be the comic *Preacher: Gone to Texas*
(created by Ennis Garth and Steve Dillon for DC Comics in 1996). This
supernatural horror western is about a Texas preacher, Jesse Custer, who
can speak in the voice of God. Full of gore, swearing and unpleasant characters, the Preacher series is a version of the superhero comic book with a
theological twist.

technological devices and such traditionally male provinces are given full reign in the superhero comic book. With the women's movement, the superheroine comic book made its appearance.[2]

Bruce David Forbes explores another dimension to the superhero comic book. He notes that there is a surfeit of religious imagery in comic books that have superhero plots and characters. DC Comics started a Millennium series in which characters called 'Guardians', who assist the superheroes, are ready to depart for another world. But before they leave they are to train an elite band of similar assistants. Episodes in the series were named after religious themes: 'The Chosen', 'The Teaching' and 'The Ascension'. When Jack Kirby returned to DC Comics in 1970, he created a whole new series, with titles such as 'The New Gods', 'The Forever People' and 'Mr. Miracle'. The series revolved around a planet that had been blown in half. One of the surviving worlds was called 'New Genesis', whose leader was called, appropriately, Highfather. Highfather was drawn as a majestic figure with a flowing robe, white hair and a great beard. In opposition to New Genesis was the evil world of 'Apokolips', ruled, again appositely, by Darkseid and his parademons. Forbes has even identified superhero comic book covers which have the hero in the crucifixion pose: five of Batman, three each of Green Lantern and Green Arrow, one of Nightwing, and one of Wolverine, all published in the 1990s. Since comic books use iconography from the *general public culture*, this is bound to include religious images. Religion provides obviously applicable language and imagery to express such contests between good and evil. The super-heroes' self-doubts are, in effect, quasi-mystical, religious quests for meaning (Forbes n.d., http://www.wacconline.org.uk/404.php).

Theological versions and twists to horror, superhero or science-fiction are not new strategies. Even Dracula—that most 'other' of all monsters—Timothy Beal has demonstrated, has been described in Biblical terms (Beal 2002: 124–29). In women-centred comic books, we have an entire range of theologically-informed tales and characters. In *Warrior Nun, Areala*, Areala descends from Valhalla (in the year 1066—an interesting date for those who know European history) and sets up an order of—believe it or not—sword-carrying nuns. Avengelyne is the daughter of a god, and works in tandem with a priest to save a church from demons. Lady Death battles Lucifer.

However, there has been a tendency to 'humanize' the superhero while simultaneously demonizing the monster. For instance, Spider-man's self-doubts render him recognizably human. The Fantastic Four squabble among themselves. Stan Lee, once editor-in-chief of Marvel Comics, suggested that the humanization was essential. No one in the 1960s and 1970s could see the individualism of the superhero as a reality (qtd. in Lang and Trimble 1988: 165). Thus even Captain America, as noted earlier, joins the administration to show that the individual can work best when part of an organization. The Justice League of America (appearing first in DC Comics in 1960) was a move to give a sense of *family* and *community* to superheroes (the Justice League's core members include Superman, Batman, Wonder Woman, the Flash, Green Lantern, Aquaman and the Martian Manhunter).

Lang and Trimble speak of a 'progressive demythification' of the superhero (ibid.: 166). The hero must be made fallible so that the tale could get more interesting and new challenges could be 'created'. Kryptonite as a threat to Superman is not simply a weapon—it reveals a human-like vulnerability of the superhero. He has to be diminished and humanized for the suspense to work. Lang and Trimble list the process of demythification of Superman:

> Clark Kent is no longer a wimp (he lifts weights); Superman is no longer all-powerful, and he needs to hold his breath in the strato-sphere; Krypton itself has not been destroyed. (ibid.: 171)

It also, as Berger points out, helps us relieve the anxiety caused by the presence of a power that cannot be controlled (1973: 159).

Women and the superhero comic book

The representation of women in comics (both comic strips and comic books) has come in for sustained critical attention. Trina Robbins, cartoonist, cultural critic, historian, and the author of *From Girls to Grrrlz: A History of American Women's Comics from Teens to Zines* (1999), points out that from the early decades of the 20th century, the 'funnies' invariably portrayed the male as 'cartoony' and the woman as pretty (2002). Animal comics—including Mickey Mouse—often exaggerated the secondary sexual characteristics of the female (recall Minnie Mouse's long, fluttering eyelashes? On comics with themes of sexuality, drugs and violence, like Zap Comics, Manhunt, Snatch Comics or El Perfecto, see Estren 1987 [1974]).

In superhero/superheroine comic books, the bodies of both women and men are flawless. The male superheroes are basically about hyper-masculinity. Jeffrey Brown, reading the body of the superhero, writes:

While the superhero body represents in vividly graphic detail the muscularity, the confidence, the power that personifies the ideal of phallic masculinity, the alter ego—the identity that must be kept a secret—depicts the softness, the powerlessness, the insecurity associated with the feminized man. (qtd. in Klock 2002: 111)

During World War II, comic books developed a different sexual orientation. Women in distress were common to comic book covers. These inevitably showed a scantily clad woman in chains, at the mercy of a leering Axis villain. In the background was an American hero moving (struggling) forward to rescue her (see Savage 1990). 'Girlie' comic books, of course, constructed an ideal teen girl, who had hopes and dreams of marriage and family (Perebinossoff 1975). Trina Robbins argues that with the 1990s the female body gets altered—with larger breasts and clad in fewer clothes (mainly sprayed-on body suits, emphasizing, specifically, the size of the breasts). *Wild C.A.T.S X-Men* (Marvel Comics) is a good example of this kind of altered woman's body purveying to the male voyeur. Robbins puts it succinctly when she describes the male and female bodies in the comic books of the 1990s:

The males sport enormous muscles, most of which don't exist on real human beings, necks thicker than their heads, and chins bigger than the rest of their heads. Their expressions consist of gritted teeth and a permanent scowl. The females, on the other hand, possess balloon breasts and waists so small that if they were real humans they'd break in half. Their legs are twice as long as the rest of their bodies, and they affect an exaggerated pose: breasts and rear both thrust out. The noses of both male and female characters are very short and their eyes are long, often without pupils. Both genders are fantasies for young male readers, the women representing sex fantasies of adolescent boys who have little or no experience with real women.

(2002, http://www.imageandnarrative.be/gender/trinarobbins.htm)

Superheroine characters include Barb Wire, Catwoman, Wonder Woman, Supergirl, Lady Justice, Lady Death, Spider-Girl, Witchhunter, Avengelyne and others.

The emphasis in even superheroine comic books is on the woman's body. Where the male superhero is portrayed—as Robbins points out in the quote above—with bulging biceps, square jaws and legs like tree trunks, the woman is reduced to legs and breasts. The cover of *Wonder*

Woman (1995) shows her profile, with the focus entirely on breasts and thighs. In *Silver Surfer* (Gotham # 17, 2002), Silver Surfer lets Nova win their race through space, and she realizes this, commenting: 'Just like a man! Letting me win'. Later, Silver Surfer—haunted by memories of Shalla Bal, the woman he had to leave behind when he rebelled against Galactus, the planet-devourer—thinks of Nova in Shelleyean terms: 'Not since my beloved Shalla Bal have I known a female so fair of form and blithe of spirit.' The woman, who is endowed with similar powers as the superhero, is finally reduced to 'fair form' and 'blithe spirit'.

There is a certain soft-porn quality about the visualization of the woman in such heroine-centred works. Admittedly there is no sex in the comic book, and the overdrawn sexiness of bodies is a kind of sublimated image for the actual act. The heroine of the eponymous *Promethea* (from Alan Moore and J.H. Williams III, starting in 1999) is an exception to the general portrayal of big-breasted, small-waisted women in superhero comic books. With women cartoonists and women's comics, things are changing in the representation of women. Men and women are drawn similarly in *Artbabe*, *Action Girl*, *Tank Girl* or *Castle Waiting*. Comments on women, sexuality and sexual relations are, however, couched in terms of banter or jokes. For instance, General Fury, head of S.H.I.E.L.D., describes his job thus: 'the money's good and the girls are pretty' (*The Ultimates* # 02, 2003). The sexism of the superhero comic book is quite clear.

Another version of the superhero comic book is the horror comic book, exemplified best by Alan Moore's *Swamp Thing* (DC Comics, 1986 onwards). Here Alec Holland is a botanist who is working on an experimental plant formula when the whole laboratory blows up. This transforms Holland into the Swamp Thing. The Swamp Thing has the plant equivalent of human organs—yam kidneys and a non-pumping heart. The Swamp Thing blurs the barrier between plant and human, like Poison Ivy—played to perfection by Uma Thurman—in *Batman*. Geoff Klock argues that Moore's creation is not of a man transformed into a plant, but a plant that—altered by Holland's experiments—thinks it is a man (2002: 191–92). Klock identifies a new genre, the pop comic, which is no longer about superhero adventures alone, but takes its inspiration from MTV, and contemporary media culture (advertising, fashion). The *Ultimate X-Men, New X-Men, Marvel Boy* are examples of this new genre (ibid.: 172–77).

The superhero comic book is thus essentially about monsters who seek to take over the world. These monsters—who represent the otherness *within* ordered society—are battled by superheroes who are themselves freaks, armed with powers and talents beyond those of ordinary men. In the case of the superhero, the talents are utilized to save the world. The only reason why Batman's violence keeps him out of prison—or possibly a mental asylum as a homicidal maniac—is that he kills people who are beyond the pale: *homo sacer*, a man so outside the pale that his killing does not constitute murder (Agamben 1998).

❑ BUILDING IDENTITIES: *AMAR CHITRA KATHA*

The *Amar Chitra Katha* (translated as 'immortal pictorial classics' by *ACK* itself) series of comic books was conceived and continues to be edited by Anant Pai of India Book House (IBH). Launched in 1967, it has sold, according to the 2004 catalogue, 80 million copies of its 400-plus titles—the website announces that it has sold 100,000 issues every fortnight—in various languages (a 1992 catalogue says '38 languages of the world'). With this kind of sales, publicity and popularity, *ACK* is surely one of India's prominent forms of public culture for the English-educated, urban children in its towns and cities. In postcolonial India, with all its problems of secessionism, communalism, linguistic and cultural chauvinism, there is still the discourse of ONE India, best captured in India's favourite catch-line: 'Unity in Diversity', a kind of 'pasteurized multiculturalism', as Satish Deshpande termed it (1998). *ACK* is central to this construction of a postcolonial Indian identity. Its influence, especially among non-resident Indians, has been remarkable, as a recent news item in the *Times of India* reveals, and it is even seen as 'an ambassador for Indian culture' ('Amar Chitra Katha Spurs Research', 5 July 2004, http://timesofindia.indiatimes.com). Karline Marie Mclain, researching 'Amar Chitra Katha and the Construction of Indian Identities' in the USA, argues that Indian mythology and legend have become more accessible to both Indian children in the USA and Americans because of *ACK*. *ACK* comics, she says, 'are distributed to students pursuing courses related to Hinduism and Indian culture' (qtd. in Rajnish Sharma, 'Amar Chitra Katha's Westward Voyage', May 2002, http://supra.websitewelcome.com/~little/may2002/htm). The importance of the series thus extends far beyond its consumption within India.

The stated intention of the series is described on the homepage as follows:

Although initially targeted at children, the Amar Chitra Katha series also served to fill the lacuna left by grandparents in the smaller nuclear families in urban areas. In the olden days, grandparents would regale the children of the household with these tales from folklore and epics … Amar Chitra Katha stepped in to fill the void and gave parents and children a simple, colourful window into the past. It made the names of Shivaji and Abhimanyu, Shakuntala and Savitri, Kabir and Tulsidas as familiar as they used to be in joint families of the past. (http://www.amarchitrakatha.com, 4 December 2004)

The comic book is thus a substitute for the grandparent and the storytelling traditions of joint families. In a recent interview, Anant Pai states: 'Children all over the world love stories and stories with pictures are even more popular. India has a great tradition of story telling' ('Amar Chitra Katha fascinates foreigners', 6 August 2004, http://sify.com/news/pioneer/fullstory). What is not mentioned is that the comic book format that *ACK* uses is a Western one (though Pai has always tried to deny this, protesting that only the speech balloons are alien. See Sircar 2000 and Rao 2000 for a critique of the format). Further, as Frances Pritchett points out, the purpose of *ACK* is not the same as that of the traditional comic book. The purpose is not entertainment but education (Pritchett 1995: 96). *ACK* steps in as both a transmitter of cultural values and a mnemonic device. This makes the series a powerful tool for the propagation of ideology, because stories are perhaps the best mechanism for delivering ideas and notions of identity, history and culture. *ACK* has often stressed its role in education. In one number it states on the inside front cover:

Comics are welcome in schools but only Amar Chitra Katha because Amar Chitra Katha

- Acquaints children with India's cultural heritage
- Develops the habit of good reading
- Supplements school education

(*ACK*, Bumper Issue # 10, *The Story of the Freedom Struggle* 1997: inside front cover)

The *Dasha Avatar* issue (# 10002, 2004 [1978]) suggests: the 'Avatars enable the common folk to speak of or listen to stories of divine doings' (inside front cover).

I am concerned in this chapter with the ideological and political sub-texts of the works in the series, arguing that *ACK* enables a construction of a certain kind of Indian identity: an Aryan, upper-class/caste, Hindu identity, which is projected as a secular 'Indian' one.

ACK occupies a peculiar position in Indian children's literature. Arguably, English literature—both 'high' (as in 'classic') and popular—is privileged over regional Indian literatures. In post-Independence India, English is the language of power and of the dominant culture/class, as numerous cultural critics have demonstrated (Joshi 1991). This means that *ACK* and other children's literature in English are not really directed at the working classes or the masses (which is the target audience for 'popular' literature in the English/European context). In the strictest sense of the term, then, these works in English are not really 'popular'. What is important, however, given the secondary status accorded to children's literature in India, is the fact that comic books and writing for children (even in English) can be a dynamic site of contestation and productive tension. Ironically, the 2004 catalogue uses a quote from *Eve's* magazine (of January 1993) as a publicity line: it describes Pai as the 'Disney of India'—quietly ignoring the capitalist, exploitative and consumerist ideology that informs and drives Disney's culture industry.

Partha Chatterjee's (1986) influential account of the nationalist dis-course has demonstrated how the nationalist movement served bour-geois ideology and interests. What this discourse did was project a certain pan-Indian identity, in which *every* Indian was oppressed by the colonial ruler. A homogenization of classes and castes was achieved in such a nationalist project of constructing one INDIA. This construction elided crucial differences between classes, regions and castes, and was predicated, in a large way, on the image of the woman. Reforms, political struggles, nationalist consciousness, all utilized a certain pre-Islamic, Vedic Hindu, middle-class 'model' of woman who was projected/deified as an *Indian* woman (see Tharu and Niranjana 1996 for a detailed dis-cussion of the issue of gender in colonial and postcolonial India). Nationalist discourse automatically excluded, *under the sign of 'Indian'*, non-Aryan, working- and lower-class, 'lower'-caste people and cultures. In the case of the freedom struggle, for instance, the role of the 'lower' castes gets assimilated into that of the urban, middle-class upper-caste, Hindu role. Dayananda's efforts at assimilating 'untouchables' into Hinduism—specifically Brahminism, he is shown distributing the 'sacred thread' (# 624: n.p.)—are highlighted. Only *one* panel is allotted to showing Brahminical oppression of 'lower' castes, while the *assimilation* of these castes into mainstream Hinduism—there is no discussion of tribal/Dalit lifestyles at all—gets four.

ACK subtly extends the nationalist discourse of Indianness in its retellings of 'classic' tales by glorifying certain cultural practices, ideals of womanhood, and ideas of the 'nation'. Excluding other forms of Indian culture—I hesitate to use the term 'alternative'—*ACK*'s discourse legitimizes one dominant image/iconography of India.

One begins with the catalogue of titles *ACK* has developed over the years. The titles are organized into the following categories in the 2004 catalogue: 'Mythology', 'Teachers and Saints', 'Ancient Indian History', 'Monuments and Cities', 'Tales from the Epics and the Vedas', 'Medieval Indian History', 'Regional Classics', 'Folktales and Legends', 'Buddhist Tales', 'Sanskrit Classics', 'Jain Tales', 'Freedom Struggle', 'Sikh History', 'Panchatantra' and 'Hitopadesha', 'Makers of Modern India', 'Saints of Modern India', 'Travellers to India'. In addition it has the following two series: Pancharatna Series (stories from Indian mythology, epics, Jatakas, and accounts of freedom fighters, 'brave Rajputs' and 'great rulers of India', among others) and Special Issues (on the Ramayana, Jesus Christ, Sanskrit plays, Indian emperors, Buddhist tales, etc.). The 1986 catalogue had some interesting series too: 'Poets and Musicians (seven titles), and titles organized around dynasties/communities: 'The Rajputs', 'The Marathas', 'Great Women of India', 'Scientists and Doctors', 'The Mughals and their Adversaries', among others. Several of these are missing from the 2004 catalogue, suggesting that they are not being reprinted.

Perhaps the most dominant image of India projected in the series is that of Vedic, pre-Islamic India. The tag-line for the new runs of the *ACK* titles is 'Route to your roots'. It is therefore crucial to understand two things here: (*i*) the exact nature of the 'roots' to which one can return; and (*ii*) the problematic notion that one can return to some kind of uncontaminated 'past'. Often, the past/roots turn out to be a Vedic Indian one. So was there a pre-Vedic civilization at all? Was there a southern Indian history worth mentioning as 'roots'? The term 'roots' somehow conflates with northern Indian, Hindu originary moments in this discourse of public culture.

India, then, is more often than not reduced to Hindu culture and identity. For instance, India is described as 'the land of Rishis' (# 599, *Vishwamitra*). The catalogue for 2004 shows a montage of covers from various titles—every one of them is from a title that deals with Hindu mythology/history/legend, with only one exception from the Jataka tales. One can identify, easily, Krishna, Arjuna, Meerabai, Shankara, and some Brahmin priests on the covers. Inside the catalogue, the series' role is described thus: 'inspiring interest in India's great heritage'. Taken in conjunction, the three quotes/descriptives suggest that a great 'Indian' heritage is an ancient Hindu one of Rishis, Hindu gods and saints alone. It is significant that the very first title in the series was *Krishna* (# 501), and three of the first 10 issues were stories from the Ramayana tradition (*Hanuman*, # 502; *The Sons of Rama*, # 503; *Rama*, # 504). Most of the titles in *ACK* foreground this sense of heritage by having a legend on the cover: 'Amar Chitra Katha: the glorious heritage of India.' What is interesting is that some titles belonging to another series within *ACK* do *not* carry this legend. *Babasaheb Ambedkar* (# 611) and *Sultana Razia* (# 725), one dealing with the life of a reformer/thinker and critic of Hinduism from an 'untouchable' caste, and the other with the life of a *Muslim woman* (albeit a queen), do not carry this legend. Are these figures and moments not a part of India's glorious heritage? The omission is worth noting.

Hinduism is swiftly merged into 'Indian', even when speaking of non-Hindu figures as in the *Guru Nanak* issue (# 590). The story of *Jesus Christ* (# 10003), writes Cardinal Lawrence R. Picachy (President, Catholic Bishops' Conference of India) in his prefatory note, 'is another witness to the general truth that the life of Christ is a restatement of the permanent values of human living, the brotherhood of man and the need for charity and right action in society'. It concludes with: 'Whether one is a Christian or not, one cannot fail to be drawn to this man who spoke of goodness with wisdom and power, and brought comfort and peace to men of goodwill.' Here Christ's teachings are projected less as a separate (non-Hindu) faith than as a 'general restatement'. What or whose faith Christ's teaching *re*-states is left ambiguous. Presumably the ideal of universal human values is far less threatening than the notion of a non-Hindu culture/faith. In *Chaitanya Mahaprabhu* (# 631), the comment on Chaitanya's vision in the prefatory note is as follows: 'Chaitanya not only stemmed the tide of conversion to Islam, but also provided a new life force to Hindu religion.' In the case of the reformer Narayana Guru (# 403), the ideal of a casteless society is transformed into a vision which is 'universal in nature'. Here again, the critique of Hinduism implicit in Narayana Guru's vision is translated as 'universal', so that it gets blunted *as* critique. In *Shankar Dev* (# 229), the teacher-saint's greatest achievement is described thus:

> But for the 'Ekasharana Dharma', the Vaishnava movement initiated by him in Assam, the several tribal communities of that region would never have been drawn into the mainstream of Hindu society. (Inside front cover, Prefatory note)

'Separatist' movements (such as Guru Nanak's, which sought to create a separate Sikh faith) are either (*i*) extensions/offshoots of Hinduism; or (*ii*) secular faiths. That is, they are not accorded a status as the totally/wholly 'other' of/to Hinduism. In the prefatory note to *Rama*, the editor writes:

> Ramayana is an integral part of our heritage such that our apparent diversities are reflected in slightly differing versions written in various languages. The Ramayana of Kamban, Tulsidas, Kirtivas and Tunchan, are variations of the same theme. (# 504)

Nowhere in *Guru Gobind Singh* (# 588) is the *break* from Hinduism mentioned.

Titles such as Savitri, Shakuntala, Rani of Jhansi or Vikramaditya have just the title on the cover. However, there is a significant variation in the case of other titles. *Kannagi* (# 666) has as its tag-line the following legend: 'Based on a great classic of Tamil Nadu.' *Subramania Bharati* (# 708) carries the tag-line 'The Story of the Poet-Patriot of Tamilnadu.' *Bikal the Terrible* (# 667) is identified/tagged as 'Folktales from Madhya Pradesh'. *Noor Jahan* (# 701) has 'the most powerful Mughal Queen' inscribed under the title. The prefatory note to *Shivaji* (# 564) expends considerable space describing Mughal/Islamic cruelty, stating: 'even the zeal of such fighting races as the Rajputs had been suppressed by centuries of slavery under Mughal rule' (inside front cover, prefatory note). *Kochunni* (# 173) has this line as subtitle: 'the beloved bandit of Kerala'. The prefatory note to this tale states:

The man who made it [Kayamkulam town in Kerala] famous was neither a poet, nor a statesman or a soldier. He was a Muslim bandit called Kochunni. (Inside front cover, prefatory note)

Why are Muslim or regional figures highlighted even in the title/on the cover? And why does the issue of Bankim Chandra's *Ananda Math* (# 655) gloss over the novel's anti-Muslim sentiments? There is, I suggest, a distinct categorization at work here, where 'national', 'Indian' figures are not named/identified, but regional ones are. Vikramaditya or Savitri are pan-Indian: indeed, it is not necessary to identify the 'category' at all. 'Indian' is inscribed *over* and through these figures. On the other hand, regional characters or Muslim queens need to be described/captured in a term or phrase, or they may not be identifiable as 'Indian', perhaps? Even English-educated, urban Indian children would identify Shakuntala and Savitri as 'Indian', though in the case of Kannagi they require help with the identification. More significantly, in *Rama* (# 504) we are told:

This sublime theme is embodied in the character of Rama and Sita—the highest ideals of 'man' and woman'.

Thus two figures from Hindu mythology come to stand in for the entire human universe. In *Dayananda* (# 624), we are told: 'to give a wide base to his teachings, he traveled all over the country and addressed a number of meetings' (p. 26). The next panel shows Dayananda looming over many people. The caption runs: 'He won unprecedented ovations and a large following in the Punjab.' Around the enlarged figure of Dayananda in the panel we have 'Amritsar, Lahore, Multan, Gurdaspur, Jullundar' inscribed (p. 27). 'All over the country' in the previous panel does not provide a listing of places. But the cities/towns of the Punjab are detailed. Somehow, 'country' gets compressed into one section of north India here. Further, as Srilata points out, in the attempt to construct a pan-Indian woman, 'the clothes of a local heroine from the south, say Kannagi, is very often like those of the clothes of heroines from the North, like Padmini of Chittoor' (1992: 69).

There are other codes that enable the construction of such a pan-Indian, Hinduized identity. The representation of 'Indian' heroes and heroines is invariably through an iconography of fair-complexioned, muscular men and ultra-feminine women. Visual representations in *ACK* have been inspired by Raja Ravi Verma's paintings, as critics have pointed out (Sircar 2000). The visual culture that *ACK* represents is an example of what Philip Lutgendorf terms 'intericonicity' (2003: 87), where *ACK* art must be seen in relation with poster images and other visual media such as television, cinema, and even personal photograph albums. Kajri Jain has argued that 'calendar art' and 'bazaar art', the visuals in comic books, advertising, hoardings, cinema, television and packaging are all about 'framing pictures'. Such visuals 'impart different valencies to the image as they traverse it' (2003: 34. Also see Uberoi 2003 on calendar art, and Balamani 2003 on family/personal photograph albums). *ACK* combines aesthetic frames with ethical and commodity values. There is the attempt at an aesthetic appeal, while catering to commercial purposes. The highly decorative surfaces of the image in *ACK* books on gods—with a focus on the face and expression—suggests this imbrication where the sacred is combined with decorative styling. Rama's physiognomy (# 504) is more often than not cast in beatific expressions, for instance. (For the changing iconography of Rama, from benignity to 'ugra' after 1992 and the Babri Masjid controversy, see Anuradha Kapur's brilliant 1993 essay. For recent studies in the iconology of nationalism, see Pinney [2003], Ramaswamy [2003] and Uberoi [2003], among others. The consumers of *ACK*, as noted earlier, are English-educated urban children. It might be interesting to see how they respond to *ACK* visuals and such popular art forms as calendars or posters.)

The only figures who are dark-skinned are the evil *rakshasas/asuras*. All gods are fair, and all evil comes in dark colours. There is a significant difference in physiognomies and bodies too. Asuras and rakshasas are grotesque in appearance, as opposed to the well-formed 'devas'. They are also cannibals, according to tales such as *Ghatotkacha* (# 61). Since devas are symbolic of virtue, it follows that forms of embodiment—such as well-formed and ugly—are codes for moral states (as I have argued about the evil monster in the superhero comic book). The moral is mapped onto a north Indian body (since a fair complexion is associated mostly with north Indians), and contrasts with the darker-skinned, evil *asuras*, who synecdochically stand for the south Indians. Sandhya Rao has noted that in the Akbar–Birbal tale, 'The Most Beautiful Child in Agra' (*Birbal the Clever*, # 558), the dark-complexioned, thick-lipped, langoti-clad child is from the 'lower' caste, and he is poor, ugly and undesirable (Rao 2000: 34). The 'villains' are always with grimacing, frightened, lustful or contorted faces, while heroes carry beatific, quiet and smiling expressions. Subtle codes in the narrative persuade us to read the portrayed situations in specific ways. Thus in *Abhimanyu* (# 533) Kaurava warriors are described as 'forgetting the code of war conduct' (n.p.), though Arjuna's mode of killing Bheeshma (by concealing himself behind Shikandin, once a woman, is glossed over in *Bheeshma*, # 534). Thus the iconography of the Pandavas as true, honest heroes is retained, while the Kauravas are slandered. J.R.D. Tata, the business genius, is described on the cover as 'the quiet conqueror' (# 735), linking, subtly, martial and corporate exploits (as worthy of emulation?).

Such visual representations code a certain ideology about aesthetic appeal and the caste system. The visual representation of humans/gods in *ACK* thus suggests a distinct bias in favour of the north Indian cultural/racial ethos and contexts. As Sandhya Rao puts it: 'in the world of the ACKs, physical beauty is paramount, and anyone who does not possess it is ugly and therefore wicked' (2000: 34). Hanuman and the apes in popular representations (see Lutgendorf 2003 on poster art and Pritchett 1995 on *ACK*) seem to be hybrids: ape-like in appearance, but clothed and capable of human speech. What is important is that there is a distinct anthropomorphing in representations not only of animals, but also of gods and *rakshasa*s. Wearing animal skins or jewellery, they may possess superhuman traits and strengths, but they are also shown with human expressions: animals crying, gods with faces twisted in anger, and the *asura* with a maniacal grin are common features of *ACK* comic books.

One index of the influence of such visual rhetoric on children can be gleaned from Gotham Comics. In its Digest Issue # 10 (2002), Gotham Comics announced the winners of a superhero contest. The first prize went to a 16-year-old who created 'Lion'. The superhero is described thus:

> Discovering a mysterious golden belt in a jungle temple in Central India, our hero Raj is transformed by the power of the spirit Bagh Dev (Lion God) … Raj … the Lion now dedicates his life to fighting crime and injustice throughout India. (n.p.)

Another superhero created was 'Cain', who, with an ability to extend his roots over considerable distances, was dedicated to saving wildlife. Other superheroes designed by Indian children included: 'Sher Khan' (an 'animal warrior'); Garudaman (the son of Hanuman); Balzabar (the 'natural guardian of the Himalayas … choosing non-violence he protects the mountains from it's [sic] human defilers'); 'Surya'; and 'Captain India'.

The combination of Indian/Hindu mythology and Western superhero traditions is quite interesting.

In terms of gender, the ideology is clearly patriarchal. Women are temptresses (Menaka, Rambha), in need of protection (Sita), or upholders of (Hindu) ideals and customs (Shakuntala, Padmini of Chittoor, Savitri, Uloopi). Draupadi is described with a kind of left-handed compliment: 'the total woman; complex yet feminine' (# 542, prefatory note). In *Savitri* (# 511), a narratorial comment is made: 'then to the growing girl came the knowledge of pain ... of separation'. In Savitri's speech balloon in the same panel, we see this: 'Father! My friends say a girl must marry and go away! I will not go anywhere' (n.p.). Later she tells her father with lowered eyes: 'All right, father! I shall do what you say' (n.p.). While Savitri's tale is one of chastity/devotion-as-virtue, the visual representation in the comic emphasizes her beauty and virtue in almost every panel, an *ACK* hallmark. Even heroines such as the Rani of Jhansi are 'muted'. For instance, the Rani is described thus (# 539): 'She was not aggressive by nature and it was only when the British threatened to annex her small kingdom that she took up arms.' This prefatory note is to prevent any interpretation of the Rani as a non-feminine figure (since aggression is the male's province). She is aggressive only when aggravated—otherwise she would be a typical Indian woman, docile and quiet. And, of course, they are good mothers/daughters/wives. The Rani of Jhansi is shown performing the 'haldi-kumkum ceremony', thereby suggesting that she may be a warrior, but she does not abandon her 'spiritual' or religious duties (p. 17; it can of course be argued that such a representation seeks to present as complete a picture of the Rani's life as possible—domestic, familial and political). The fact that Chand Bibi is a woman before she is a ruler is constantly emphasized. When she appears on the ramparts of her Ahmednagar fort, a soldier remarks: 'how beautiful she looks' (# 685: 7). Noor Jahan is described as 'famous for her beauty and wisdom' (# 701, prefatory note). *Sultana Razia*, after detailing her abilities and political competence through the text, chooses to end the tale of her life with the historian Ferishta's quote: 'She had no fault but that she was a woman' (# 725: 31). Mirabai is described as 'the true Hindu wife' (# 535, n.p.).

The Tamil tale of Kannagi comes from Ilango's *Silappadikaram*. All the first images of Kannagi show her with lowered eyes, like a 'good' Indian/Hindu bride. The first few pages show her to be dutiful in her various roles. When the husband suggests that they take a walk by the river, she responds with 'as you wish, my lord' (*Kannagi*, 666: 4). And when he announces that she shall be the mistress of the new house, her response is that of a daughter-in-law: 'does that mean we have to leave your parents?' (p. 3). Eventually, through a series of disasters, she proves her feminine 'heroism'—often through the tears of a 'wronged woman'—and a temple is built to honour her 'divinity' (p. 32). Two things are emphasized through the tale: her devotion to her husband, and the purity which borders on the divine. The deification of the heroine, as *Kannagi* demonstrates—is also the result of a social gaze. Patriarchal Hindu society approves of Kannagi's devotion to her husband-god. The deification is an acknowledgement that she has been a good wife. By fighting for her marriage (she waits for her husband, even though he has gone away to another woman), she proves her purity and fidelity. By bursting into tears (frequently) she fulfils her 'role' as a weak woman. By demonstrating heroism—she accuses the King of being 'unjust' (p. 25)—she shows how a virtuous woman need have no weapons other than her purity. In each of these three cases, the *ACK* focuses on her purity.

The woman-centric tales selected emphasize the feminine in Rani of Jhansi, Chand Bibi, Ahilya Bai Holkar and Kannagi. What is projected as the 'Indian' woman is invariably, then, a particular kind of woman who, even when she is ruler/soldier, remains a devoted mother/wife, and whose sense of duty always involves religious rituals, mother- or wife-hood, and fidelity to the family. In *Dayananda*, when he sees the Maharaja of Jodhpur with Nanhijan, a dancing girl, the speech attributed to Dayananda goes thus: 'What! A street-walker in a lion's den' (p. 29). The derogatory label attached to the woman—but no stigma attached to her male patron—is of course not commented upon, just as the treatment of Ekalavya was not commented upon in another tale.

Sanjay Sircar points out that *ACK* has a 'preponderance of historical themes, more mythic than folktale material and more emphasis on traditional narratives than on modern original novels' (2000: 35). However, the selection of stories is itself open to ideological critique. For instance, Anant Pai has consistently refused to do an issue on the newest popular goddess on the Hindu scene: Santoshi Ma. Pai's argument is that the theology of Santoshi Ma is retrograde: she punishes her most faithful worshipper, and is a punitive god (Pritchett 1995: 80; the *Adarsh Chitra Katha* comic book series from Argus Enterprises, modelled after *ACK*, did have an issue devoted to Santoshi Mata, # 15, where she is described as a 'universal mother').

There are other, subtle modes of constructing identity through elision. In narrating the story of Ekalavya, for example, there is no comment on the injustice of Drona's action in asking for the archer's thumb. Instead we are told: Ekalavya is 'steadfast in the path of truth' (# 337: 17–22). The fact that a Dalit boy has been deprived of his crucial thumb—effectively ruining his career so that an upper-caste boy can achieve glory—by a Brahmin is erased out of the tale. In subsequent works, there is a glossing over of the discriminatory and oppressive character of the caste system in Hinduism. Yudhishthira tells Sanjaya: '[every] varna ... should adhere to its own dharma ... [If anybody] takes recourse to the dharma of another caste ... his conduct is thoroughly reprehensible' (# 381: 28). In *Ghatotkacha* (# 61), Bheema and his family leave Hidimba (his wife) and their young son, Ghatotkacha, in the forest and proceed on their way. There is no comment made on the manner in which Bheema absolves himself of any responsibility for his wife/family. As Frances Pritchett points out, *ACK* seems to be 'claiming exemption from its usual concerns ... to take seriously its "lasting impact on impressionable minds"' (p. 89).

ACK launched 'The Epic of New India: The March to Freedom', a six-volume edition in 1986. This included *The Birth of the Indian National Congress* (# 348), *A Nation Awakes* (# 350), *The Saga of Indian Revolutionaries* (# 360), *The Call for Swaraj* (# 364), *The Salt Satyagraha* (# 368), and *The Tryst with Destiny* (# 372). There is now one bumper issue (# 10) titled *The Story of the Freedom Struggle*. The very fact that the freedom struggle described is termed 'epic' has serious ideological connotations. To begin with, India has two major *Hindu* epics: the Ramayana and the Mahabharata. By sliding the freedom struggle under the same rubric, there is a subtle imbrication of the freedom struggle with the *Hindu* epics, which is then called *Indian*. The shift from freedom struggle to epic to Hinduism to 'Indian' is a problematic ideological move. In *Dayananda*, there is one panel where British officials are shown to be conspiring against Dayananda. It is described thus: 'The British who were suspicious of the Swami's role in the rise of Indian nationalism ...' (p. 30). Dayananda, the text has repeatedly emphasized, had preached a return to the Vedas. There is only one reference to his objection to alien rule prior to this (in one panel on p. 26). Then, suddenly, his suggestion of the return to the Vedas becomes 'Indian nationalism'. As subaltern historians such as Gyanendra Pandey (1995) have pointed out, there is a subtle 'equation of the history of the Hindus with the history of India' (p. 369), and *ACK* may be consciously or unconsciously echoing this theme.

The tale is also careful enough to point out that the Congress, when founded, was an 'organization of English-educated loyal subjects of the crown' (Bumper Issue, 1997: 15). There are other problematic moves the tale makes. Rand's actions in quarantining people suspected of carrying plague are described as 'brutal' (p. 17). The 1857 'mutiny', we are told, 'grew into a revolt [in which] our farmers, traders, professionals, rajas, nawabs all, all joined the struggle against the British' (p. 9). The 1857 events were restricted to parts of north India. Further, 'all' did not join the 'rebellion'. Finally, numerous rajas—from Wanarputy to Scindia—pledged allegiance to the British. By no stretch of the historical imagination can 1857 be read as a struggle where 'all India' participated, though it did bear signs of a popular struggle (Mukherjee 1984).

The discussion on Savarkar, known for his description of the events of 1857 as 'the first war of Independence', the glorification of Mangal Pandey, armed struggle against the British, *and* the propagation of Hindutva, is silent on the last one, focusing instead on his struggle and deportation (Bumper Issue # 10: 41–42). Indeed, the issue on Savarkar (# 309) edits out everything except his 'In the Andamans' (the subtitle of the book). The Bhagat Singh issue is at pains to prove that 'Bhagat Singh and his comrades were not blood-thirsty, trigger-happy terrorists. They were waging a war against a relentless colonial power' (# 234, inside front cover). In the 1986 catalogue, 'Indian Revolutionaries' listed five issues: *Bahga Jatin* (# 156), *Bhagat Singh* (# 234), *Chandra Shekhar Azad* (# 142), *Rash Behari Bose* (# 262) and *Veer Savarkar* (# 309). Subhash Chandra Bose is slotted in 'Makers of Modern India' rather than in 'Indian Revolutionaries'. Nehru and Gandhi got their issues much later. Rajaji and Patel do not yet have their own issues.

There are two major gaps, as Pritchett has noted (1995: 95), in the 'makers of Modern India' series (which includes Vivekananda, Ambedkar, Vidyasagar, Tilak, Shastri, Gandhi ['the early years'], Narayan, Jagadis Chandra Bose and Nehru). The list does not have a *single* woman. The exclusion of Sarojini Naidu, Kasturba, Durgabai Deshmukh and Vijaylakshmi Pandit is truly strange. It also does not have a single Muslim leader/thinker on it. On the cover of the bumper issue (# 10), *The Story of the Freedom Struggle*, we have a montage. In the centre, there is the profile of a hanged man, white against a red background. Around it, arranged in four 'panels', are: the Jallianwallah Bagh shooting scene, Subhash Chandra Bose taking a salute, Lokmanya Tilak in court, and Gandhi preparing salt at Dandi. There is no Muslim leader or south Indian on the cover. In the course of the narrative, the following figures are mentioned and stories detailed: Mangal Pande, Vasudeo Balwant Phadke, A.O. Hume, the Chapekar brothers, Lokmanya Tilak, Bipin Chandra Pal, Tagore, Surendranath Banerjee, Kaliprasanna Dasgupta, Aurobindo, Subramania Bharati, Prafulla Chaki, Khudiram Bose, Hemchandra, Savarkar, Rash Behari Bose, Bagha Jatin, Bhagat Singh, Nehru, Sarojini Naidu, Surya Sen, Chandrashekar Azad, Subhash Chandra Azad, Subhash Chandra Bose and Gandhi. The only Muslim leader shown is Jinnah, and that too as a dour, uncompromising man who propagated the 'Islam in Danger' and 'Two nations' slogans (pp. 66–67). There is no mention of any other Muslim leader. There is mention of the Kakori conspiracy of 1925, with Ramprasad Bismil and Asfaqullah (p. 53). The exclusion of figures such as Sayyid Ahmad Khan, Khan Abdul Gaffar Khan, Maulana Azad and Zakir Husain is a serious omission. As for south India, Subramania Bharati is the only representative. The editor's note at the *end* mentions Alluri Sitarama Raju.

While it may seem churlish to point only to exclusions, these are, I believe, omissions that must be taken cognizance of in the larger context of subaltern historian arguments regarding the elitist, Hinduized historiography of the freedom struggle.

The comic book as an integral component of public culture, as I have demonstrated, becomes a vehicle for ideologies and cultural opinions. Like the cinema or the television serial, the comic book conveys particular images of race, gender, class and caste. This chapter has only dealt with two genres. Much more work needs to be done with other genres such as the horror, adventure, war, and the science fiction comic book. Consumers of these texts—mainly children and young adults—while reading entertaining stories of monsters, gods, demons and superheroes, also imbibe the ideologies that inform them.

❏ NOTES

1. Amanda Macdonald has analysed the link between the verbal image and the graphic image—what she calls a 'graphic echo of the image line' in Hergé's Tintin corpus. See Macdonald (1998).
2. For an interesting reading of the subversive potential of superhero and other comic books, see Jeff Williams (1994).

❏ FURTHER READING

Barker, Martin. 1989. *Comics: Ideology, Power and the Critics*. Manchester: Manchester University Press.

Inge, Thomas M. 1990. *Comics as Culture*. Jackson and London: University Press of Mississippi.

Sabin, Roger. 1993. *Adult Comics: An Introduction*. London: Routledge.

Saraceni, Mario. 2003. *The Language of Comics*. New York and London: Routledge.

Savage, W. William, Jr. 1990. *Comic Books and America, 1945–1954*. Norman and London: University of Oklahoma Press.

4

Cabinet Culture
THE
MUSEUM

This chapter looks at a significant feature of contemporary public culture: the museum. It concerns itself not only with the museum's ways of ordering objects (artifacts, consumer products, lives), but also with the modes of perception, reception and interpretation of these objects. That is, it concerns itself with the cultural politics of display.

In the West, there has always been a close association between the museum and the projection of a national identity. The first national museum was the British Museum (1753). The first public museum in the USA was the Charleston museum, in South Carolina (1773). In 1793 the Louvre museum declared itself as the 'Museum of the Republic' (the Louvre really marks a turning point in the culture of museumization and displaying—the collection becomes a public display). India has various kinds of museums: the National Museum of Natural History (New Delhi), the Rail Transport Museum (New Delhi), the Birla Science and Technology Museum (Kolkata), the Visveswaraya Industrial and Technological Museum (Bangalore), the National Children's Museum (1963), and the National Gallery of Modern Art (New Delhi, 1954) are among the larger ones. In addition there are State museums in various states in India, private museums, university museums (such as the Bharat Kala Bhavan at Banaras Hindu University), the Archaeological Survey of India (ASI) site museums and historic monuments, local self-government museums such as Allahabad or Sanskar Kendra (Ahmedabad), and the various state archives. Specialized museums include ones such as the Calico Museum of Textiles (Ahmedabad), or the Shreyas Museum of Gujarat Folk Arts (Ahmedabad), the National Defence Academy Museum (Pune), the National Crafts Museum (New Delhi), the National Gallery of Modern Art (New Delhi), and the Asutosh Museum of Indian Art (Kolkata), among others.

The term 'museum' comes from the Greek *museion*, meaning the temple of the Muses, the gods and goddesses of arts and science. The 'musaion' founded by Ptolemaies I (who died in 283 BC) in Alexandria was the centre for learning and scholarship in the ancient Greek civilization. The 'musaion' was located in the centre of the town, and was housed in a huge building. Between the 9th and 12th centuries the museum was almost always a house of relics, with a predominantly religious function. The Church stocked relics and used these to influence the masses. Antiquarianism, which concretized in the form of the Antiquarian Societies in Britain from 1572, represented a curious mix of historical theory and the aesthetics of the souvenir. In the 18th and 19th centuries 'curiosity cabinets' and societies of scientific knowledge focused on collecting specimens from around the world as part of the European Enlightenment's quest for knowledge. The museum as we recognize it today is a 19th-century phenomenon, when privately owned collections were made 'public'. By the 20th century museums had moved from being private collections for private viewing to collections for public viewing.

The Indian Murdaghar, Ajayabghar and Jadughar were similar collections (some of these terms are still current). Early Sanskrit texts such as *Vishnudharmottara* (6th century) refer to 'chitraśālās'. Such *chitrashalas*, *vithis* and *alekhyagrihas* attached to the mansions of the privileged and the royalty were not open to public viewing. Sanskrit plays such as Bhasa's *Pratima* and Sriharsa's *Naisadhiyacarita* speak of permanent and mobile exhibition galleries attached to royal courts. The *pata-chitras* (scroll paintings) were intended for public enjoyment and instruction in ancient and medieval India. The relics of the Buddha were collected and preserved inside the stupas, thus bestowing a certain 'museum effect' (Svetlana Alpers' [1991] term, to which I shall return later), with the stupa itself functioning as a treasure house. Devotees would travel to see these relics, which thus become instances of public display (Bhatnagar 1999; Morley 1981). The fairs, melas and exhibitions, so common to rural India for centuries, are versions of what we now call 'exhibition-cum-sale'.

The first Indian museum in its present form was founded in Calcutta in 1814 under the aegis of the Asiatic Society of Bengal, with Dr Nathaniel Wallich as honorary curator. The Victoria Museum (now in Karachi, Pakistan) was set up in 1851 and the Trivandrum Museum in 1857. Today there are some 400 museums in India.

The cultural study of museums involves reading the museum at two levels: the physical structure of the museum (architecture, display techniques, organization, modes of viewing, visitor movement, period rooms), and the discourse of the museum. This second level is the *narrative* of museumization itself. Museums need to be treated as sites of cultural or national narratives, of political or pedagogical projects. Thus the Indian museum of the second half of the 20th century must be seen as inheriting not only the tradition of the chitrashala of ancient India, but also the colonial technology of collection and display (Cohn 1997: 76–105), since the India Museum in London and European models provided the paradigm for post-1947 museums in India. We need to look at the governing ideology—of feudalism, of royal power, of colonialism, of nationalism—that informs the collection, display and popularization of certain forms of art and artifacts.

People both perceive—as in 'see'—and experience museums and exhibitions (I use the term interchangeably here, fully aware of the variations between them. There exist numerous kinds of exhibitions: permanent gallery, temporary or periodic, special or thematic, educational and circulating). What is common to both is the discourse, poetics and politics of *display*. What we consume in the museum, or when acquiring a model/replica/simulation of a monument/sculpture/painting in the museum store/shop, is not a material object alone, but its symbolic meaning.

Broadly, a cultural study of the museum as public culture looks at the four structuring concepts of museums: the object, the context of its display, the public it purports to serve, and the reception of the objects. All museums are built around certain ideas and ideologies of these four elements (Sherman and Rogoff 1994: xii–xiv). A study of the public culture of the museum and the exhibition consequently addresses four major areas.

First, the political ideologies informing the choice of objects, and their classification as 'art' or 'utensils' or 'sacred relic'. What exhibits are displayed? Are they adequate representations of the complexity of that society? Is there something of every cultural ethos and context in this public space of consumption? Do all groups have equal practical as well as theoretical rights to what is displayed—do they contribute to the displays or are they passive consumers of whatever is displayed? Is the 'heritagization of space' (Kevin Walsh's term, 1992: 70–93) central to the democratization process of equal representation for all citizens? Does the artifact 'captured' and 'museumized' adequately reflect the functional and productive processes that create(d) the tool/object? The object in a museum is dissociated from all its original functions when placed in the display cabinet or the period room. Hence the selection, classification and presentation of objects within the museum suggests the political ideology of the present time rather than the time of the object itself.

Second, studies of the context of the museum need to draw attention to: (*i*) the complexity of *relations* between corporate sponsorship, museums and the national/global economies that frame them; and (*ii*) the actual *forms* of museum exhibitions—from banners to frames, labels to layouts, display cases to invitation cards, as agents of ideological persuasion and technologies of framing the museum experience. Public museums exemplify a 'statist' or 'official' approach to culture itself.[1] Is culture being used and appropriated as an 'educator' for social engineering? Museums in India invariably see themselves as educators, and hence the kinds of cultural artifacts presented, and the ways in which these are presented, are of critical importance. We need to carefully isolate the elements that go into making this public space a space for the public.

Third, it is important to see how the museum addresses its public. The museum's strategies of display involve the assumptions of the community or public it addresses. Thus, in India, the visitor to the museum is already aware, to a greater or lesser extent, of Indian history through school textbooks, TV programmes, and such. Further, the visitor is also aware of themes such as 'unity in diversity', local history, or concepts of national unity popularized through mass media when s/he comes to the museum—there really are no totally 'uninformed' visitors. Since questions of the public involve questions of subjectivity and experience, we need to look at the ways in which the museum organizes the *museum experience*. What are the techniques of behaviour management in museums? We need to remember that the museum is a much more formalized arrangement of objects than the fair or the *mela*. The silence that the museum demands, the 'do not touch' signs, demarcatory ropes and cordons, the security personnel (and, in the Western world, video cameras) are as much modes of regulation as they are structures of seeing. Thus, what do the new modes of museum experience, such as the 'hands on' technique, mean? The visitor is directed along certain routes, prodded into pausing at certain spots. Thus highlighted displays, free standing sculptures, niche mounted paintings, extra security arrangement for particular objects, and such techniques common to all museums highlight the significance of that particular object for the visitor. Further, the visitor is invited to explore in certain sequences through maps, signboards, directions and named collections. The overall environment of the museum seems to acquire greater importance than the artifacts inside. There is a certain ceremonial and ritual element to the museum experience: the organization of the building with its high ceilings, the marked-off spaces of exhibits, the silence as necessary to contemplation and learning (Duncan 1995: 10). In sharp contrast to fairs where exhibition and commerce are closely aligned, the museum discourages commercial transactions except in *designated* areas.[2] The museum shop is integral to the display, and is frequently attached as an annex, or an extension of the display areas. The purchase of souvenirs is integral to museum visits. The guide leaflet to Westminster Abbey, London, provides a footnote on the last page. The note, distinguished typographically from the main text by a demarcatory line, reads: 'As you leave by the west door be sure to visit the Abbey Bookshop. There are many interesting things for sale.' A place of worship, a museum, and a merchandizing outlet, all rolled into one! The British Museum advertises *five* different shops on its website (http://www.britishmuseum.co.uk/default.asp, 6 May 2004). The monument souvenir shop is the commodification of simulated heritage and history, and is central to the artificial modes of memorialization (Stewart 1984). The past, and cultural histories, are now mediated by the market. The museum with its (i) information techniques, classificatory regime and showcasing of 'heritage' and 'culture'; (ii) the shop merchandizing artifacts; and (iii) spaces of tourist visit, the summer 'treat' for children, the site of leisure trips, is situated at the intersection of three crucial discourses and contexts: nationalism and cultural identity formation, consumerism and commodification, and leisure-tourism.

Fourth, questions of the public address of museums cannot be separated from the reception of this address. The museum constructs (wo)man as both subject and object of knowledge. The space of representation of the museum—in anthropology, history, art—constructs the visitor as situated at the end of evolutionary development. The visitor is seeing the past while herself/himself situated at the culmination point of this process of development. The exhibitionary practices rely on this invisible narrative whereby we perceive our past as *where we came from*. The visitor is thus at a spatio-temporal vantage point from which to command a view of the past. The primitive, the tribal, the rural are taken to represent an earlier (even uncontaminated) stage of today's civilization. How do members of these cultures react to such niches of their culture, made available for general consumption? Does it in any way reinforce the subject–object relation where the tribal is always the *knowable* for the urban *knower*? What is the reception of such 'objects' as tribal art by urban consumers and the purveyors of ethnic fashions or politically correct citizens?

Fliers, guide books, occasional papers, documents, brochures, tracts, websites embody the ways in which a museum represents itself. All these, together, organize the space of the museum. This is the *discourse* of the museum, of the museological mode. The museum is a site of the complex interplay between social histories of collecting, classifying, displaying and entertaining—all of which are informed by certain governing assumptions, politics and ideologies. I have chosen to organize this study around certain elements of this discourse of the museum: museums and knowledge, display and viewing, the 'discipline' of the museum, and the museum-narrative. These four elements of the discourse incorporate the four structures of the museum—objects, context, public, reception.

Today the museum, with much of the entire floor plans, catalogues, information, visual images of the artifacts, voiceover commentaries and visitor services available online for free access, is visited even before actual, physical arrival. The experience of the museum, the viewing of the exhibits, must be seen as starting with this online exploration itself. It is therefore necessary to see the technology of museumization as beginning with such promotional material, which, along with the physical structure of the museum and the display, constitutes public culture. A metropolitan tourist now almost never visits a museum: s/he re-visits it, having already 'seen' it as a virtuality. The physical visit actualizes the virtual experience. Thus the Dastkari Haat Samiti creates craft maps of India, available for purchase even before one sets out to explore Indian culture. Here Indian heritage and crafts is already mapped, even before it is viewed in a museum. The museum-shopping experience has begun.

❏ MUSEUMS AND KNOWLEDGE

M.L. Nigam, former Director of the Salar Jung Museum, Hyderabad, opens his textbook, *Fundamentals of Museology* (1985 [1966]) thus:

> Museums today intend to play a lively role not only in collecting and preserving the art and culture of a particular region or community but also in presenting the social and cultural development of mankind by way of exhibiting the original evidence of man's creative genius and his control over nature. The collection and preservation of such material is one of their functions, no doubt most essential, but the *interpretation and use of this material for the*

advantage of modern society is no less a condition which the museums of the modern age are obliged to observe. (p. 1, emphasis added)

Note the theme of authoritative and reliable interpretation of objects in the museum. The definition and programme sketched out here links several themes in the discourse of the museum.

At its 1974 General Conference in Copenhagen, the International Council of Museums (ICOM) defined a museum as 'a non-profitmaking, permanent institution in the service of society and its development, and open to the public, which acquires, conserves, researches, communicates, and exhibits, for the purpose of study, education and enjoyment, material evidence of humankind and its development' (Bhatnagar 1999: ix; Morley 1981: 92–93). In the *Guide Book to Victoria Jubilee Museum, Vijaywada* the museum is referred to as a 'laboratory' (Avadhani 1976: n.p.). The Museum of Modern Art, New York, defines itself as a 'laboratory for the study of the ways in which modernity has manifested itself in the visual arts' (MOMA 1999: 16). Museums are the means by which a society represents its relationship to its own history. They seek to present a useable past, and therefore constitute an important mode of memorialization—committing to the *collective* memory and recording of social change. In fact the British Museum's special exhibition, 'Museum of the Mind: Art and Memory in World Cultures', 2003, described the museum itself as a 'receptacle of memory' (http://www. thebritishmuseum.ac.uk, 6 May 2004). Histories and critical studies of the Western museum (Bennett 1999 [1995]; Hooper-Greenhill 1992) pay attention to the ways in which the museum has worked at organizing, systematizing and presenting knowledge about the past. The term that is often associated with the museum, especially in the context of manuscript collections, is 'archive'. This term's connotations offer us the political dimensions of the culture of archivization. The term comes from 'archeion', which in Greek meant a house or address of the superior magistrate (called 'archons'). Because they were publicly recognized figures of authority, documents were filed in their houses. The archons were thus the guardians and interpreters of the documents. This act of guardianship and interpretation, which was localized and circumscribed to a particular space, became the archive. The museum, therefore, functions as the space of guardianship and first interpreter. The issue of authority—and of power and the politics of interpretation—is thus never far from the very idea of a museum or an archive. Appadurai and Breckenridge argue that in India, many museums do not provide sufficient information to the visitor, and s/he is 'free to assimilate new objects and arrangements into their own prior repertoires of knowledge, taste, and fantasy' (1992: 50). In India, ASI monuments, which are usually in the open, are frequently unlabelled, with little description available. In this instance Appadurai and Breckenridge are right to point out that the visitor is free to interpret the object in any which way. However, what is ignored here is the fact that formal *enclosed* museums do carry some information. Also, in the case of open-air monuments—and this is what Appadurai and Breckenridge ignore—labels and banners (information) are more often than not vandalized and erased. This erasure of knowledge is *as much* a part of public culture as the codification and presentation of knowledge. Stephen Greenblatt in fact points out that rarely do museums preserve attempts at vandalization or damage, preferring to 'repair' these as soon as possible. This, to him, is an important aspect of museum culture (1991: 41–43.) To me this damage to state-sponsored knowledge at ASI monuments and other such sites is a comment on civil society's negotiation with such knowledge technologies. Just as graffiti is integral to the public culture of a city, the wilful or playful distortion, erasure, or damage to knowledge-carrying structures is integral to display culture.

Adapting Ludmilla Jordanova's model (1989: 23), a study of the link between museums and knowledge in India involves (*i*) analysing the *darshanic* mode of gaze; (*ii*) the intersection of museum-gazing with mass media, Indian poster and calendar art; (*iii*) the structure of museums, their spatial arrangements and display methods; and (*iv*) the differences between ASI monument work, science museums, and state and private museums.

The museum plays an important role in the cultural ethos of a country through collecting, organizing, displaying and popularizing artifacts, the past, and the cultural heritage of the country, region, locality and peoples. Thus the museum is not simply a collection of material objects: it is a whole way of ordering and presenting culture and history itself, and, as such, has political implications. Thus the catalogue of 'masterpieces' from the National Museum, New Delhi, describing the stone sculptures of the Mauryan period, writes: 'It is possible that the exquisite polish or the bead-and-reel motif and acanthus motif were introduced in Indian art because of the cultural interaction with West Asia' (p. 18). (Cultures have always travelled and mixed [see Hoerder 2002: 117–22]). The comment seems to echo what the catalogue to the National Museum makes about medieval Indian art: 'the similarity in art forms could be explained in terms of migrations of people, bifurcation and expansion of families of traditional *sthapatis* or architects, and frequent intercourse amongst these kingdoms through cultural exchange and marriages' (p. 20). The visitor to the museum has to take for granted that such an interaction did indeed occur: the exergues, the 'outworks' that frame this reading of the past—the politics, the military, the economic, the cultural, the communitarian—are assumed to exist outside the frame of viewing, a frame decided on authoritatively by the 'expert'. Thus, digging for proof of a temple beneath Babri Masjid, the ASI experts 'discovered' satisfactory evidence at one 'level' in the ground. Hence the excavation is taken to have 'conclusively' proved the original 'heritage'. The point is mighty simple. Why did the excavation stop at *this* level? Why not dig further, beyond the so-called 'conclusive' evidence? What if, on further digging, we discover yet another heritage, a counter-cultural site? Public awareness is sought to be restricted to one level of proof. Counter-proofs or contestatory anecdotes/evidence that complicate the present acceptable and politically useful narrative cannot be made visible. Hence the narrative is told only up to the point where it is useful for ideological or political reasons. The tale is not pushed further back. Thus the reconstruction of the narrative of heritage is a socially symbolic and politically-mediated act. It is ultimately a matter of narrative interpretation sanctioned by a community of readers, who decide what is acceptable and what is not, what is beautiful and what is not.

In a post-9/11 and post-7/7 world, cultural identities are being constantly called into question and are assuming the status of the most significant narratives of our times. As the Parekh Report (2000) on the future of multiethnic Britain documents, there does exist an anxiety on the part of both whites and ethnic minorities about the shifting demographics, cultural mixing and political rights in contemporary Britain. In a world that is becoming increasingly multicultural, museums such as the British Museum, with its colonial ancestry, seek to be politically correct in the way it frames, defines, and offers up Other cultures. It is in this context that the British Museum declares: 'The museum is committed to improving *public awareness and appreciation* of Asian cultures of both past and present, and working with Asian communities in Britain' (http://www.thebritishmuseum.ac.uk, 6 May 2004, emphasis added). Ted Tanen, the executive director of the Indo-US Subcommission on Education and Culture, which is the principal organizer of the Festival of India, USA, said: 'India has been woefully neglected in this country and we hope that as a result of this festival, there will be many more opportunities and more people taking advantage of a better climate for exchange' (qtd. in Wallis 1994: 268). It appears as though the purpose of the festival was to showcase Indian culture as a preliminary to structuring beneficial political and business relations.

Here is the Introduction to a printed collection, *Masterpieces from the National Museum Collection*, published by the National Museum, New Delhi, in 1985:

> Out of this vast collection [of 150,000 works of art in archaeology, sculpture, paintings, epigraphy, numismatics, decorative arts, jewellery, textiles and anthropology], only 368 art objects have been chosen for this exhibition [originally scheduled for 1984] .... Every possible attempt has been made to *select some of the finest examples covering different areas of our collection.* (p. vii, emphasis added)

This statement needs to be read in conjunction with the Director's Foreword to the volume:

> While other institutions and commercial publishers have published their [the Museum's curatorial staff's] works, the National Museum has not undertaken publication of manuscripts and catalogues of Museum's art collections prepared by them. Those by outsiders were given preference. This anomaly needed to be rectified ... Keepers and Heads of Sections were assigned responsibilities to select the finest exhibits from their respective collections, keeping in view the limitation of space available in the special exhibition gallery. They were also asked to write catalogues, preceded by a short introduction, concerning their exhibits, assuring that their academic contributions will be published in their own names. It was felt that this catalogue would not only remain as a documentary evidence of this exhibition, but will also serve as a handbook for the general public. (n.p.)

The Introduction to the volume emphasizes two things: the physical constraints of exhibitions, and the process of selection. The second point is of particular interest here. Of the 150,000 items, a few hundred were selected as the 'finest' specimens. But what were the standards of comparison and measurement? Such questions remain unanswered, and one has to conclude that the cultural politics of display is an insidious one, since the end-result alone is available for viewing. Museums organize knowledge, evaluating some artifacts as historically, aesthetically and culturally significant, while relegating others to the margins. The narrative of the museum—its organization and display technologies, control over the sequence of arrangements and viewing—is what achieves the 'museum effect'.[3]

The display in the exhibition is thus governed by a set of principles known only to the curatorial staff. The selection is then passed off as a reliable and natural one in terms of appeal, significance and value. Like technology, where the user is rarely aware of, or made aware of, the actual mode of working of the product, there is a 'black box' of museum display.[4] The *expert* curator decides, using certain scales, that some objects are worthy of being selected as the 'finest' examples of an entire genre, category, history. The 'finest' is the climactic moment of a long historical narrative. The viewing is thus governed by principles set out and coordinated by the expert. The problem is further compounded because we are given information about the artifact alone, and not its position in the room/gallery, or the processes by which it was allocated its present space. Visitors, therefore, are *not* encouraged to see the room/display/gallery as either (i) a set of arbitrary decisions taken by 'experts'; or (ii) as a careful, theatrical and staged construction. We are asked to see the position of the artifact as *natural*—just there.

The exhibition becomes a venue where the curators' interests can be displayed and (perhaps) appreciated. There is no reference to the public which an institution of this kind is supposed to serve. How is the public to benefit from a particular mode of display? Is the selection of displays based on any perceived *need* of the viewing public? Neither of these questions even begins to be addressed here. Then there is the issue of *authoritative* writing on the actual items in the Museum's collections. The Director notes that 'outsiders' have published catalogues of these items. What or who constitutes the 'outsider' is not defined. The rhetorical tension posited here between 'outsider'/'insider' can very well be interpreted as a tension regarding rights of description/display between the insider-expert and the outsider-non-expert. It sets up a binary between the authorized wielder of knowledge and the non-authorized one.

Divisions and classifications, which are integral to the museum (Bennett 1999 [1995]: 2; McQuat 2001; Stewart 1984: 153), are based on specific decisions: the existing divisions between objects, the curatorial practices of a particular institution, the actual physical condition of the object, and the interests of the curator(s). Classification can be at several levels. The entire museum may be placed in a category such as 'natural history' or 'fine arts'. Then a museum may be organized around internal groups: pre-historic, 'modern', or styles (*kangra, bidri*). Finally, at the level of individual objects, labels and catalogues provide the context for reading that particular object. Classification imposes order and histories. This order or history is *external* to the object itself. Thus the various classifications of the object—as 'natural' or 'primitive', as distinguishing a particular school or style, as belonging to a specific locality or place—are the contexts in which the visitor views the object displayed. The categorization allows the collection, historical time, and events to be finite, encapsulated. Spatial divisions are based most often on conditions of visibility, narrative (the chronological sequence, for instance, within a particular set of objects), and the condition of objects (those which can be exposed to the atmosphere, for instance, or others such as parchment which require more controlled environments).

What must be kept in mind is that there is always an effective distance between the spectator and the curator. The Museum of Modern Art, New York, states: 'collections ... are all the result of discrete decisions made by individuals .... The result of this reflects the unfolding pattern of the Museum's history in a highly nuanced collection that is inflected and altered by the particular tastes and ideas of individual directors and curators, and the responses those tastes and ideas engender in their successors' (1999: 19). The exhibits, the narrative are all the effect of a considerable degree of 'discretion' and power. Curators are invariably 'invisible' to the spectator, and their presence is perceived as effect: the museum's narrative. The visitor thus sees the effect, and not the process of selection or the justification offered/debates conducted before the object is displayed. Curators are thus in positions of power, ordering the viewing for the visitor, knowledge obtained by the visitor is carefully constructed through such invisible practices. There is a clear distinction between the private, curatorial space of the museum and the public section.

A cultural study of the museum must pay attention to the ways in which curators, guide books, brochures and fliers issued by the museum, and the labelling, descriptions and presentations available to the visitor organize knowledge for public consumption. The museum as an emblem and organizing centre of public culture is enmeshed in issues of knowledge and power.

The history of the museum may be read against the grain. It can be fruitfully located within a history of practices and counter-practices of power relations that have structured/governed the acquisition, organization and dissemination of knowledge and objects. Thus, looking at museums in India from the second standpoint, we need to be aware of

(*i*)   the ways in which traditional fairs, exhibitions and wandering shows have been absorbed, rejected or modified by the arrival of the Western-type museums;

(*ii*)   the arrival of the Western mode of object acquisition, modes of taxonomy and classificatory regimes with the Asiatic Society, the India Museum (London, the last years of the 18th century), and such;

(*iii*) the political structures that informed and created the organizational networks that govern museum functioning. Thus the antecedents of the ASI, the ethnographic collection of materials by colonial Britain in India, are to be explored. Thus for example, the ASI, mapping its own origins, writes:

> No spectacular event inaugurated the birth of archaeological studies in India. It had a much humbler beginning. Sir William Jones, formed, on the 15th January, 1784 the Asiatic Society, an institution for enquiring among many other things, into the History ... the Antiquities, Arts, Sciences and Literatures of Greater India.
>
> Once started, the Society thrived rapidly and contributions commenced pouring in it from all quarters announcing new finds or new interpretations of materials already known. A journal, the *Asiatic Researches*, was started in 1788 to make public the results of these new efforts and a museum was set up in 1814 to house the objects collected by the society's workers. The start was made in Bengal which was soon followed up in other parts of India. (http://www.asi.nic.in)

Notice that there is no mention of the close link between the disciplinary regime of colonialism—ethnographic and demographic studies were used to police cultures and populations, as writers such as Bernard Cohn (1997) have demonstrated—and the aesthetic and cultural practice of such surveys and enquiries. Attention must be paid to the ways in which such enquiries, collections and knowledge were used for colonial purposes.

(*iv*)   The ways in which Indian identity begins to be enmeshed within its 'displays' in 'national' museums.

(*v*)   The modes by which post-1947 India tabulates, commodifies, represents and organizes knowledge about its various cultures both within and outside India. The Festivals of India in the USA (1985–86)—over 100 exhibitions, dances and performances in 38 museums, 90 cities and 37 states, a $15 million event—the art exhibition (*India! Art and Culture 1300–1900* at the Metropolitan Museum involved 350 objects spanning five centuries) are good examples of the latter. The Festival of India was widely advertised in the department store, Bloomingdale's, which itself was thus drawn into the culture industry through the sale of 'official' and 'indigenous' Indian products (Wallis 1994: 268). The world-famous Selfridges of London had a special India festival in 2002. As part of the attractions (merchandize?) were Amitabh and Jaya Bachchan, Dimple Kapadia, Yash and Karan Johar, and Shah Rukh Khan. The overwhelming circulation of Indian films and film personalities (as they participate in and stage shows abroad, for example) enables a globalized condition—of consuming India through its films. Globalization works in a two-way mode, of course.[5] It is important to note that the Festival of India held abroad became *indigenized* as Apna Utsav from 1986. Such 'national' festivals can be seen as a nation's narrative where ethnic/cultural factions and differences are temporarily glossed over or subsumed under a pan-Indian identity. Thus the cultural nationalist ethos is at once a public culture for Indian consumption and ideological assimilation, as well as international recognition.

Each of these contexts becomes visible through discourses that circulate in the public domain.

❑ MUSEUMS AND DISPLAY

In India the *darshan* has been a central mode of the spectacle, as Diana Eck (1986) has demonstrated. A typology of the *darshan*, with specific reference to museum practices, can be suggested here.

(*i*) Relics in temples were museumized as sacred objects. Devotees and believers sought *darshan* on particular days and in certain seasons. There has not been a complete separation of sacred objects from the objects of everyday life (Appadurai and Breckenridge 1992: 38–39). However, this is not a particularly Indian phenomenon. The guide book (leaflet, actually) to the Westminster Abbey, London—one of the most popular tourist spots within the UK—begins thus:

> The Abbey is a living church that enshrines the history of the British nation. It is not a museum, although there are many things worth seeing.

Here one notes the distinction, highlighted in the brochure, between a museum and a 'living' space of worship. One cannot see 'history' as separate from its religious and sacred structures. On the very next page this leaflet suggests:

> Pause and ask: 'What was the faith that made people build like this?' Remember in your prayers today's leaders of the nations.

This comment, set off in a red font from the black font/lettering of the rest of the text, is both a command and a direction on how we need to perceive a nation's history itself: as the history of its *faith* and as the history of its great *leaders*.

(*ii*) The palace functioned as a treasury—a storehouse of wealth, power, values and cultural heritage of the people.

(*iii*) The museum also functioned as a space where the entire heterogeneity of social life and culture could be captured and framed for a single, unified consumption.

All three religious and secular modes of *darshan* exist in contemporary museums. Palace museums in Mysore or Jaipur are windows into the past. They ostensibly store the treasured 'values' of a past lifestyle. The museum asks us to move from the objects to the people who used the objects. Further it asks us to gauge and imagine the values attributed to the objects by their users. Finally, it asks us to visualize the value systems of the users themselves. It forces us to ask: what kind of people would have used this kind of object? It codes the history of that community in terms of the objects they used *and* the values they espoused. The museum suggests that the past community's values may be perceived 'in' the objects themselves. Thus the showcasing of objects of culinary or feasting events *codes* a culture/community's value or key feature: hospitality. Eventually, the history of that community becomes associated with that particular value of hospitality in a kind of twisted semantics of the objects. Simply put, the museum constructs both the objects and its values, while making an implicit connection between a culture's objects and the culture's values of/for that object.

In contemporary museums, serious attempts are made to present the cultural diversity of India. National Museum, New Delhi, now has a North-east section. The museum announces with evident pride:

> The Gallery of Tribal Life Style of North-East India includes a total of 327 excellent traditional exhibits of dresses, appearls [sic], ornaments, basketry, wood carving and personal adornments etc. of several tribal groups inhabiting the 'Land of Seven Sisters' are on view. (http://nationalmuseumindia.org/)

The public space is now meant to represent, in as complete a manner as possible, the diversity of India. Museumization is a safeguard against complete ignorance about these regions, while also being a weapon against the erasure of local cultures under the onslaught of globalization. The National Culture Fund, set up by the Government of India in 1996, states in its preliminary document: 'the pace of change poses unprecedented threats to the continuity of that cultural heritage. Aware of these threats, societies everywhere are expressing a growing demand for cultural preservation and renewal' (n.p.). The suggestion of continuity is, of course, crucial, and I shall return to this theme in the section on the museum's narrative.

Discourses of national identity, cultural heritage, conservation and a homogenization that erases 'conflicts' all presuppose and embody power relations that achieve these 'effects'. The Museum of Modern Art begins the introduction to its *MOMA Highlights* (1999) thus:

> In 1929, its founders dreamed, and its friends, trustees, and staff have dreamed since, that its multiple meanings and potential would ultimately be resolved into some final, fully formed equilibrium. (p. 16)

It is significant that the museum hopes to 'resolve' the connection and relations between the objects. Disparate objects have to be codified and arranged in a way such that they relate to each other. They should not be at odds, but must exist in 'equilibrium'. Multiple meanings must neatly dovetail into each other. The curators, authoritative—and authoritarian— interpreters of the objects' meanings, will discover the links, and present them to the (uninformed) visitor. What the visitor perceives as the 'natural' sequence or connection between objects is actually the carefully constructed, artificially forged narrative between them. The description emphasizes the politics of optics—the ideological or political imperatives that drive this narrative link between objects.

Conservation is itself a phenomenon where conservatives/conservationists seek to maintain what they consider 'traditional' or worthy of representing that which best signifies the idea of nation (Walsh 1992: 70). Thus, a news item in the guide book/leaflet to York Minster, York, UK (2001), states:

> Restoration and conservation work on the Chapter House Vestibule is in progress. The Minster's own Stoneyard team are working to stabilise the buttresses. Original masonry is conserved wherever possible but restoration with new masonry is undertaken if it is considered essential.

Conservation in many cases involves an entirely new building, with new materials. What one sees as 'conserved' is the result of careful re-building with new materials in such a manner that it becomes impossible to discover the difference between new and old. Further, the degree of reconstruction is almost always unknown to the visitor. This reconstructed fiction of an older 'reality' is in itself a cultural politics. Smita Baxi, formerly Director of the Crafts Museum, New Delhi, refers to the museum exhibition as a 'sample of reality' (1980: 7). The museum is reality captured and, ironically, re-*created*. Another such leaflet, *Jorvik News* (Spring 2001), states:

> Resurrected inch by painstaking inch, the skeletal frames of the 10th century home-steads and backyards are gradually being moulded into place, following the exact plans of archaeologists who have laboured to analyse the thousands of finds excavated at the original Coppergate dig over 20 years ago. (p. 4)

It goes on to add, in supreme irony:

> Viking builders and inhabitants would have no difficulty in recognizing the Jorvik they knew 1000 years ago, as plant-life, door-hinges and even the positions of walls and doors are faithfully recreated. (p. 4)

The emphasis is on the reality-effect which museum techniques and conservation strategies are supposed to achieve.

However, this also results in what may be called the 'niche effect' of the museum or cultural conservationism: the different classes, ethnic communities and cultures are to be preserved in their separate niches so that there is no possibility, or threat, of cultural mixing or boundary crossing. The tribal or the aboriginal, the worker or the woman is captured and placed for study here: to be stared at and analysed. Here the body of the aboriginal is itself the object that is on display and is viewed. Ethnic dances and live performances at exhibitions—and even at academic seminars/conferences in India where they are presented as 'local flavour'—are now ubiquitous. An essential part of the tourism industry, such body performance is a complex interplay of voyeurism, consumption and display. The exhibition of a 'different' body—in terms of colour, physique, dress, behaviour—is as old as the history of exhibitions (see Richard Altick's groundbreaking 1978 work, *The Shows of London*). The body codifies difference—which is what makes tourism, tourism: the exploration of difference. The body of the tribal man/woman in native costume, in the space of the museum or tourist show, provides the basis for knowledge—what Jane Desmond terms 'physical foundationalism' (1999: xiv). Such exhibitions package difference. The body of the tribal/aboriginal is taken to be 'primitive', while positing the viewer/visitor as being at a level different from that of the object displayed. Through this 'staging of the natural' (ibid.: xv–xvi), the audience/visitor gets a taste of the 'authentic' folk experience, rural life, and such. Now, the location of these objects in their 'natural' settings—the weaver's hut, the temple background, the farm land—converts them and their way of life into spectacle, but erases—or sterilizes—the actual political, economic and social history within which this life is lived. Thus the question to be asked is: how do visitors respond to such instances of staged authenticity, sacredness (the latter in the sacralization of sites as places of worship in former ages), and life? This is why museum visitor studies are of crucial importance. How many aboriginals/tribals actually visit these exhibits? How do *they* react to these niches displaying their culture, made available for general consumption? Does it in any way reinforce the subject–object relation where the tribal is always the knowable, the object of analysis, the focus of the analytic gaze, and the (upper-caste, middle-class, literate, metropolitan or semi-urban) visitor the knower?[6]

Kings and rulers, with their royal pageants, durbars and great tours through the country, provided 'shows' for the subjects. In a way the spectacle conditioned the population to the role of subjects, and emphasized the power relations that informed the subject–king relationship. The durbar, with its hierarchic arrangement of spectators, the monarch on the elephant, and court festivals—such as the Mysore Dussehra, which even today involves the Palace and the 'monarch'—was a mode of articulating specific roles. The continuing spectacularization of the film *into* public culture through stage shows, film awards ('spectacles' where stars perform, in the flesh, so to speak), and even the coverage, in film magazines, of the Holi celebrations at Amitabh Bachchan's Juhu bungalow, which involved almost all the Bollywood stars, involves the philosophy and poetics of the *darshan*.

In a museum the primary poetics is of display and viewing. This involves what Svetlana Alpers (1991) terms the 'museum effect'. The 'museum effect' 'turn[s] all objects into works of art ... it isolate[s] something from its world, to offer it up for attentive looking and thus to transform it into art like our own' (ibid.: 26). This fracture between the origin of a particular object and its 'display' turns the object into what I shall term an 'art-effect'. Adapting Alpers' argument, I suggest that the neighbourhood of the display cabinet, the colour of the wall on which the painting is mounted, the frequently tasselled/brocaded ropes, curtains, carpets, all generate the art-effect: and part of this art-effect is the object that is the centrepiece. V.H. Bedekar recommends that the visitor 'should be in comparative darkness' so that the object is clearly visible without 'distractions' (1980: 13). In these descriptions the surroundings, of formal arrangements, renders the object an artifact, something special to be contemplated in clear light, without intrusive elements. And this is the art-effect, which can transform a useless thing into an artifact. Central to the very premise of the museum is the notion that artifacts should be separated from their original context—of ownership, use, manufacture—and redisplayed in a different context of meaning. That is, the museum is regarded as possessing a superior authority when it comes to interpreting and representing the artifact, and as a space where the artifact can be safely preserved against the wear and tear of daily use (Smith 1989: 9). In any case, what is at stake here is the spectacle: the ability and facility to draw attention to particular scenes, people and events. The leaflet announcing the Jorvik Story of the City of York (UK), published as part of promotional material for the Viking Festival, declares:

> Jolablot 2001 ... The Jorvik Viking Festival ... Imagine ... It is the first Millennium. Jorvik throngs with visitors who have come to celebrate the wedding of a prominent Viking Lord to a young Anglian bride. However, a hostile force is approaching and the great warlord King Erick Bloodaxe must prepare his troops for battle .... The annual epic adventure that is Viking Festival commences on Saturday 17 February 2001 promising dramatic combat and a chance to get as close as you dare to Viking warriors and their colourful households. (*Jorvik News*, Spring 2001)

Like the royal pageants of yore, which drew attention to conquests, victories, marriages and births, or simply to royal power through spectacles, the museum's art-effect generates a spectacle for consumption.

A more permanent feature than royal pageantry, the museum involves a related but different set of exercises. The visitors to the museum are to be educated in their cultural heritage—much like subjects created by the sight of royalty—so that they go away as bearers of that heritage. Anupama Bhatnagar thus mourns the fact that 'the traditional museum has failed to establish link between the members of the community and their rich cultural and natural heritage' (1999: 39). I suggest that what the pageant achieved in ancient times, the museum performs in a different way today. It transforms the visitor into an active tool for the propagation of culture. The visitor, on her/his part, acquires cultural capital through museum visiting. Museum visiting becomes, in the case of certain classes, a matter of lifestyle. As an educator—and every museum emphasizes this role above everything else—the museum instils in the visitor a sense of belonging to an Indian culture/identity/Republic. School children, taken on museum visits as a mandatory part of their education, are forcibly treated to glimpses of Indian history and culture. They learn their lessons in history or civics or geography in these spaces. Museums thus function as sites of enforced and organized education. Heritagization is an educational projects where the museum/state instils (or seeks to instil) notions of cultural identity and belongingness through displays of particular objects and events in that culture/nation's part. However, as Bhatnagar suggests, this agenda of education and heritagization has been betrayed. Of course, Bhatnagar does not specify what she means by 'natural heritage', or the power equations that inform such transactions of heritagization. The problem is that period rooms often emphasise ruling families and palaces in all heritage conservation work and museum displays (this occurs across the world). Thus, the Victoria Coach Station (London), in its *Guide to London, Winter 2000/01*, writes:

> London also has many wonderful art galleries, the Tate and the National being perhaps the most famous, and many historical homes, offering a fascinating insight into the lives of some of *England's most important people* and the furnishings and styles of the times. (p. 13, emphasis added)

This promotion of a ruling-class history of the nation, from various 'periods' such as the Maurya, the Chola, the Vakataka, the Vijayanagara, the Mughal, actually means that the everyday past of the majority of Indians is marginalized in favour of these glorious 'moments'. Indian history here is not the history of the artisan or the farmer down the ages. Museums are organized—like school history books—around dynasties, ruling clans, kingdoms, great scientists or statesmen/women. We do not have 'A History of India' that starts with peasant life in ancient times and 'concludes' with the village in late 20th-century India. Village or even semi-urban life, the life of peasants and workers, are *adjuncts* to the 'main history'—which is that of the great kingdoms that have ruled India. Thus such a museumization of the past achieves an imposition of the concept of nation, while eliding the differences that existed in the pasts of different places. *Jarrold's Guide to the University City of Oxford* (1997) opens thus:

> Crammed into a tiny space less than a mile square is one of the greatest collections of buildings to be seen anywhere. Moreover, these buildings have been home to an extraordinary number of statesmen, kings and saints, and over eight centuries Oxford University has educated philosophers, poets and scientists who revolutionised the way we see the world. (n.p.)

The space of the heritage centre or the museum here is highlighted as the space of success alone. The history of a place, clearly, is the history of its successful, great women and men. The reconstruction of Oxford University's history therefore never pays attention to the toilers, the poorer students, the students who did not 'make it' in the world. It is no surprise, therefore, that among the portraits on the first page of the *Oxford Story Exhibition Leaflet* we recognize Bill Clinton, Tony Blair, Margaret Thatcher and Lewis Carroll.

It is important that one views this mode of creation of an imagined nation as part of a larger 'technology' geared towards organizing public culture. The reconstruction of an Indian past through museumization should be read in *conjunction* with mass media images and technologies of image-making such as TV serials: *Yatra*, History Channel documentaries, Discovery and the National Geographic programmes, the telecast of the *Ramayana, Mahabharata, Akbar*, and others. The middle classes, which constitute a major presence in dissent from vote-bank politics to Public Interest Litigations, and which constitute, because of their economic status, arguably the bulk of museum visitors, have to be trained in ways of seeing Indian history. And museums play an important role here, as they contribute to definitions of what India is, and what Indians are. In a global context larger museums such as the Smithsonian or the British Museum perform similar defining and classifying functions for entire national cultures and ethnicities. Here, for instance, is the British Museum's self-declared purpose (as formulated in 2002): 'In looking towards 2003, the 250th anniversary of its founding, the British Museum will preserve these distinctive commitments to access, scholarship and care of the collections, whilst *redefining* them for the new millennium' (http://www.thebritish museum.ac.uk, 6 May 2004, emphasis added). What form does the redefining take? Are the members of the various ethnicities 'captured' as material objects within the Museum consulted during this process? How does the narrative of the museum capture the social, economic, political and other changes in the societies even as it represents their *pasts*?

However, one cannot assume that the museum simply imposes knowledge. When visitors come to the museum they bring with them prior knowledge, semantic systems and interpretive frames—about their history, cultural icons, and the way history is told. The visitor is alert to the ways in which Indian history is being represented in the museum because there exists, through mass media forms such as TV serials or school history books, prior knowledge, however limited, of, say, the great empires in Indian history.

The museum thus presents itself as a provider, custodian and organizer of knowledge, albeit one that relies on pre-existing knowledge and frames of reference. Grace Morley, former Director, National Museum, New Delhi, describes museums as 'custodians of objects' (1981: 95). The

National Rail Museum, New Delhi, calls itself 'The *custodian* of the glorious heritage of Indian Railways ...' (http://www.railmuseum.org, emphasis added). The sense of discipline, power and control is, perhaps unconsciously, embedded in such representations. As noted earlier, the issue of power—to acquire, display and interpret—is closely aligned with the very structure of the museum or the archive.

One more point before moving on to the poetics and politics of display. In earlier ages the chitrashalas were meant for private viewing. Pageants were meant to underline the power of the sovereign. During the Raj the grand 'durbar' was used to instil in Indians the feeling of being subjects of the British crown (a theme discussed in several histories of the Raj, and therefore one that need not detain us here). What purpose does display serve when such private spaces are converted into public spaces? The state, in post-monarchic cultures, is not given over to a transcendental principle or focus, but to a multiplicity of objectives. It is not the prince, the royal family or the solitary, concentrated power of the sovereign that is highlighted through such displays. In the case of India, it is the narrative of its civilization, heritage and the famous 'unity-in-diversity' theme that is celebrated. With Independence, the need to project a 'national' identity became paramount. The National Museum declares:

> National Museum, New Delhi, today, has in its possession over 2,00,000 works of exquisite art, both of Indian and Foreign origin covering more than 5,000 years of our cultural heritage. Its rich holdings of *various creative traditions* and disciplines which represents a *unity amidst diversity*, an unmatched *blend* of the past with the present and strong perspective for the future, brings history to life. (http://www.nationalmuseumindia.org, emphasis added)

The National Culture Fund writes in its preliminary document:

> India has witnessed, in the millenia that are past, coming together of peoples from various places, of distinct racial stocks, of different religions, of diverse cultures and ideas, and this interactive togetherness has created a unique plurality—plurality of religions, of languages, of dress, of architecture—that yet draws upon and strengthens the same resource that has acquired eternality namely the 'Indianness', quintessentially. (http://ncf.nic.in/htm)

The display, description, and promotion of various cultures from various regions of India must serve to highlight this diversity, which is its

'Indianness'. Indian culture, united (at least spatially) under one roof, is to be organized around this narrative principle. It is important to understand the emphasis here. The shift from private ownership/collection to public viewing is also, simultaneously, a shift from monarchic spectacle to democratic participation. The state's role in the democratization of culture—with its attendant power relations—is captured in the website of the Government of India's Ministry of Culture. This is how the Ministry describes itself:

> The Department of Culture, Government of India was set up with the objective of developing ways and means by which basic cultural and aesthetic values remain dynamic among people. It primarily deals with the tangible and intangible heritage. In a larger perspective, it also addresses the issues relating to history, values and beliefs in conjugation with several other Ministries and Departments like Tourism, Education, Ministry of External Affairs etc. (http://www.indiaculture.org, 8 May 2004)

This is the state's own way of organizing culture. It decides on the 'aesthetic values', the definition and constituents of heritage, and the nature of 'basic' cultural values. This 'statist' culture is then treated and presented as 'natural' and democratic, for *all* Indians to consume. The National Museum website has a line, directly under the heading, which reads: 'Ministry of Culture, Government of India', thus making it clear that it is a legitimate museum, and the exhibits are part of state-sponsored culture. This is what Tony Bennett terms the 'exhibitionary complex' (1999 [1995]: 61).

In the narratives of the Indian public museums it is *India*—as nation-state, as a 'unified' culture, as a set of people with shared and mutually recognizable traits and history—that is emphasized. Here it is significant that private collections such as those by Salar Jung were 'nationalized', seamlessly merged into the grand narrative that is 'India'. Further, the identification and classification of sites as 'heritage centres' is a move towards transforming little known sites with limited spectator access as well as privately-owned ones into 'Indian' spaces with mass access. Here state power works with cultural rather than juridico-political power. The effect of display in national museums invariably follows the 'unity-in-diversity' and multiculturalist theme. In India, museums such as the Salar Jung or the National Museum construct an ongoing narrative of Indianness that ties up with similar narratives in forms of public culture such as the cinema or television, all of which are to be imbibed *repeatedly* by citizens (indeed, citizenship may very well be defined by this act of consumption). A whole new public representation of the Indian past—ancient/medieval/modern, Buddhist/Hindu/Islamic, and others—with its own hierarchies and exclusions is organized here.

Displays in museums are frequently accompanied by descriptions, labels, fliers, occasional (scholarly) publications, and now vast amounts of information on the websites, all of which are *public* documents. Such documents, however, have a definite purpose, and function mainly as supplements to the displays. Grace Morley writes:

> The art/archaeology museums staffs did, however, recognize the need to provide a sort of frame-work within which even master-pieces of archeology or art could be viewed, which might result in a greater understanding on the intellectual level, as well as in the aes-thetic pleasure .... Ways were accordingly devised to provide intro-ductory labels, often accompanied by maps, charts, diagrams .... In the case of an exhibition of similar artistic works or of the works of a group of artists associated in an art movement, such introductory labels assume the importance of a separate introductory exhibition of supplementary and reference material .... Such introductory labels, or exhibitions are, of course, of the greatest possible assistance to the general visitor .... (1981: 101–2)

Vinod Dwivedi likewise emphasizes that the registration of objects con-stitutes the museum's 'brain' (1973: 22), suggesting the *intellectual* role of such information. The 'introduction' here is basically a way of framing the view, limiting the approach to be adopted during the view, and the act of interpretation. The description and information is the prism through which the object needs to be 'read'.

The collections allow objects on display to not just be seen, but *seen through* into some invisible but palpable 'thing' behind them. Thus 'history' as both affect and effect is what lies behind the object. The viewer must see beyond the immediate object—with the assistance of the documentation—in order to grasp this history. In earlier times, this access was meant for certain classes of people with the taste and ability to perceive the 'truth' behind the object. Such elite viewers at art galleries were privileged, and thus distinguished from the 'uncultured' peasantry or working classes. It is therefore significant that the National Museum's publications were all, initially, in English. But now, the Museum declares:

'Of late, the efforts have been made to provide the material in Hindi as well, for the benefit of *common people*' (emphasis added). This suggests a division among the audience for which the exhibits are intended: the elite who can follow English commentaries, and those who cannot. V.V.S. Avadhani in his Preface to the *Guide Book to the Victoria Museum, Vijayawada* writes:

> Catalogues published by the department [of Archaeology and Museums of Andhra Pradesh] were mainly of scientific nature and have been useful only to the researchers. There was persistent demand from the general public for a general guide book of the museum objects so that the objects displayed in them may be better understood. (1976: n.p.)

The aim, obviously, is to reach out to the public—though the insistence on publishing such guide books in English remains a peculiar problem.

What the collections (at national, regional and local levels) with their documentation and commentary seek to achieve is a sense of the history of India or a particular region, and the history of its art. Thus Kangra paintings, Mughal architecture and Chola Natarajas all contribute to the narrative (that is) of India. The aim is not to merely catalogue rarities, but to be as *representative* as possible, and for the representativeness to be captured within the museum for ready consumption. The eclecticism of the 'national' museum is aimed precisely at developing such a varied, popular narrative where the uncultured, the regional and the local can be initiated, integrated and homogenized, at least temporarily, into a 'national' mass. M.L. Nigam recommends: 'a national museum should collect the supreme examples which illustrate a particular discipline nationally. The regional museum with its specialist staff and good planning should house all unique material of a regional character' (1985: 51–52). What is consumed is India, or Andhra Pradesh, as a whole, in a nice little package. It is therefore important to note that entries to most of these spaces are either free or priced very nominally. Public access to a museum is educational, and aids in the construction, in Benedict Anderson's influential thesis, of an 'imagined community' of India and Indians. The museum display is not for the indulgence of the curiosity of the elite few, but for the many (though, as I have pointed out above, the language of commentary, labelling and the accompanying information suggests a divisiveness in the museum itself) seeking to be educated, cultured and absorbed into the narrative of India.

However, heritage is not the only emphasis in a modern museum. The Guwahati declaration on the 'new museology' (1988) stated the new agenda explicitly when it suggested that 'in the past, museums were concerned primarily with heritage without simultaneously relating it to the on going struggle for socio-economic progress'. It therefore suggested that the museum must adopt a wholly different approach to organizing itself. This 'new museology' appropriates the concept of trusteeship, where 'museums ... are to be established, maintained and operated as trusts in the hands of representatives of the concerned communities'. This involves opening up 'new channels of two-way communication with various sections of the community so that they themselves participate and support museums to attain the self chosen goals of integrative conservation of heritage' (qtd. in Bhatnagar 1999: 63–64). This idea of the museum as trustee—which is exactly how the world's oldest museum, the British Museum, advertises itself: 'The British Museum holds in trust for the nation and the world a collection of art and antiquities from ancient and living cultures' (http://www.thebritishmuseum. ac.uk, 6 May 2004); we know that at least 10 per cent of the British Museum's treasures have been legitimately acquired!—is a significant development. It suggests that the people have a role to play in the creation and preservation of their heritage. However, while the democratization of museums is a welcome move, it remains to be seen how the process can be actively practised. Community museums in the USA, as I have pointed out, appear to come close to the ideas of the Guwahati resolution. What the new approach can achieve, if effectively implemented, is a *local* narrative of the specific region/community that does not seek integration with and/or homogenization into a 'national' heritage or culture. The *Oxford Story Exhibition Leaflet*, University of Oxford (UK), describes the Exhibition thus:

> Recognised as an excellent introduction to Oxford, the Oxford Story Exhibition captures the very essence of the University's and the City's fascinating and enigmatic 900 year history.

The emphasis on 'essence' captures the purpose and politics of exhibitions. This essence, produced by local authorities and organizations, provides direct and reliable access to the place. The leaflet claims that the story is narrated by one 'Magnus Magnusson (Jesus College 1948–1951)'. The information provided thus is meant to suggest authenticity.

Such local museums/exhibitions link cultural practice with the political economy of the place. This revisits, of course, an old debate in display cultures: whether to 'privilege the context or the object, whether to highlight the aesthetics of objects or prepositional knowledge about them or whether a curator's message about the history of an object and its original context is more authentic than the provenance of the object itself' (Karp 1991: 12). Rather than a 'museumized' and 'mummified' culture which de-links the artifact from its social conditions, we require a more politically aware museology. Further, such spectator-participation makes the process of display, and the means of representation, more transparent. James Bradburne (Director, Museum für Kunsthandwerk in Frankfurt am Main, and UNESCO advisor on museums), describes the museum experience and role thus:

> The role of the museum is to create an informal environment where the visitors can explore the ways in which they can actively modify their relationship with culture, by enhancing their knowledge, piquing their curiosity, by honing their critical judgement. In the museum, visitors should be in control, and they should be encouraged to chart their own course. (2000: 387)

The phenomenon of conservation is primarily a 20th century one in the Western world. The notion of 'heritage', closely linked with conservation, began to assert its influence on cultural policy in countries such as Britain in the 1960s. Kevin Walsh estimates that at least 60 per cent of English Heritage's (or Historic Buildings and Monuments Commission) annual budget is spent on historic buildings (1992: 80).

Extending this point to international exhibitions and museums, we need to ensure that the exhibits are organized according to the aesthetic categories of the cultures from which they derive. Thus exhibiting Indian art in the Smithsonian or the British Museum runs the risk of rehearsing and repeating traditional Western ways of organizing experience. Anglo-European visitors to this exhibit will respond in the ways in which they are trained. Hence, the San Francisco Asian Art Museum, which organized the 'Essence of Indian Art' exhibition in 1986, chose and arranged the exhibits according to the various *rasas* of Indian tradition (see Goswami 1991).

Displays are meant to be viewed. There is an entire technology of seeing in a museum (with variations for different kinds of museums). Michael Baxandall notes two aspects of the museum visitor: (*i*) S/he comes partly to look at visually interesting material and objects. A large part of the activity consists of looking. (*ii*) S/he is usually interested in the purpose and function of the artifact s/he sees. In both these cases the response to an object is culturally conditioned (1991: 33–34).

There is a 'technology of the series' (Bennett 1999[1995]: 44) at work in the viewing of artifacts and other objects. The series, based on schools, or ages, or even regions, denies the very idea of a masterpiece. The National Museum's archaeology section has a note about its 'nine thousand art objects representing all major regions, schools and periods'. What the series does is to provide a narrative that *sequences* the particular object with its past and lateral relations. Thus groupings such as 'Kangra school' or 'Mughal miniatures' suggest a relationship between the various items in the collection, and is characteristic of the representational strategy of the museum.

In addition to the organization of the objects and the documentation, there is another mode of organizing viewing. The visitor is forced to perform a *programmed* itinerary of the rise and development of a particular school of art. There are designated rooms, arranged in such a way that one leads into another as the visitor literally 'follows' art. The Louvre museum guide book, for instance, adds a footnote to its instructions for the department of Greek and Roman antiquities: 'In each room of the department visitors will find, hanging on the wall, a notice commenting on the artistic evolution of the exhibits' (p. 13). Or later: 'Having descended the little staircase, the visitor will turn to the right into the Salle Romane (1) where the visit logically begins' (p. 163). This is a performance, one that is organized for the visitor by the museum's space and spatial practices. The route the visitor takes is integral to the narrative that the museum seeks to deliver. Thus, it is important to recognize here that the narrative of the museum has two significant components: the spatial practice of walking through rooms, halls, viewing galleries, and the mental/intellectual one of seeing, experiencing, assimilating the information being given to us. Here is an example of how the narrative and the visitor's performance constitute a museum:

The monumental image of Surya from the world famous Sun Temple of Konarak greets the visitor *first*. Eight pillars, surrounding the Surya image, present beautiful female figurines standing in different postures. While five of them belong to Mathura art (2nd cent. A.D.) the remaining three are the products of 10th–12th cent. A.D. Four railings pillars from Mathura carved with various damsels performing various functions are Khadganrtya, a lady taking bath under a spring. Ashokadohad and the mother carrying the child. The fifth one is Sri Lakshmi, the goddess of plenty and prosperity. Carved in marble, the statue of Jaina Saraswati from Pallu (Rajasthan) is a highly sophisticated and delicate work of sculptural art. She is the goddess of music, learning and intelligence. Alasakanya from Khajuraho region and the lady playing with ball from Nagda are other attractions. *On either side of the reception counter*, the visitor sees two well-known sculptures of Indian art— a superb image of Shiva in vamana form from Mansar (5th cent. A.D.) and a rare exhibit of the Yaksha from Pitalkhora, Maharashtra (2nd cent. B.C.) carved by a goldsmith, Kanhadasa, as is evident from the epigraph.

Maurya-Shunga Gallery: *After crossing* the Indus Valley or Harappa Gallery, the *visitors step into* the gallery of Maurya-Shunga-Satvahana art (3rd cent. B.C. to 1st-2nd cent. A.D.) and see a few Mauryan Shungan stone sculptures and terracottas. The Mauryan art was followed by a simpler style. The sculptures of Shunga period (2nd-1st cent. B.C.) were used primarily to decorate stupas at Bodh Gaya, Bharhut, Sanchi etc. They depict life scenes of Buddha or the tales of his previous births (Jatakas). The folk deities like Yaksha, Yakshi, Salabhanjika etc. are also very important items of Shunga art, but with a difference. Besides, the Yaksha and Yakshi images from Mathura, Mehrauli, Amin and Bulandshahar are also fine specimens. In the Deccan, the patronage of Satavahana Kings and support by lay-disciples produced a large number of rock-cut caves carved at Pitalkhora, Bhaja, Karle, Kanheri etc. On the other hand, important structural buildings like stupas were built at Amaravati, Ghantasala etc. Both are represented here through some superb specimens looking like jewels in Indian art.

Kushana Gallery: This *leads to the next gallery* where one can view the products of three overlapping styles of art—Mathura, Gandhara and Ikshvaku—that had flourished side by side in the first three centuries of the Christian era. (http://www.nationalmuseumindia.org, emphasis added)

One notes the way in which the visitor's route is predetermined by the museum itself. In many cases one is forced to complete a particular circuit. The general guide book to the Louvre Museum opens with a description of the 'Greek and Roman Antiquities'. Here is the opening statement of this guide:

> We advise the visitors to follow the plan during the visit to this department for, as the rooms are not numbered, we have adopted some fictitious numbers to make this difficult circuit easier. (p. 12)

The references to routes, access and viewing positions in such detailed instructions (the Louvre text refers to itself as a 'practical guide') are meant to control the viewer.

Thus, while the museum is a public space, it is also a technology of spacing this public space. Visitors are regulated, their movements controlled and modified so that they access the objects in the 'right' order. What this suggests is that the older notion of cultivated capabilities in viewing works of art persist in even democratic spaces today. The visitor has to be trained to see in particular ways, to see the right things at the right time, and to be made aware of the sequence in, say, the history of Indian art. The museum juxtaposes individual time with historical time. The individual is both transcendent to and within historical time: part of the history s/he perceives, yet outside it. This is the purpose of the museum, which has a particular disciplinary regime informing its representational practices. Like schools and educational apparatuses such as textbooks, TV programmes and the cinema, the museum must be seen as one of the institutions of social training. Capturing the past, and delivering it in particular ways (the narrative), the museum depicts an evolutionary scheme: past to present, where the viewer, if s/he follows the programmed sequence, will be a witness to human development in history (organized as significant events, people, places or dates, but always in evolutionary sequence).

The 'discipline' of the museum

The exhibitionary complex was constituted in Western museums, and in colonial ones such as the Asiatic Society, by the arrival of a range of new disciplines: anthropology, biology, history, archaeology and art history. The relations between these disciplines informed the space of representation. Each discipline within the museum sought to represent a type. The rise of a 'historical frame' (Stephen Bann's phrase, qtd. in Bennett

1999[1995]: 75) in Europe is linked to the development of practices that demanded and enabled the life-like reproduction of an authenticated past and its representation in a series of stages leading to the contemporary. Thus the museum's historical frame was connected to the development of the historical novel, or the history-writing genre.

The catalogue, *Masterpieces from the National Museum Collection* (New Delhi), for instance, writes:

> Contemporary to the Guptas were the Vakatakas in the Deccan. Here too art reached its zenith as is evident from the creation of works of art in the Ajanta and Ellora caves of great fame. The sculptures made in round, like Siva Vamana, shared a number of Gupta characteristics.
>
> The legacy of the Gupta art was carried on by the Maitrakas of Vallabhi in Gujarat, by the early Chalukyan kings in the Deccan and by the Pallavas in the south. The Maitrakas (6th-8th century A.D.) produced beautiful and elegant works of art marked with delicate modeling. Samalaji images are the finest specimens of Maitraka art.
>
> Chalukyan works of art of monumental proportions could be seen at Badami and Aihole in which the Gupta idioms lingered on to a significant extent. During this period the famous rock-cut Kailash temple of Ellora, Maharashtra, was built by the Rashtrakutas.
>
> But the simplicity of the Gupta art soon merged into the heavy ornamentation of the Medieval art in northern and southern India. (p. 20)

The introduction to *State Museum, Hyderabad: A Folder* comments:

> There has been a continuity in the religious history of India, and South in particular .... Here there has been continuity and contacts between the art styles prevailing in different parts of the country and we see great number of influences working behind in evolving some common understanding among the various styles. (p. 5)

The gallery, with its emphasis on seamless progress and evolution, and the period room marked important developments in the museum. Here is an example of how the museum narrative seeks to convey this sense of progress, continuity and sequentiality. Here the narrative of the catalogue—and I am not suggesting that this narrative is an exact equivalent of the museum, only that it is a public domain document that seeks to represent a narrative about Indian culture—suggests a sequence of movements and influences that appear to merge into each other. The narratives rarely mention alternative art forms, artisan guilds and royal/ political patronage, the economic conditions in which artists and arti-sans worked. The seamless movement mapped for the reader/visitor— 'contemporary to', 'legacy carried on', 'merged into'—suggests this sense of continuous history. The National Culture Fund's document states:

> The heritage of a community is essentially its resource for growth— a threshold for a forward movement even if that is rather evolution-ary in character. It not only constitutes the spiritual resource of the community as also of individuals it is an essential source of an iden-tity deeply rooted in the past. (http://ncf.nic.in)

The emphasis here is on continuity, an evolutionary scheme from past to future, and the present identity is firmly located in the past. The scheme does not, of course, interrogate whether this version of the past-as-identity will also look at and exhibit caste oppression, class and gender inequal-ity, or whether it will only showcase the glorious Hindu, feudal, bour-geois past. What elements of this past will be retrieved? Who decides? The process of deciding what constitutes Indian culture and its seamless progress from the ancient times to the present is what makes up the pol-itics of display and museum narration.

In newly formed nation-states, where national history is crucial to the general education of the population, the chronological sequence of the gallery is important. Grace Morley writes:

> After Independence, New Delhi, the Capital of India, began devel-opment of museums appropriate for its status. The National Museum was the result of a large exhibition of Indian art held in London in 1947–1948 .... At the suggestion of India's leaders a good number of the loans were secured for the new museum, while a vigorous acquisition programme was launched. (1981: 64–65)

The museum enables the construction of a national imaginary through its representation of the collective past of the nation and its people. Collections of national materials are represented as the culmina-tion of the progress of civilization. The narrative of the museum goes by continuities rather than breaks. The aim is a seamless history, with minor, but not startlingly disruptive, digressions. The National Museum at New Delhi announces that its collections represent 'more than 5000 years of our cultural heritage'. Further, the Museum declares that its collections provide 'an unmatched blend of the past with the present and strong perspective for the future' (http://www.nationalmuseumindia.org), thus suggesting a chronology that not only culminates in the here and now, but one that is also directed at the future.

One of the major features of the discipline of the museum is its clear disjunction of the product from the process of production. The disciplinary apparatus of the museum retains the product, but not the conditions, processes, or contexts of its production. The narrative of the production conditions of the object is available only in retrospect, in the form of a narrative that works its way backwards from the object on display. And here the museum shop enters the discourse. The products in the museum shop—the souvenirs—are attached to locations and experiences which are themselves not on sale, but whose ghostly presence adds the value (and price) to the object we purchase in the museum shop. In fact, as Susan Stewart (1984: 136) points out, the object we hold in our hand or the object framed in the museum becomes the point of origin of the narrative, which then extends into the past. These objects of yore become commodities. This is especially the case with 'expositions', where we are asked to admire the *finished* work. However, expositions in India are increasingly seeking to demonstrate skills, and pottery, weaving and tribal manufactures are 'performed' within the space of the exposition. This of course turns the process itself into a commodity for the spectacle. The visitor is given a glimpse into the way it is done, but in controlled conditions. The dirt, suffering, or financial contexts of the village or tribal economy are cleansed out in the discipline of the exposition. Art supposedly captures the material conditions of existence here. The annual fairs at DWACRA or Shilparamam in Hyderabad are cases in point. The simulated village or *tanda* in expositions (such as 'tribal crafts fairs') functions as an anthropological museum. Thus Arun Chatterjee writes of tribal art exhibitions and collections:

> The tribal art is to be understood in its own context even if it is detached from the cultural and natural environment and placed in museum show-cases. Utilitarian they are, no matter, whether they originate from the magico-religious or secular urge. It is quite clear that the economic consideration has never been the ulterior motive behind the production of varied art forms. (2001: 72)

The disjunction of economic considerations from 'art' here reinforces the utilitarian/aesthetic divide in evaluating artifacts, and corresponds to the elite/tribal distinction. Further, Chatterjee does not describe how one can access the original conditions of a tribal artifact when it is in a museum. Finally, to argue that there were no economic considerations behind the production of the artifact is to ignore the actual conditions in which these were produced.

The public museum's disciplinary apparatus is a curious combination of the very elite temple of arts (*chitrashalas*) and the utilitarian instrument of democracy. They seek to showcase the 'finest' specimens of ancient Indian art, while also suggesting that students, scholars and the lay public can learn from these exhibits. Documentation enables this disciplinary apparatus to function both as the elite space of art appreciation—the privilege of the connoisseur or the learned elite—and the public, free space of education. School trips for children, a standard component of education in India, combine the two very effectively. And it is here that the third function of the museum becomes visible.

The third function is of the museum as a disciplinary space. Knowledge is organized (the conducted tour, the museum guide accompanying the students) into packets in what is presumed to be the best way to educate the visitors. Not all objects in the museum are made available, nor are the children allowed 'free' access to exhibits. The education in and exposure to the great arts of India must be performed under— and this is the third function—controlled conditions of viewing, description, commentary. The students are under surveillance, and are not really free to explore as they like, what they like. The combination of the visit to a great temple of arts such as the Salar Jung Museum (I remember being herded through the bewildering array of rooms and exhibits!) and the compulsory schooling with that of a disciplinary and disciplined 'performance' renders the museum a strangely democratic space.

The irony of this discipline of the museum is linked to a set of contradictions that Tony Bennett identifies in them (1999[1995]: 102–5). The first is that there is a disparity between the museum's universalist aspirations—where its exhibits and rooms are representative of Indian civilization itself—and the obviously selective nature of its representations. Thus, how do the great museums represent tribal or aboriginal culture? What does the aboriginal/tribal see when s/he visits such exhibits? The suggestion of evolution here—from the primitive to the civilized, the ancient to the modern—is rarely in favour of the tribal or the rural. The sense of progress is invariably from country to city, from the hand loom to the machine. This rhetoric of progress thus posits an evolutionary scale where the aboriginal is (*i*) at the lower end, and (*ii*) completely different from the present viewer. These artifacts still figure as curiosities. Alpers' 'museum effect' argues for a museum's 'way of seeing'. Alpers suggests that serial displays ('Kangra Art', 'Lambada Craft') 'establishes certain parameters of visual interest' (1991: 28). The objects' *difference* from what is ordinarily seen is what generates the sense of craft (one can extend the point to suggest, perhaps frivolously, that whatever is seen in a museum assumes the status of 'artifact', including the wall-mounted fire extinguisher). John Urry, writing about the 'tourist gaze', argues that 'potential objects of the tourist gaze must be different in some way or other. They must be out of the ordinary. People must experience particularly distinct pleasures which involve different senses or are on a different scale from those typically encountered in everyday life' (1998 [1990] 11–12). Tribal pitchforks, awls and grass-cutters become exhibits and generate a pressure on the visitor to treat them as artifacts rather than everyday, utilitarian objects of that tribe or subculture. It is here that the issue of the museumization of subcultures in order to retain their difference from 'mainstream' (bourgeois, upper-caste, metropolitan) culture becomes integral to the study of the museum. In a sense, this retains the classic hierarchy and differentiating structures of class, race, ethnicity and caste. If categories such as these were once used as markers of difference, exploitation and oppression, cultural tourism—of which the museum and the exhibition is an integral part—uses culture. However, the underlying grid is the same—particular races/ethnicities/ castes give rise to particular cultures. We do not speak of looking at different 'races' or 'castes'. Rather, with the museum, we speak of looking at different 'cultures'.

The second contradiction is between the avowed democratic nature of the museum and the cultural politics of differentiation. Visitor studies are urgently needed in order to understand how a museum organizes its viewers. Leisure studies will reveal the class, income, age and other markers of museum visitors, since museum visits have to be seen as 'parts of a larger cosmopolitan world of leisure, recreation, and self-education for wide sectors of the Indian population' (Appadurai and Breckenridge 1992: 42).

If museums are meant to be democratic spaces, do visitors have greater rights over what is exhibited (in terms of both the objects and the narrative linking the objects)? The museum, as I have demonstrated, treats the visitor as a passive recipient of the entertainment or education it offers. Both take place under controlled circumstances, and visitor behaviour is strictly regulated. How is such a space popular or democratic? Since a museum is a part of civil society—even if funded by the state or the private corporate office—shouldn't ethnic groups, minority subcultures, voluntary associations and professional societies have a right to challenge the representations in the museum? Are these museums also spaces for other histories? Will there be, some time in the future, a museum of communal riots in India, or at least a section in history museums devoted to this? Will the atrocities against Dalits in Chunduru (Andhra Pradesh) be incorporated into 'standard' museums of history? Would labour unrest be museumized? Or scandals such as the fodder scam, or the stamp paper one? Does a museumization of riots alter the visitor's comprehension of Indian culture, history and politics? For those like me, growing up in Hyderabad with curfew-informed 'annual holidays' during school time, communal riots are an integral, if deplorable, part of this city's history (along with power cuts, dirty water, chaotic traffic). Why can we not have a museum that captures the dissenting voices within Indian civil society itself? For instance, would Kancha Ilaiah's critique of the Hinduized Indian culture be taken into account when exhibiting 'Indian' culture in museums? Would the Naxalbari movement's ideas and representations of culture—especially their views on land ownership or state power—be 'subjects' for a museum? Can the Civil Rights movements, or the Human Rights Commission's indictments of state power, be museumized for public consumption as a part of modern Indian history? Museums, as noted above, are places for defining what people are. But can such a space not be used to represent resistances to these definitions? The statist museum sanctions only certain versions of history. The cultural politics of the museum renders it schismatic: democratic but selective, open yet secretive, free yet disciplinary. The Other is not an exhibit here, except as a curio. Or a deviant.

❑ MUSEUMS AND THE NARRATION OF THE PAST

Jarrold's Guide to the Historic City of York (2000) lists museums in the city of York. Here is a catalogue:

York Castle Museum ... contains entire reconstructed Victorian and Edwardian streets ....

Fairfax House, a superbly restored Georgian town house ....
Jorvik Viking Centre ... where a Viking Village has been created
underground ....
National Railway Museum ... gleaming railway carriages and
immaculately restored carriages .... (pp. 22–25)

What emerges is the fact that every single element is reconstructed or
restored here. The organization of history and heritage is clearly based
on present interpretations of the past.

The museum is a space for the cultural organization of the past as text.
Material objects and their symbolic meanings—the central narrative of
the museum—are integral to the ways in which the past is made available
for present consumption. How does the museum organize the past *as*
past? What are the modes by which this organization is achieved? What is
the degree of transparency involved here? Does the visitor see the object,
or see through the object at the story/past behind it, and the space/time it
comes from? How does the narrative of the museum effect this transparency? These are some of the questions we need to ask of the museum.

An important component of the museum, especially archaeological
ones, is historical reconstruction, and simulations of bygone ages and
cultures. The question to be asked is: does the (re)production of sites
(house, markets, streets, material objects) work on the principle of
recapturing the 'essence'—that is, with the same meaning as it once possessed for its original users—of the earlier model? Reconstruction of, say,
Harrappan cities, suggests that the reconstructed model is a facsimile of
the past. In the case of objects placed within (history) museums, it is the
objects that are made to tell the story of their own past, but in a way that
makes sense to the present.

Heritage sites, now an important aspect of cultural tourism, and hence
of state patronage, are thus curious spaces. They must mean something
to the present which organizes them, and yet they convey a sense of the
past. The label is the 'intellectual space', which the viewer establishes
between the artifact (and its maker, who is usually *not* present) and the
exhibitor (the museum). The label not only delivers information about
the object concerned, but is also the space which is the source of the
viewer's activity (Baxandall 1991: 37–38). This means that the viewer
moves between the object and the information, and thereby *alters her/his
first culturally conditioned responses to the object after consuming the information on the label.* This is why the narrative of the label, the flier, the

guide book, or the brochure becomes central to understanding the cultural politics of display.

What I am suggesting here is that the 'heritage zone' is a space that is heritagized precisely because it is publicly *demarcated* as such. It becomes a symbol of antiquity, forgotten culture and other such 'wonders' because it is *represented* as such. That is, the objects, spaces and models exist only as narrative reconstructions, definitions and legitimization *as the past*. It is narrative that links objects and things into a story. Official gestures, signs and descriptions delineate the space as 'heritage', as 'ancient India', as 'art'. The boundaries are thus clearly set out: the labels separate the past from the present, the viewer from the viewed. The label or the guide book is what designates the past as past, and hence all heritage is ultimately the effect of the organizing narrative, and is invented. Legislative frameworks (starting with the Constitution of India, which refers to a citizen's cultural rights, and the duty to protect [designated] national symbols and monuments) and administrative procedures create this past for consumption.

One of the features of the ASI site museums is their reference point: pre-colonial India. Anupama Bhatnagar argues that 'during the colonial rule, the cultures of these counties [Asia and Africa] got distorted, disintegrated and replaced by the cultures of the colonial powers'. As a result, these countries in their post-independence state 'felt the need to rediscover their past and to assert their cultural identity'. She goes on to suggest that in this phase subcultures and minority cultures—and she mentions tribals and the downtrodden—needed to be 'preserved' in order to 'enrich' the national culture (1999: 41. Also see Basa 2001: 14). This is the kind of museology that informs ASI efforts at a hyper-Indianization of the past (though ASI does pay attention to British buildings, the emphasis is predominantly on ancient India). As the National Museum website and other publications indicate, this past is itself being pushed further and further back in time, right back to India's tribal and indigenous cultures. With the 'Aryan invasion' controversy simmering beneath cultural debates in India, such efforts are major contributors to the way in which India represents itself. Thus the histories of aboriginals, women, the working class or peasants are now being included, expanding the 'notion' of India itself. The political dimensions of such a preservation of the past—selective and authoritatively described, interpreted by 'scholars'—in the name of a 'national heritage' are severely problematic.

It suggests a cultural politics where Indian identity is defined and delimited by a select group of professionals who have assigned themselves the right to identify and 'preserve' threatened subcultures. This nationalist identitarian agenda behind museumization is emblematized in the (UNESCO convened Round Table) 'Santiago Resolution' of 1972. The resolution passed declared:

> That museum should intensify their work of recovering the cultural heritage and using it for social purposes so as to avoid its being dispersed and removed from Latin America. (Qtd. in Bhatnagar 1999: 52)

What is interesting is that cultural identity is *reduced* to material culture. The British Museum describes itself as a 'social enterprise' where 'cultures can be seen, experienced and studied in depth or compared and contrasted across time and space' (http://www.thebritishmuseum.ac.uk, 6 May 2004). How does one study ancient, distant and Other cultures? The answer apparently is: through specimens of their art work, their material culture. The British Museum, by being the world's oldest (dating back to 1753) repository of material objects from over the world, becomes a centre for the study of entire cultures (which, as even a naïve reading would tell us, is more than just its 'objects'). In one of its more specialized exhibitions, 'The Museum of the Mind: Art and Memory in World Cultures' (2003), the British Museum suggested that '60 key *objects* illustrate the subject of memory across different cultures and time' (http://www.thebritishmuseum.ac.uk, 6 May 2004, emphasis added). How does an object illustrate the experience of memory, individual or cultural? The curator, interpreter, anthropologist, psychologist and behavioural scientist read objects as texts that reveal subjective, internal processes. Similarly, objects can be 'read' as direct signs of cultural processes and experiences. What is therefore required is a genealogy of the ways in which material culture and cultural identity have been enmeshed in contemporary public culture, a genealogy which pays attention to power relations that mediate between the two.

- Sources of funding in the acquisition of material culture are crucial. Who acquires, or can afford to acquire artifacts of Indian culture? (The latest event in this line is Vijay Mallya's acquisition of Tipu's sword, 2004. The related question is also, of course, why *now*?)
- The appointment of 'experts' in museums.

- The process of display, and the regulation of viewing are to be taken into account here. (For a reading of this genealogy in the British context, see Hides 1997.)

The museum, the heritage centre, the theme park actually say more about us and the present than they do about the past—since it is we who select from the past whatever makes sense for us today.

Thus the narratives of the museum need to render the invisible past visible. The visitor witnesses the scene that s/he has never been in. The narrative of history is here replaced by the narrative of the collector-subject. And this second narrative is taken to be the narrative of history itself. In other words, the museum is another mode of illusion like the cinema, where visualization techniques which use physical artifacts rather than screen images enable the visitor to step into another world. Tony Bennett adapts the term 'backteller' from T.H. Huxley to refer to this function of the museum and the museum visitor (1999 [1995]: 178). The museum visitor uses signs and material evidence to reconstruct the story of the past: 'what happened *then*?' tracing her/his way *backwards* through the narrative—which includes a range of textual devices: objects, icons, descriptions, labels, chronological sequencing, history books, dates and important events inscribed alongside—in order to understand the past. The narrative originates *not* with the context of an object's origin, but *with the object itself*. This narrative is based on the premise that the artists' original vision of the artifact is the true one, and that the artists were unaware that they were setting the object forth on a long journey at the end of which (in the museum) both its appearance and meaning may be changed. Reconstruction seeks to reverse this process and return the artifact to how it used to be (Smith 1989: 20). The part is seen to stand in for the whole. What this means is that any culture, past or present, is seen as *the sum total of the material objects*, whose meanings have supposedly been *retrieved* and presented by the museum. Museums are thus spaces that create meanings. The antiquarian—and by extension the museum visitor to the antique—both distances and appropriates the past. The lived experience of these objects, their sentiments and affects are *not* captured in either the objects or the museum's narrative. What is achieved in the reconstruction is a way of assuming that 'this is the way they experienced life, as is visible in their objects'. The object and its narrative (or perhaps we should say the object created *within* the narrative) generates what Stephen Greenblatt terms 'resonance'—the 'power of the displayed object to reach out beyond its formal boundaries to a larger world, to evoke in the viewer the complex, dynamic cultural forces from which it has emerged and for which it may be taken by the viewer to stand' (Greenblatt 1991: 42). The urn, the utensil, or the sword extends beyond its time, place of origin, and even function to work its effect upon a contemporary viewer, who feels some of the dynamics of that object reverberating in the viewing. Such a narrative has two components: (*i*) the metonymic displacement of part for whole (a statue stands for an entire culture, school, civilization); and (*ii*) the invention of a system of classification which defines space and time in such a way that the world is accounted for by the solitary, serialized elements of the museum's collection. This might also involve projecting our notions of aesthetics, taste and beauty onto objects produced centuries ago. For instance, the guide book to the 'masterpieces' of the National Museum, New Delhi, writes about Harappan and pre-Harappan objects in their collection:

The works of art and craft selected for the exhibition are notable for their elegance of naturalism combined with subtle imagination .... Each exhibit is a masterpiece and it proves that it was the creation of a highly urbanized and complex society where freedom of expression was cherished more than in any other society like Egyptian or Mesopotamian. (p. 3)

Lala Aditya Narayan, the then Deputy Keeper (Prehistory) at the National Museum, New Delhi, states: 'the stone tools themselves are least attractive. Moreover, most of these are so small in size that they can hardly catch anybody's attention' (1980: 25). Here the attribution of taste, beauty and such features must be carefully problematized. One, it begins with the very process of selecting certain objects as representative. Two, it attributes beauty or functionality to an object without possessing any exact or reliable knowledge about how this object was treated/received in its original culture. Three, it assumes that *our* standards of beauty or use can be applied *backwards* in time to describe the object at hand. We need to remember that beauty or ugliness is not an inherent or immanent feature of the object: *these are always ascribed by the viewer*. Since the object has been removed from its original setting, such descriptions can only generate narratives about them from our perspective—which may or may not have anything to do with that culture's evaluative principles or signifying systems. The narrative that is given to us, then, is the narrative represented by the arrangement of objects, labels and information: an arrangement that is the curatorial staff's projection rather than (*a*) the original (irretrievable) contexts of the object, or (*b*) the visitor's construction of history. The objects are *made to tell a story* by the arrangements—and hence become 'subjects' of the poetics and politics of such arrangements. Thus the Museum of Modern Art announces:

> Our goal is to suggest new and imaginative ways of understanding the different works of art that constitute the Museum's collection ... it endeavors to juxtapose works from different parts of the collection in surprising, revealing, and sometimes arbitrary ways .... By locating objects and people in time as well as space, the Museum is constantly mapping relationships between works of art and their viewers, so that the space of the Museum becomes a site of narration where many individual stories can be developed and realized. (1999: 20–21)

S. Ramakantam, in his introduction to the *Folder to the State Museum, Hyderabad*, writes:

> [The collections] shall make the lay citizen more aware of his cultural heritage .... This could be brought about only if the material is *arranged in a scientific manner* in a museum. (p. 1, emphasis added)

The emphasis on arrangement in these museum documents (which I take to be illustrative of the *discourse* of the museum), and the admission of the experts' discretionary powers in deciding the arrangements and terms of representation make it clear that the narrative the visitor reads is an effect generated according to rules laid down elsewhere. This makes it a subject for Cultural Studies, since authority—which is what such control over representation essentially means—is always a question of power.

The visitor to the museum, I believe, is, however, far more sophisticated than is generally assumed: s/he is competent enough to realize that this 'resonance' is a fiction—that there is a boundary between the real and the fictional reconstruction of the past. Thus, museums where processes of craft or manufacture are displayed represent the exhibit as real. This is different from reconstructions of historical events that are merely convenient fictions. In both cases there is a politics of selection and authority.

As already noted, the narrative has both its physical-spatial (walking, viewing) and intellectual components. The narrative of the museum organizes the walk and the sights in particular ways, usually in a sequence that posits the viewer as being located at the climax of an evolutionary movement. From this vantage point the past can be viewed and made sense of. However, occasionally, this narrative falters when the links in the chain are broken, or when the object in question does not quite fit the sequence.

The museum concretizes the past through a cultural politics of selection, display, epistemological authority and spatial organization. What is important is to realize that the museum, in addition to reconstructing the past for present reasons (political or otherwise)—and here I am thinking mainly of history museums—is an act of nostalgia. The museum is a narrative that seeks origins. The objects in the museum have no functional use for us: what they represent is a past functionality and use-value. Hence, phrases such as 'capture/visit the glorious past', often used to describe museums, are inscribed into this poetics of longing. Indeed, it is precisely because these are in/from the past that they possess value. The distance is, literally, what makes the heart grow fonder, and the museum thrives on the management of distance. The appeal of the primitive or the antique or the exotic arises, Stewart points out, not in the conditions of the primitive culture itself, but from the 'analogy between the primitive/exotic and the origin of the possessor' (1984: 146). Since the primitive represents my/our own past, my/our own anterior moment ('childhood', in Stewart's formulation), it appeals to me/us. In addition, the experience of the museum, with the ceremonial silence and viewing, the mapped routes and contemplation suggests a space where individuals step back from their everyday lives and look at their world. The suspension of time that the museum embodies creates what the Louvre curator George Bazin once called 'momentary cultural epiphanies' (qtd. in Duncan 1995: 11): a revelation and unveiling of the past in coordinated splendour.

❏ NOTES

1. State funding for museums apart, there are other ways in which the government clearly organizes cultural viewing. The museums are generally governed by Boards of Trustees, appointed by the government. This means that the state does not involve itself with the day-to-day running of the museum, but retains power.

2. The amusement park or exhibition is an interesting genre among museums. The fair was different from the official exhibition for various reasons: the carnival atmosphere, the more participatory, user-friendly stalls where objects could be handled, the commercial slant to exhibiting goods, and so on. In the early years of the 20th century amusement parks were regulated through harsher measures in order to bring them in line with the official exhibition and the museum (Bennett 1999 [1995]: 75). Appadurai and Breckenridge (1992) contrast the museum with the department store. In the former the 'Indian viewer's visual literacy is harnessed to explicitly cultural and nationalist purposes.' In the latter one gazes, but buying is the normative goal. The problem with this distinction is the fact that almost every museum merchandizes models of its exhibits. Palace museums, for instance, allocate a separate space for a shop—in the Amer Palace, Jaipur, the shop is within the Palace itself—often owned by the state government. In other cases, stalls immediately adjacent to the museum retail relics, models and postcards. Thus viewing is almost always tied up with buying, even in the museum.

3. It is also important to note that every museum has its own 'little narrative', which has to do with the type of museum it is (archaeological, natural history, or science and technology). However, every museum is also part of the larger narrative of museums in general. The intelligibility of a particular museum depends on its being viewed as part of a sequence of museums. Thus heritage tours, for instance, link what is generally called 'places of interest', 'places of historical significance', and such, thereby inserting the viewer into a whole chain of narratives. Souvenirs and miniatures of monuments transform heritage into objects of consumption. It transforms the past itself into material culture. Variations in the narrative of museums are also dependent upon museums housed in buildings and structures designed for museum purposes, and spaces such as palaces that have been transformed into museums.

4. It must be pointed out that almost every museum has its 'rare' or valuable sections that are not on public display. A certain elitism is retained here, where such collections are meant to cater to the scholar or the distinguished visitor. For example, the Keeper of Zoology at the British Museum, Edward Gray, suggested in 1858 that there should be a 'study-series' as distinct from an 'exhibition series' (Bennett 1999 [1995]: 41).

5. There is also another link worth exploring—that between the trading of art objects, especially from aboriginal cultures and 'Third World' societies, and museums of natural history in 'First World' nations. See Benthall (1987) for a brief sketch of the issues involved. A brilliant study of the commodification of 'Third World' culture and artifacts in the 'First World' is that by Graham Huggan (2001). Huggan points to the staging of the exoticism of 'native' cultures by both 'First' and 'Third World' nations, and its direct link with the global market.

6. Visitor studies would include various aspects. Treating museum visiting as a cultural phenomenon, Nick Merriman looked at the visitors to heritage museums in Britain, using, among several others, the following criteria:

   (i) Age, status (high, middle, low), education (minimum to tertiary), activity status (full-time, unemployed, retired).
   (ii) Reasons for last museum visit.
   (iii) Attitudes towards museum.
   (iv) Museum's image as institution. (1989: 149–71. Also see Merriman 1991).

❑ FURTHER READING

Bennett, Tony. 1999 (1995). *The Birth of the Museum: History, Theory, Politics.* London and New York: Routledge.

Bhatnagar, Anupama. 1999. *Museums, Museology and New Museology.* New Delhi: Sundeep Prakashan.

Hooper-Greenhill, Eilean. 1992. *Museums and the Shaping of Knowledge.* London and New York: Routledge.

Karp, Ivan and Steven D. Lavine (eds). 1991. *Exhibiting Cultures: The Poetics and Politics of Museum Display.* Washington and London: Smithsonian.

Vergo, Peter (ed.). 1989. *The New Museology.* London: Reaktion.

Brochure Culture

TOURISM

This chapter looks at the culture of travel. Tourism is the organization of travel for commercial purposes. By the last decades of the 20th century and early years of the 21st, with faster transport and communications and easy availability of information, tourism had attained the status of a major industry. The World Tourism Organization predicts that arrivals will reach 1 billion by 2010, and international arrivals will reach 1.6 billion by 2020, thus spending more than $5 billion everyday. Currently, of the 698 million international arrivals in the world, India gets a share of 2.64 million, which translates into a measly 0.38 per cent, though it constitutes 9.5 per cent of the *total* percentage of exports (10th Five-Year Plan document of the Planning Commission, http://www.planningcommission.nic.in/plans, 7.5: 820, 7 September 2004). The Tourism 2020 Vision predicts that by 2020 one out of every three trips will be a long-haul journey to another region of the world. India recorded a 27 per cent growth in June 2003, as compared to the same month in 2002, according to data supplied by the Marketing Division of the Ministry of Tourism (*Incredible!ndia* newsletter, Vol. 17, September 2003). For the period January–May (2004), the foreign exchange earnings stood at Rs 84.56 billion. This is in comparison with Rs 63.81 billion for the same period in 2003, and Rs 57.49 billion in 2002. The increase is by a whopping 32.9 per cent. All these statistics suggest that tourism is one of the largest industries in the world. Tourism and travel emerges as one of the greatest cultural features of the human race.

This chapter analyses the rhetoric, discourses and cultural politics of travel. Treating travel and tourism as cultural commodities, product and affect, it seeks to unravel the constituents of this discourse. To this end I have used tourist brochures and promotional newsletters from the Ministry of Tourism's *Incredible!ndia* initiative as the subject of analysis, but have excluded travel memoirs and travel diaries. This is so because as cultural artifacts, the brochure and promotional literature are more visible and more in the public domain than the travel book. The brochure is what is picked up, free of cost, at any information booth. These brochures are also kept as mementoes of the trip, sometimes for years! Since this book is about public culture which circulates between and among the high cultural classes and the masses, the brochure is what requires more sustained attention. I shall demonstrate how promotional material and guide books conceal a deeper cultural politics of travel, destinations and the tourist.[1] The informing assumptions are two-fold: (i) The creation, representation (and promotion) of a place, whether as a tourist spot or for local use, is a social process; and (ii) one never travels to a completely unknown place: one always knows something about it in advance. We look up public documents such as a railway time-table, gather information about places of accommodation, inquire with people, and so on. In this sense travel and tourism is always a visit that occurs *after* we have visited it through these channels. Thus promotional literature and informational material prepare one for the experience of travel, and constitute a significant moment of tourism itself. The brochure is as important as the actual act of travel.

❏ PROMOTIONAL CULTURE

The tourist brochure is essentially promotional culture, an advertisement for a particular place. Promotional culture combines—and the tourist brochure is one of the best examples of this—information and art. But, as Andrew Wernick has argued, it is actually neither information nor art, but rhetoric: the art of persuasive speech (1994 [1991]: 27). In the case of tourist brochures the purpose is three-fold: information, entertainment and commerce. The brochure is usually available free of cost and they are read out of choice. That is, we can assume that the readership is an *interested* readership, actively seeking information from the brochure. The rhetoric of the tourist brochure—which is my interest here—is calculated to project a certain image of a specific site, evoke a set of responses (emotional, intellectual, sensory, mnemonic and, especially, desire) in the potential traveller, and persuade the reader/viewer that the site is worth a visit.

All promotional culture has 'hard facts' and a hidden rhetoric of sales, and tourist brochures are no exceptions. A simple way of understanding what promotional rhetoric does is to look at what it omits, the way in which certain human values are generalized and projected, and the form of address (impersonal or personal, factual or ornamental). What I am trying to emphasize here is that all promotional rhetoric is ideological. It is ideological because it automatically defines and treats the reader/ viewer as a potential consumer/buyer, and seeks to persuade/influence this reader/viewer favourably towards the product. The tourist brochure thus assumes that each of its readers is a *potential* tourist.[2] Brochures belong to different genres depending on the clientele they seek and the destinations offered.

Brochures, in most cases, adopt a common format. There is almost always a visual on the front cover/page, with a few lines of publicity material, a catch line. This may be a single large visual or a series of smaller ones arranged as a collage. Following this are pages of information, cautiously interrupted by visuals (that may be smaller in size than the first or lead visual). Finally there will be boxed items of information about where to stay, addresses and websites of the organizing authority, and such on the last page/cover.

The kinds of visuals used depend on the destinations. Beach holidays, for instance, feature beaches and sand. They also depend on what the state chooses to project. Pondicherry Tourism, for example, projects the city as 'Peaceful Pondicherry'. The opening visuals are the sea, and a bit of the deserted waterfront in the foreground. There is a speck on the horizon. The second visual shows a section of the coast, with five boats (empty) tethered, and two others in the distance. The emphasis is on the selection of visuals that complement what the brochure 'sloganizes' about and what the state seeks to project—in this case, serene emptiness and peaceful locale. The *Chardham* brochure of UP Tourism's Hills Tourism concludes with a series of boxes listing package tours and general information (pp. 21–23). Facilities and special deals may often be in small print. Colour photographs are, of course, a must. There is no author mentioned, and often, as mentioned earlier, it is a form of literature for which you do not pay.

❑ TRAVEL AND TOURISM

In India tourism policy has had five stages (Richter 1989). From 1949 to 1966 tourism received little support from the government. The Tourist Traffic Branch of the Ministry of Transport was formed in 1949, and in

1958 a separate Tourism Department was established. The second phase starts around 1966, when the Indian Tourism Development Corporation (ITDC) was created, followed by the Ministry for Tourism and Civil Aviation. Tourism is now a concurrent subject, where responsibility is shared by both the Centre and the states. The Centre concentrates on attracting foreign tourists, and the states develop local programmes and structures. The *Incredible!ndia* campaign, the newest attempt to project India as the ultimate tourism destination of the century, is supplemented by similar campaigns at the regional/local levels by State Tourism Boards. Phase three was the period of the Janata Party government. The emphasis shifted from elite, 'star' hotels to Janata hotels. 1980 (the fourth phase) declared the 'Year of the Tourist' and marked by the 1982 Asiad, saw a massive expansion in infrastructure development. The fifth phase began in 1984. In 1986 India saw over 1 million international tourists, and earned over Rs 18 billion. Allocation for tourism grew from Rs 33.3 million in the 2nd Five-Year Plan (1956–61) to Rs 29 billion in the 10th.

Before reading the rhetoric of tourist brochures and the ideology of tourism, it is necessary to identify the key features of travel and tourism that form the subject matter of these brochures.

Travel is the displacement from one site to another, however temporary it may be in terms of time. One travels to school or work everyday (and comes back 'home'). One travels to visit another city (and comes back 'home'). One may even migrate to another country for good. Travel suggests a movement from one place to another, a point of departure and a point of arrival, a point of origin and a point of return (usually coterminous with the point of origin), separated by another space (the space of transit). It suggests also a movement in time, where the time spent on travel is crucial to defining a tourist. Travel thus has both a temporal and a spatial dimension.

Tourism is the business of organizing travel for commercial purposes. Tourism is almost always a leisure activity that seeks to provide pleasure and experiences outside the realm of everyday life and work. Thus Rajasthan Tourism (1997) claims: 'if you are looking for an out-of-the-ordinary experience, start out to discover Rajasthan' (p. 5). The suggestion is of an alternative to the everyday. The Kerala Tourism brochure goes on to elaborate this alternative:

> In a world of fast foods, fast cars and oxygen bars, life is a far cry from good old nature. So, when contemporary lifestyle takes its toll on you, journey to a land where nature is still an integral part of everyday life.

Here nature is contrasted with the culture of everyday life, and tourism is meant to be recuperative rather than entertaining. As the 10th Five-Year Plan document notes, there is a large increase in the numbers of people seeking 'wellness' and 'health' holidays (http://www.planningcommission.nic.in/plans, 7.5: 818, 7 September 2004).

Tourism is almost always geared to a place which is unconnected with the place of work. 'Get away' is a favourite image in tourist brochures. The Andamans, in fact, advertises itself as 'floating in splendid *isolation*' (emphasis added) in its brochure (things are now very different after the tsunami of December 2004; there are, however, reports of 'disaster tourism' and a 'volcano tourism' phenomenon; see *The Times of India*, 7 January 2005). Pondicherry recommends that you 'give time a break'. *Travel + Leisure* announced a number on '50 Romantic Getaways' (February 2002).

Integral to this choice of place is the promotional culture about various places. Tourist brochures promote places for people to choose from: the form of travel, the form of experience they wish to have. They draw attention to the features of a place and construct an anticipation of a different experience (I shall return to this point). In short, travel and tourist brochures construct, in *advance* of the actual travel, the experience of the place in the traveller's imagination.

People travel for various reasons. A short list of the forms of travel is as follows: leisure travel, adventure travel, medical travel, pilgrimage, nature travel, business travel, research travel, personal travel, cultural travel, election/political travel, immigration/refugee/exile travel, etc. Travellers can, therefore, be of various types: young/old people, families, business travellers, vacationers, pilgrims, etc. Since travel involves movement from one place to another and a temporary 'immersion' in an Other place/culture, and because it requires the coordination of more than just the traveller (the ticketing agent, the tour operator, the hotels, and the shops …), travel is irreducibly social. It is socially organized and promoted. Travel is a feature of public life, even if the traveller is solitary. Any writing or promotional culture that explains, defines, or informs a person as a potential traveller is firmly located in the public domain, even if the information comes from another individual and not a public document. The act of communicating about another place is a public cultural act, since it promotes another *public space through a shared set of attributes, values and signs.*

Tourism, as diverse thinkers (MacCannell 1976; Urry 1998[1990]; Veblen 1994 [1899]) have demonstrated, is a leisure activity. As such, it is closely linked to the social conditions of work and living. The sociology of leisure argues that leisure displaces work from the centre of modern social arrangements (MacCannell 1976: 5). On the other hand, *lifestyles* combine both work and leisure, and lifestyles become the basis of social relationships. Cultural Studies is interested in the ideology of leisure and/or tourism. Tourism and its rhetoric represent society, leisure, places and people in specific ways.

I am interested in the ways in which the tourist brochures construct places and the experience of tourists to those places. Following John Urry's suggestion (1998 [1990]) that the tourist 'gaze' is socially organized and produced, I argue that the rhetoric of tourist brochures constructs, like the museum, not only objects/sites of seeing, but *ways* of seeing them. There is, therefore, a poetics and a politics of the brochure. Tourism and the tourist brochure is a collection of signs about a place, and they construct the (individual/collective) tourist's gaze. The brochure involves the individual reader in an exercise of the imagination, in order to create a degree of attraction about a particular site.

- The poetics is the rhetoric of the brochure—its visuals, its coded and structured information, its appeal to sentiments, emotions or values.
- The politics is the *construction* of the other place as commodity, the tourist as consumer, and the interaction of the two.

In a larger sense the politics of tourism is linked to global geopolitics. Tourism in 'Third World' nations thus cannot be separated from the merchandising of the 'Third World'.

The tourist brochure, like a piece of travel writing, is both a *descriptive* and a *prescriptive* geography. It codes the individual experience as personal, though it is carefully constructed through social and public 'technologies' of representation. It transforms publicly and socially crafted (commercial) interests into a one-to-one appeal.

Hereafter I shall use the term 'tourist' rather than 'traveller' to convey this dual movement: of the individual's experience and the public/social structures that inform, mediate and define that experience. The tourist experience is, however, not a simple one-way absorption of whatever is staged. The tourist works under what I call a 'tourist imperative', where s/he is asked to participate in certain rituals (seeing, admiring), activities (consumption, shopping) and behaviour (non-routine playfulness).

The tourist imperative may be discovered in the pages of the brochure, exhorting you to do this and that.

The tourist market is mainly organized around class lines in terms of both 'taste' and cost. One index of this distinction along class lines is the variety of brochures and information material to suit various needs. Newspapers in India carry advertisements for package tours on a regular basis. Note the differences between these and the advertisements in *Outlook Traveller* or the up-end travel magazines. The package holiday is standardized: offering sun, sand and sea to all. It is aimed at the mass market (like the pilgrimage tours offered in Uttaranchal and other tourist areas in India). It is not for the 'discriminating' tourist of the upper class.

Incredible!ndia, the Indian government's newest initiative, states in its opening lines in one of its online newsletters:

> From culture to heritage to wildlife to adventure to pilgrimage to nature, whatever the theme of your travel may be, India has the perfect destination for you. (Vol. 20, February 2004)

The newsletter has effectively listed the *forms* of tourism available in India. Larger categories of tourism, as documented by the 10th Five-Year Plan, include long-haul travel, neighbouring country tourism, rural and ethnic tourism, 'wellness' and health tourism, cultural tourism, spiritual tourism, eco-tourism, and sport and adventure tourism (7.5: 817, 818–19, www.planningcommission.nic.in/plans, 7 September 2004).

There are three principal types of tourism today.

1. Cultural and Ethnic Tourism: There are actually three related forms of cultural tourism: high or institutionalized culture, which includes museums, exhibitions, visual arts, literature, science and technology centres; folk or popular culture, which includes film, entertainment, shopping, sport, mass media, customs and traditions; and ethnic symbols, which include folkways, local/vernacular architecture, education, transport, dress and language. Ethnic tourism depends on first-hand experience of other cultures, and the ethnic tourist invariably seeks an authenticity of experience. Cultural tourism induces social, economic and political changes in the society that functions as the destination of the cultural and ethnic tourist with the arrival of the structures of tourism itself: the corporation, the hotels, the transport and communications infrastructure, the advertisement, and guide

companies. Dances and art forms originally designed for particular religious or social purposes take on the role of entertainment for tourists. A related term is 'heritage tourism', where heritage is taken to mean history, culture and the land on which people live. It includes historic buildings and monuments; traditional landscapes and indigenous wildlife; language, literature, music and art; traditional events and folkloric practices; sites of important events like battles; and traditional lifestyles including food, drink and sport.

2. Rural Tourism: The 10th Five-Year Plan envisages the promotion of Indian villages as 'the primary tourism product of India' (http://www.planningcommission.nic.in/plans, 7.5: 826, 7 September 2004). This is a popular form in Western tourism, especially in countries like the UK, which highlights the glories of 'ye old England' and its famous, presumably unchanged, villages and countryside, and often links up with *heritage and cultural tourism*. York city advertises itself in the Jarrold's brochure and city guide (2000) thus:

> Eboracum to the Romans, Eoforwic to the Anglo-Saxons and Jorvik to the Vikings, York has almost two thousand years of recorded history and a wonderful collection of buildings of all ages, contained within the finest remaining length of medieval walls in England. (p. 1)

The emphasis on time past is meant to suggest that tourism is about a mythical Golden Age of culture. Then there is the set of activities associated with rural life: farming, community living and the 'simple life'. In India, the major tourist circuit should integrate the metropolitan centre with the non-urban.

3. Eco-tourism: UP Tourism's brochures often carry the following write-up as a special, clearly noticeable boxed item:

> Awesome, serene and inspiring snow bound Himalayas of Uttar Pradesh are one of nature's most beautiful gift to mankind. As a visitor please make sure to respect local traditions and culture, help maintain local harmony and protect the majestic natural environment.

This is followed by a list of 'Dos and Don'ts', which include eco-friendly advice/instructions about cooking, and culture-friendly ones about seeking permission before taking photographs. The

Incredible!ndia campaign promotes 'responsible tourism', where travel is linked to conservation and value for nature and local cultures. This is how it describes 'responsible tourism':

> If it actually enhances wildlife values
> If it is able to improve the lives of locals
> If the facilities are ecologically sensitive
> If it is understood that tourism should serve wildlife and not the other way round. (Vol. 22, April 2004)

Today this is also called 'sustainable' or 'eco-tourism'. Closely aligned with *wilderness tourism*, eco-tourism is travel to relatively undisturbed natural areas with the specific objective of studying and enjoying the scenery (including plants and animals), as well as cultural aspects of those areas. Sustainable tourism operates within a region's capacities for regeneration and future productivity. It recognizes the contribution of local cultures and seeks to provide an equitable share in the economic benefits of tourism. The natural environment—coastal resorts, national parks, tropical rainforests, mountain resorts—which mixes natural beauty with safety and comfort, has proved to be one of the most popular tourist destinations around the world. This includes components as diverse as the aesthetic (the appreciation of wild nature), the escapist (relief from urban life), the challenge ('roughing it' with minimal facilities, and endurance), the historic/romantic (re-living the 'frontier' or 'primitive' life), solitude (being alone in the 'lap of nature') and others.

The various sites of these forms of tourism include craft centres, museums, centres of industry, science-based attractions, religious sites, military features, primary production centres (fishing, mining), older villages and towns, resorts, monuments to historical events (battles, deaths, suicides), 'natural' settings (jungles, rocks), film locations, historic homes, places associated with famous people, and, finally, places that offer specific pleasures and entertainments (sex, adventure, gambling, entertainment—Disneyland, South-east Asia's sex tourism, Las Vegas and its casinos, Mediterranean yachting).

It is important to understand that tourism and leisure also involves work. Holiday-makers and tourists may be escaping from their daily chores, but their leisure and relaxation involves the labour of workers in the tourism industry. Some people have to work hard at providing leisure to others.

Tourism, postmodernity, globalization

By 1984 there were nearly 30 million tourist arrivals worldwide, and international tourist receipts had increased by about 48 times over the 1950–84 period (Urry 1998[1990]: 47). This is what Urry terms the 'internationalization of tourism', where the tourist patterns of countries cannot be read separately from the developments in other countries (ibid.: 48). What occurs is that different countries begin to specialize in their tourist appeal: Singapore as the futuristic city, England for its 'old world' charms, India for its colourful places, and so on. The package holiday tour has become the standard mode of tourism for most people. However, there has been an increasing trend in 'free and independent travel' or FIT (Hart, qtd. in ibid.: 49). The rise of hotel consortia has enabled the spread of international tourism because a certain uniformity of standard is now made available to the tourist wherever s/he goes. The internationalization of tourism has also meant a similar growth in tourist-related services. Food and restaurant chains (McDonalds) and theme parks (Disneyland's branches worldwide) are the most immediately visible forms of this development (on theme/amusement parks see, among others, King 1981; Nye 1981).

Such worldwide tourist development has economic, social and cultural impacts. The routing of places, building of structures and policies about entertainment centres are politico-economic decisions with socio-cultural effects. Tourism is thus a cultural condition that affects both guests and hosts. Urry notes that the growth of tourism in developing countries—expecting and creating 'safaris' in African nations, for instance—is almost never linked to the 'native' social/economic/cultural processes of that society. It is linked, on the contrary, to externally-imposed factors such as hotel chains, travel agencies, investment from the outside, and so on (1998[1990]: 61–64). A host culture is thus transformed by another, often for self-aggrandizement. The tourist's culture, or at least a few aspects of it, are decontextualized, essentialized, indigenized and recontextualized. A process of what Mary Louise Pratt famously termed 'transculturation' occurs in this context. Pratt used the term to describe the ways in which subordinated and marginal groups select and invent from materials transmitted to them from the dominant or metropolitan culture (1995 [1992]). The adoption of Levi's jeans or the arrival of the digicam in a suburban Indian town is an example of tourism's transculturational effect. The tourist, likewise, takes away ethnic clothes, food, or artifacts to adorn her/his walls. In both cases, the 'local' culture cuts across boundaries and moves beyond the point of origin into another field where it can be reinterpreted. Levi's, for instance, can very well stand for 'modernized' or Westernized India. Transculturation is thus the semantic reorganization of artifacts through tourism.

Transculturation is also one of the challenges faced by local communities. In addition to the obvious one of changing demographics, local communities face numerous challenges from tourism, such as being able to maintain their regular lifestyles in the presence of visitors, the commercialization of their culture and customs, continuing to perform their rituals and customs under the shadow of commercial exploitation, and such. The cultures—both host and tourist—lose their 'natural' relation to geographical and social territories. The tourist's culture stretches across time and space, and is thus 'deterritorialized'—that is, it loses its specificity when it is adopted by another. (For instance, American popular culture is increasingly global today. This has a lot to do with the material structures of marketing and the power held by transnational corporations that spread American culture.)[3]

In other cases tourist production and display may be the central process in the reconstruction or reassertion of an ethnic identity. For instance, the community may emphasize their unique features (even those elements that were forgotten or lost) for tourists. This in itself is an assertion of identity, in the sense that there may even be a retrieval of cultural features for the sake of the tourist. The creation of this public image by the host community for tourist consumption recreates traditional culture (Friedman 1996 [1994]: 111).

Increasingly, international tourist attractions tend to blur the distinction between reality and illusion. Tourism is, of course, based on spectacle, since it is primarily a visual practice. Much of what is experienced in the tourist's gaze today is mediated through photography. What we see when we stare at the Taj Mahal is an actualization of the image that we have already seen before. Advertisements and brochures prepare the image for viewing even before the trip. What is *seen* is a representation that has been internalized. This postmodern condition where the image (say, a photograph) merges into the object of the image/photograph, means that there is a problematic fusion of reality and representations of that reality. Further, one of the features of postmodern tourism has been that anything and everything can become a tourist attraction.

One of the central features of the post-industrial world is the growth of the service sector as an industry in itself. The service class, as a result, expands. It is this class that has a greater concern with 'culture'. This is the class—constituted by youth working in banking services, the media, call centres, the fashion industry and hospitality services—which now spends more money as consumers. It is also the class that travels, and seeks new experiences and places. International and domestic tourism has been considerably altered with the arrival of this class in the category of 'tourist'. The National Tourism Policy of 2002 foregrounds the significance of this new class of tourist:

> A new class of young tourists, with marked preference for adventure and distant destinations, in hills, caves and forests, is emerging, this class is not looking for 5-star accommodation but only for simple and clean places to stay. The requirements of this class of tourists should be met and guest tourism encouraged through Panchayats and local bodies and associations. (p. 5)

Another central feature of postmodern, globalized tourism is the widespread media coverage of everything: from celebrities to events. What this means is that people with access to the Internet and television also have access to alternative lifestyles, fashions and cultures. The class I have described above has all of this. As a result of such 'institutionalized voyeurism' (Urry 1998[1990]: 91), younger tourists and groups are able to adopt or imitate other lifestyles easily. This means that a kind of refracted cultural tourism occurs when borders between different social groups, ethnicities, and even nationalities are transgressed. From the consumption of Mars bars at a supermarket to wearing a piece of ethnic jewellery from sub-Saharan Africa, the cultural package now available to the new youth is connected to international tourism, the globalized economy, and a new cultural condition of postmodern boundary-breaking.

What is also important is the political economy of international tourism, and the close links between the travel of global capital, labour, skills and tourism. Tourism, especially from the last decades of the 20th century, has been structured around geopolitics that may or may not have anything to do with culture. The demographics of global travel is invariably skewed—from the 'First World' to the 'Third'—and immigration (one of the worst forms of travel) from the 'Third World' to the 'First'. That is, the politics of travel is aligned with and informed by the system of exploitation and domination that structures the global economy and culture. The critic John Frow in fact sees tourism as a mere 'extension of commodity relations, and the consequent inequalities of power between center and periphery, 'First' and 'Third World', developed and underdeveloped regions, metropolis and countryside' (qtd. in Huggan 2001: 177). The structures of differentiation/exploitation are naturalized into tourist spectacles and drama for consumption, and thereby hide the actual conditions that create a 'Third World' tourist destination.

In such a heavily media-ted postmodern tourist set-up, we have a post-tourist (Urry 1998[1990]: 100). The post-tourist is a different kind of tourist because s/he can now endlessly recycle/re-experience the tourist experience through the images beamed from various technologies. A flick of a switch or the click of the mouse can summon up endless images of the 'scene'. Admittedly, all tourist activity is a 'framing' of the event or the place. However, in the case of the post-tourist, the experience of the place is not only mediated in *advance* of the experience, it is also reduced to (or modified into) a part of popular culture with its endless repetition. I am arguing here that the extraordinary proliferation of material and images for tourists renders one a perpetual tourist, without ever having left the city. As an example I offer the rapid expansion of the Indian state's tourism programme: newsletters in the email, brochures, kiosks and offices—with unusually well-informed and cooperative staff, for government employees—and such measures have altered our perception of tourism itself. Further, the colourful tourism fair (Hyderabad just concluded one, as I write this, between 27 and 29 August 2004), showcasing the tourism departments of various Indian states, and places and events, itself becomes a tourist attraction. It is not merely a centre to dispense information: it is a destination in itself.

The post-tourist also has a greater variety of choices—from the sacred to the dangerous. There is little to constrain a post-tourist from the pursuit of pleasure, as it were. S/he can move from high culture to low, and vice versa, with little or no problems. In fact, one of the features of postmodern tourism is this very interesting mix of cultural forms: eating at a 'star' hotel, visiting the local museum, and spending an evening being entertained by/at the village talent. Star hotels also organize special regional festivals (*dosa* festivals, Rajasthani festivals, and so on; *Incredible!ndia* even promoted a Mango Festival in Mumbai in May 2002), where efforts are made to re-do everything—from décor to food, costumes to music—with elements from that particular region. This is a startling development: seeing rural Rajasthan reproduced within the premises of Best Western or the Taj (or *havelis* converted into hotels). The rural ambience is, of course, carefully free of cow-dung (or cows), gutters or flies in this case, thus rendering it a safe bucolic experience. Tourists cannot take the completely strange or new either. They need to travel and see from a safe vantage point. Thus tourism, especially in 'Third World' nations/regions, needs to create the exotic with a degree of safety. Jharkhand Tourism, advertising its wildlife tourism, for instance, describes itself as 'wild and beautiful'. In another brochure, it refers to its rivers as both 'tamed and untamed'. Since the wild is invariably awesome and the beautiful certainly tame, the brochure combines awe-inspiring danger with a more placid beauty. It goes on to add: 'ten observation towers in the sanctuary makes [sic] it all the more easier [sic] to have a closer encounter with wild life'. The distance from the wild is crucial to tourism here: danger can be experienced mainly through a safety device (the jeep safari, the window of a bus, a watch tower, and so on).

The high and the low, the urban and the rural all come together in the postmodern, post-tourist experience, in which kitsch is central. Images and replicas of all cultural artifacts are now easily available in some form or the other (photographs, brochures, souvenirs, digitized CD-versions). The replica cuts across various levels—the artistic, the commercial and the cultural.

This also makes the postmodern tourist scene a site of play. The post-tourist is aware of the kitschy nature of her/his experience. The ethnic bar or tribal costumes in the controlled precincts of the hotel are, at best, ludic. The post-tourist is involved in a game here: make-believe, instant-history, packaged adventure, and bottled 'native' culture. The ludic is integral to the idea of the post-tourist. Brochures suggest a 'letting go', a release from the constraints of managed, organized and regimented life. The sudden shift to so-called 'freedom'—stated in many advertisements and brochures—transforms the act of tourism into a *play*.

The commodification of place

The 10th Five-Year Plan lists the following 'special interests of tourist target markets', an exercise in delineating the consumer geography of India. It opens the description with the following note:

> Cultural and heritage tourism will be expanded. India has a vast array of protected monuments with 22 world heritage sites, 16 of which are monuments. The integrated development of areas around these monuments provides an opportunity for the development of cultural tourism in India.

Having said this, it goes on to list the natural and man-made features that can be marketed: beach and coastal areas, villages, adventure spots (Himalayas), cuisine, wildlife (sanctuaries such as Kaziranga and Kanha), fairs and festivals, 'rejuvenation packages' (health tourism), and others (10th Five-Year Plan document of the Planning Commission, http://www.planningcommission.nic.in/plans, 7.5: 826, 7 September 2004). *Incredible!ndia* newsletters occasionally advertise a 'crafts map' of India. What this means is perhaps best explained by the write-up on it:

The Crafts Map of India: The Dastkari Haat Samiti is a federation of Indian Crafts people which creates these artistic and informative craft maps of different parts of India. These maps are handy and useful for lovers of craft, exporters, students, Indian and foreign tourists, travel agencies, hotels, designers, entrepreneurs and voluntary organizations.

These maps inform you of production and marketing areas of the vast range of handicrafts and handlooms in the different states of India. (Vol. 15, July 2003)

The geographical or political map of India is now supplemented (supplanted?) by a 'crafts map'. The colonial administration once prepared medical geographies of India in the 19th century (examples include James Ranald Martin's *Notes on the Medical Topography of Calcutta*, 1837). The 'crafts map' provides information on the consumer pleasures— of acquiring ethnic crafts and such—that can be expected. This is the ultimate consumer geography of the age of tourism. It marks the perfect commodification of place itself.

Tourism requires careful preparation, crafting and presentation of a place. To begin with, a place must be made accessible. Places of accommodation have to be set up. Other essentials include banking, health and information centres. Peripherals include shopping, entertainment, and other centres. Finally, there is the publicizing of the place through the media. All this suggests that the place is staged, made ready for presentation and consumption. Robert David Sack (1992: 157–58) identifies the stages in the commodification of a place.

The first stage is the *discovery* of tourist potential in a place and the subsequent image-making of the place by the state or entrepreneurs. This is followed by the *development* of the place, where local authorities and entrepreneurs set up natural and cultural attractions, changing the physical appearance of the place. *Consolidation* is the stage of aggressive marketing and publicity. This stage might also be marked by some imposition of 'artificial' facilities to 'augment' existing ones. After a while the place begins to lose its clientele (*decline*). It then has to be *rejuvenated* with new attractions (Sack 1992: 157–58).

It is important to note that the commodification of a place usually involves the consumption of its own contexts. That is, a landscape of consumption may very well reinforce existing inequalities and oppressions. Thus the indigenous poor artisan or the marginalized tribal tends to be further repressed when s/he is converted into a tourist attraction. Their rituals—rooted in their lived social contexts—are transformed into commodities for consumption. They may be paid to perform these activities by the state or the entrepreneur, and this may very well alter the meaning of the ritual (though this need not happen—the presence of the tourist need not alter the significance of the ritual for the tribal or the artisan). But the poor tribal *remains* a poor tribal for the benefit of the tourist. Nowhere does one see tribals being depicted as having transformed into lawyers or doctors. One does not see them as 'outside' their immediate habitus. The tourist expedition to the Araku valley in Andhra Pradesh does not show them as anything other than tribals—unchanging, and available as spectacle (or sociological analysis, funded by 'First World' nations). They would not be tourist attractions if they were presented as tribals-become-doctors.

Another effect of the commodification of place through tourism is the homogenization of places, events, cultures and people. When tourists arrive in large numbers in places such as Ooty, the place itself becomes less a region/place in Tamil Nadu than a cosmopolitan city. This cosmopolitanism is not a feature of Ooty, but something imposed upon it by tourists from all over India. The very fact that tourist guides in these places speak various languages is symbolic of the cosmopolitanization and transculturation of the place. The *development* of a place into a tourist spot also makes for the cosmopolitanization of the place. The arrival of machinery, engineers, investors, entertainers, experts, and other associated service personnel invariably alters the demographics and cultural conditions of the place even before the tourist inflow begins.

This also means that the construction and development of a place into a tourist attraction transforms the place into a stage. The landscape, with its people, itself becomes a stage. However, the true exploitative, oppressive and unhealthy consequences of the dirt and the labour are, of course, hidden behind the fantasy, the screen and the glitter. An acceptable (sterilized) version of the labour and the mess are, however, made available on stage, as contemporary postmodern tourism makes it a point to showcase *everyday* lives: the artisan at work, the loom in operation, the mason toiling in the sun. Rural tourism, ethnic tourism and such other forms, for instance, enable the tourist to go and live with the community and participate in the activities of everyday life there. This rather odd mix of spectacle and participation, of tourism and everyday 'host' life, is a postmodern tourism condition. Thus Himachal Pradesh Tourism advertises its famous Naldehra Golf Club on its brochure. And the Corporation's catch-line is 'suburbs of paradise'. The juxtaposition of ultramodern tourism, sport and 'suburb' in the phrase reflects the kitsch. The theme park is one form of this condition, where community life is recreated for tourist consumption. Synthetic labour in these contexts becomes postmodern tourist spectacle.

Through each of these processes of staging, construction and presentation, the place becomes a commodity. Perhaps the best example of the commodification of place in tourism is illustrated by the Andhra Pradesh Tourism booklet (2002). The cover page reads:

Andhra Pradesh

The Ultimate Tourist Destination

(Product Catalogue)

Between the first two phrases and the parenthetical descriptive is the Andhra Pradesh Tourism Development Corporation's logo. Here is the ultimate commodification of a place: the place is now reduced to a 'product', and the brochure, which includes in its contents everything from pilgrimage to hotels and shopping centres, has transformed everything into a consumer product.

Descriptive and prescriptive geography

What exactly does a tourist brochure do *to* a place? As noted earlier, a brochure (re)presents a place as spectacle. However, the brochure, the travel write-up (the Gantzers' columns in *The Hindu*, for instance), the travel book (Bill Aitken's) and the travel guide are a curious mixture of information, entertainment and commercial (promotional) culture. I suggest that the tourist brochure or guide can be read as an exercise in geography.

Travel writing (by which I mean the brochure, the diary, the log book) is a *descriptive geography*, where one records and reveals information about new places. A quick glance through any travel writing will reveal its contents. The descriptive geography includes: city area (including environment); population and population density; what it contains (major industry, shops, kind of houses, parks, schools and universities); inhabitants (ethnicity, wealth, character, religion, languages and dialects, famous people); weather; history of town (including name and age); 'tourist attractions' (temples, museums, forts, statues, festivals, sightseeing tours, souvenirs); tips and hints for real fun/adventures; currency; local transport; how to get there and get away again/where and what to eat/where to stay.

This, however, is not all. A good travel piece frequently recommends a particular place or activity: 'When in ... you must ....' Or, as corollary, they may suggest a particular place for a particular experience ('Want to learn French? ... then go to Pondicherry'). This might be promotional (in the case of the brochure), or the advice of one who has tried it (in the case of the memoir or travelogue), and makes the brochure a *prescriptive geography* too. Most tourist brochures and travel literature are a combination of these two forms of geography. The first form retails information and is encyclopaedic in scope, and the second offers opinions and is evaluative.

❑ ATTRACTION, IMAGINATION, ANTICIPATION

The *Incredible!ndia* online newsletter carried this as a banner-ad:

Where you can watch Discovery on 70 mm.

Andhra Pradesh Tourism's *Srikakulam* brochure opens with the following lines:

Imagine a place where gushing rivers meet thickly wooded hills. Where the golden sands of the beaches are coupled with a variety of flora and fauna. Where ancient Hindu temples flourished side by side with historical Buddhist relics.

Andhra Pradesh Tourism's *Nagarjunasagar* brochure opens thus:

Imagine visiting a place where at one go you can have an unfettered view of the past and the present. Where the finest examples of human achievement can be witnessed. A site that once was home to a highly evolved civilisation and which is today a location that represents the high point in the evolution of construction activity.

In all these cases the potential tourist is invited to travel first *in the mind*—through the recreation of a visual, or through an act of imagination based on a verbal description. If the first example summons up an image through recourse to an already familiar visual medium, the second and third asks us to picture the place for ourselves, using the given descriptions. In both examples the act of imagination is the necessary preliminary to the act of actual travel.

The promotion of natural landscape as a version of a television channel is a truly interesting phenomenon. The image of the landscape as a visual field known from the screen is an attempt to introduce it as something already known. The potential tourist, already aware of the Discovery channel (the nomenclature of the channel/programme is worthy of debate in itself), sees the Indian landscape a second time, as it were. The brochure and the newsletter, therefore, conceal a rhetoric that anticipates the reader's response by invoking a familiar visual. By linking the landscape to the channel, the banner-ad effectively cinematizes the land, rendering it known/knowable. It suggests the new that is not startlingly new either. It invites the reader/viewer to see the place *again*.

The essence of the travel brochure/guide is the effect it seeks to create about a particular place upon its reader(s). It is a promotional device that seeks to persuade the reader to become a tourist to that place. In short, a brochure is a regime of representation, with its own rhetoric and poetics. The anticipation of pleasure at the prospect of visiting a particular place can also be through the consumption of films, documentaries (on the Discovery or National Geographic channels, for instance), photographs, and even literature. In fact, such an imaginative construction of the place and its pleasures even before arrival is central to the tourist enterprise. Here is the *Incredible!ndia* banner-ad in one of its newsletters:

Visiting India might turn to be a far more rewarding experience than going just by the written word. Till then, read on …. (Vol. 22, April 2004)

Here the reader is actively encouraged to set up a dialectic between reading about India and being there. However, the rhetoric achieves something else: it prepares the reader as a potential tourist, who readies her/himself for India by reading about the land first. The *anticipation* of pleasure is part of the tourist experience. You begin to travel even before you have booked your ticket. The importance of reading up on a place is further emphasized in this same newsletter when it states:

> According to a survey conducted by *Travel + Leisure*, the world's leading travel magazine, India ranked #1 as the ad read most in the issue (from the 75 ads featured). In fact the ad scored higher than the average ads in the tourism promotion and travel category. Just goes on to show that India is where the action is. (Vol. 22, April 2004)

This imaginative act of constructing an Other pleasure is intimately linked to the rhetoric of the brochure or the travel book, which lists and details the attractions of the Other place. With the arrival of globalized media, especially television and the Internet, the process of transculturation has speeded up considerably. The travel brochure creates an Other land/culture for the potential traveller—and thus sets up a dialectic between her/his present culture and the other one. The media offers another place to the potential tourist's imagination. Transculturation—which is essentially the crossing of boundaries (geographical, material, cultural)—is initiated from this very moment of anticipation and imagination. The tourist experience is always prepared for through this process of *imaginative transculturation*.[4] The actual ('real') physical experience is the *material transculturation*, which has already been (pleasurably) anticipated. This anticipation and imagination means that one never sees a place for the first time: a place is always already 'seen' through the process of transculturation coded as information in brochures, posters, guide books, and such. In this section I shall look at the structure of tourist attraction as constructed by brochures.

Zoos, heritage monuments, technological centres, natural and man-made landscapes, people and their habitats, are all part of tourist attractions. Jane Desmond (1999) identifies two main forms of tourism in the case of Hawaii: people tourism and animal tourism (p. xv). People tourism—my main interest here—is more commonly called 'cultural tourism', which means leaving home and routine to meet practices different from one's own. It is important, as a structural feature of the attraction, that there be a physical enactment of difference: the people performing must be performing something different from the tourist's own practices. That is, the difference must be physically manifest and embodied for it to be an 'authentic' tourist attraction. Most tourist programmes emphasize such 'live' performances for precisely this reason. In the case of animal tourism—which includes safaris, animal documentary films, zoos, animal theme parks, nature parks and eco-tourism—the attraction is higher if the animals are *doing* something. As a result performing animals are the central attractions.

Structural differentiation and the tourist experience

Incredible!ndia, in its monthly newsletters, identifies specific circuits and regions for travellers to plan their itinerary. These include: 'The Punjab Circuit, The Metro Guide, The Lure of the Jungles, The Buddhists [sic] Circuit, The Temple Trail'.

The UP Tourism's slogan and catch-line in some of its brochures is 'Uttar Pradesh: The Essence of India' (*Chardham* brochure, back cover). Andhra Pradesh Tourism's brochure on Vijaywada describes it as 'the heart of Andhra Pradesh', once again condensing the state to one focal point, and suggesting that the region can be essentialized in this spot.

Communities, nations and state enterprises organize social, historical, cultural and natural elements into a series of impressions. Tourism is the management of these elements into a series that delivers the maximum value of attraction. This organization is what MacCannell terms 'structural differentiation' (1976: 48).

To begin with, the *entire* state/region is the principal attraction. The brochure/website/flier invites the tourist to the region or state. The other attractions are *embedded* in this principal attraction. The region is therefore *differentiated* into its embedded attractions, often as a sequence that appears as natural as possible. Thus institutions, work areas, establishments, and 'natural' areas are all designated as tourist attractions. Differentiation and detail are integral to the tourist brochure, and constitute what I have called its 'descriptive geography'. While differentiation is the key to tourism, the tourist brochure often also treats certain sections of the region as *essential* to the itinerary. When UP tourism advertises the state as the 'essence of India', it has, first, structurally differentiated India into its regions and states. It then goes on to present an 'essence', a core within this selection. The structural differentiation is therefore a means to isolate certain spaces as crucial to the tourist itinerary. Structural differentiation is about selecting and grading elements in terms of what the host believes are their degrees of appeal.

Most tourist spots in the world, especially urban centres, are organized into tourist districts, communities, neighbourhoods and regions. Each is further differentiated into markets and shopping areas, restaurants and eating places, recreational spots, and people. London, for instance, has the shopping centres (Oxford Street), the museum area (Tates, Victoria and Albert), sporting areas (Lords), and monument zone (Westminster). Following MacCannell (1976), I shall isolate those elements differentiated in tourist brochures.

(*i*)   One central element differentiated and often detailed in tourist brochures is the *functioning establishments* of the area. Commercial, industrial, business and even (older) educational establishments are basic elements in many tourist brochures.

(*ii*)   Then there are the *domestic establishments*—the homes of celebrities (usually dead), with visitation seasons and such. Visiting stately homes is a major part of English 'domestic tourism'.

(*iii*)   A third element is the *group*. Groups that are distinctive in character or appearance are mentioned in brochures as 'shows' for tourists to see. This is a curious mixture of the animal and the people tourism modes—where people are exhibited for their cultural uniqueness, but can convey their uniqueness only when they *perform*.

(*iv*)   *Occupations* are also major tourist attractions. Closely aligned with the functioning establishment category, tourists are encouraged and invited to watch whisky being made in Scotland, or the tribal artisan making pots in Shilparamam (Hyderabad).

(*v*)   *Transport networks* and systems are also sometimes tourist attractions. The Metro in Kolkata, London Bridge and San Francisco's Golden Gate Bridge are actually transport 'technologies' that double up as tourist attractions.

(*vi*)   Finally there are the designated 'touristy' attractions: the museums, parks, and such.

The rhetoric of tourist attraction

I am interested in the regimes of representation that posit, present and market a place as 'tourist attraction'. A place cannot speak for itself—it must be spoken for. It is the technology of this 'speaking for' that renders a place into an attraction, creating an anticipation of pleasure and inviting the potential tourist to participate in it.

Dean MacCannell defines a tourist attraction as the relationship between a tourist, a sight and a marker (1976: 41). The sight is the object viewed, and the marker is the information about the object. These three elements of the tourist experience also constitute the rhetoric of tourism.

Sights and sightseeing

Theorists of tourism—especially MacCannell and Urry—suggest that the gaze is integral to the tourist experience. Sightseeing is indeed often used as a synonym for tourism, thereby emphasizing the visual ideology of travel and tourism. Seeing sights is, as MacCannell argues (1976: 42), a ritual that all tourists perform with great sincerity. The ritualistic factor— the tourist imperative—is emphasized when we discover that one is supposed to see things in certain ways. Thus the Empire State Building, for instance, has an observation platform from which to see New York City. New York City is a sight to be seen, and it is best viewed from the designated spot. It becomes an obligation to see it in this way. What is being 'performed' through this sightseeing is a 'sacralization of sight' (ibid.: 43) itself. This process of sacralization has certain stages (ibid.: 43–48). The sight is first marked off from other objects in the vicinity, thus distinguishing it as a 'sight' (the naming stage). The object is then 'displayed', opened up for viewing in order to enhance its tourist quality ('framing and elevation' stage). Closely related to the second phase is the 'enshrinement stage', which includes the creation of special rooms, pedestals, lighting arrangements, and viewing platforms, all of which enhance the visibility and significance of the object. The 'mechanical reproduction' stage is the production of the tourist brochure, posters, guide books, photographic reproductions, replicas, souvenirs and models of the object, all of which promote it. Finally, in the 'social reproduction' phase, cities and regions begin to name themselves after famous monuments and attractions. Stratford-on-Avon is thus known as *Shakespeare's* place.

The above discussion focuses on the structures of sightseeing. However, sightseeing, by its very term, also implies an act of seeing/ gazing. That is, after a typology of the object of the gaze, we need to move on to two other aspects of the tourist gaze: the marker which mediates between sight and tourist, and the actual gaze of the tourist.

Markers

A marker is a sign that gives information about a particular sight. It may be a map, a picture, or a plan. Plaques, signboards, inscriptions are all markers that enable a certain way in which the tourist perceives the sight.

As you open the *Chardham* brochure of UP Tourism, on page four you get a landscape photograph. This is a long shot of a settlement on a hill, with more hills and rolling clouds in the background. The descriptive line adjacent to the photograph says: 'A magnificent view of Chamba.' Here the marker and catch-line tells us how to prepare for Chamba. The view is 'magnificent' even before we see it in 'reality'. The marker is telling us how our response should be. It is a poetics that prepares this emotional and aesthetic response: 'how magnificent' is what one exclaims when seeing the actual landscape. In terms of language, the marker is both the vehicle of meaning, and the meaning. What tourists see is not simply the sight, but the picture or postcard of the sight. That is, they see the *marker* (the photograph of Chamba) come alive when they behold the object (the settlement of Chamba). How does a tourist recognize the Taj Mahal for the first time? The answer is obvious: s/he is *not* seeing it for the first time, but is only matching the 'reality' with the picture/description s/he had. I am suggesting that what the tourist perceives in the so-called wonderful or beautiful qualities of the object is the picture itself. This is a kind of transformation where the image of the object and the object merge in the course of the gaze. In fact, such a transformation is part of the tourist imperative.

What is important is the fact that the designation of the object as a tourist attraction, as a 'must-see', has nothing to do with the inherent quality of the object (aesthetic, cultural, monumental, or social) itself. The object is made a 'worth-seeing' one by the social structures, values and politics *around* it. If a tourist recognizes sights by transforming them into their markers, then society 'recognizes' places, events or people by providing the markers, which the tourist will then see. In fact, 'heritage' is only heritage in tourism terms when it appeals to the tourist. In order to make this monument or that piece of machinery a 'heritage' site, it requires a marker which *calls* it that.

In the case of travel posters, for instance, a tourist identifies with the sight by sacralizing one of the sight's markers. This is displaced recognition, especially when the travel poster or replica adorns walls and drawing rooms (and now railway compartments, where *Incredible!ndia* posters are put up). These icons and images are basically markers that enable recognition, from afar, of a 'must-see' place. Destination branding is this sacralization of places through markers, and is a key feature of all contemporary tourism. Since many places compete for the tourist's attention (and money), destinations need to create a unique identity for themselves. They need to *differentiate* themselves from other tourist spots. The 10th Five-Year Plan states the case for India's destination branding in this way:

> As there is fierce competition for tourists from India's source markets, India needs to change its traditional marketing approach to one that is more competitive and modern. It needs to develop a unique market position, image and brand, which cannot be held by any other competitor. India's positioning statement will capture the essence of its tourism product to convey an 'image' of the product to a potential customer. This image will be related not only to its ancient Vedic civilization with a cultural heritage that continues to thrive especially in its rural areas but also to its essentially secular nature. (http://www.planningcommission.nic.in/plans, 7.5: 827–28, 7 September 2004)

It seeks, therefore, to highlight India's antiquity and glorious past as a special feature.

What tourist brochures and organizations do is to associate a place with strong emotional or other overtones/appeal for the consumer. Destination branding is this creation of a set of associations for that place. Thus Maharashtra Tourism's line is 'unlimited', suggesting unending attractions and possibilities. New Zealand tourism's line has been 100 per cent 'pure', and Ireland's 'Live a Different Life'. England brands itself as a heritage tourism site, with an emphasis on history. Each destination advertises itself for one (or more) identifiable feature. What destination branding does is summon up a set of visuals and ideas about a place in the tourist's mind. Nagpur city, famous for its oranges, for instance, uses the epithet 'Orange City' under its name. Both 'Nagpur' and 'Orange City' are in a blazing orange colour on the brochure (January 2002). Likewise, Kerala identifies itself with Ayurveda and 'holistic healing'.

Destination branding is surely a lure for potential tourists. But it can also function differently: if it portrays a particular feature to render the place attractive, that particular feature can also become the basis of evaluation by the tourists. One of the risks involved in sacralization and destination branding is that the descriptive geography of a place in the brochure/flier/poster can become the framework for perception and evaluation by the tourist.

The gaze

As noted above, the rhetoric of tourism in brochures, posters and fliers links sights, markers and tourists. The tourist is here, for purposes of my analysis, reduced to the tourist gaze, though surely tourism involves more than just seeing.

John Urry (1998[1990]: 47–48, 97–98) provides a typology of the tourist gaze. The two most significant types of gaze are the romantic and the collective.

(*i*)   The Romantic Gaze: This is a gaze that proceeds from a solitary viewing of nature or objects. The emphasis here is on solitude, privacy and a personal, almost semi-spiritual relationship with the object of the gaze. This kind of 'communion' with nature, for instance, is also closely aligned with the development of niche tourism.

(*ii*)   The Collective Gaze: This necessitates the presence of a large crowd. The atmosphere is, therefore, carnivalesque, and involves a public participation in the viewing. Package tours, where people are shepherded around the places of interest in groups, museum groups and study tours constitute examples of this kind of gaze.

Obviously, both these gazes have to do with the class and other background of the tourist. The collective gaze is the effect of a democratization of tourism, a Samsung-like 'Everyone is Invited'. The romantic gaze is exclusive, privileged and unaffordable to most. On the other hand, certain kinds of tourism call for the romantic gaze itself. For instance, nature tourism, or the pilgrimage, often necessitates a solitary, contemplative mood.

❑ STAGED AUTHENTICITY

Tribal and aboriginal culture is integral to tourism today. The commodification of aboriginal, folk or tribal culture is also linked to the degree of authenticity that can be achieved through these 'presentations'.

Authenticity is the key to visitor satisfaction when viewing other cultures. Staging is the key to the aesthetization and commodification of identities and places. A place or a people is cast as a 'scene'. Note the number of descriptions that suggest this emphasis on staging and theatre in tourist brochures and advertisements: scenery, kaleidoscope, views, picturesque, sight, profiles, panorama. In fact, the term 'scene' clearly indicates a stage, since etymologically it is connected to 's-kene', meaning a tent or stage where a spectacle is to be enacted and presented. In this section I shall look at the ways in which culture, places and people are staged for consumption. I am suggesting here that tourism consists of a careful *staging* of events and people, even when the tourist is taken into the depths of houses, asked to live with a family, or given a tour of the factory.

Dean MacCannell adapts Erving Goffman's analysis of social establishments (in which he speaks of 'front' and 'back' regions) to describe the conscious crafting of 'authentic' experiences. An analysis of the means by which authenticity is delivered to the tourist includes various components.

Setting

Tourists, escaping from their everyday life, seek new experiences when they travel. As noted above, one of the main aims of the tourist experience is to see how life is lived elsewhere. Therefore, the tourist seeks the everyday of another culture/region/group. As a result, the tourist does not want mere 'performances' staged for tourist benefit. S/he wants the genuine, the real. However, it is also true that the tourist, seeking to move beyond the front regions—of the reception, the performance—into the back regions—where the intimate, the 'home', the 'real' family meets—is seeking a more meaningful interaction with the Other. Much of contemporary tourism, therefore, takes the traveller into the workings of establishments, homes and institutions. There is the attempt to reveal and demystify the 'back' regions of the house. Most of us can recall being taken to fire-stations, newspaper offices and even biscuit or confectionary factories as part of school excursions. These trips revealed to us the inner world of the factory. The issue is whether this movement into the interior of a place or culture is more authentic. MacCannell argues that this kind of tourism is meant to foster feelings of discovery and of being an 'insider' (1976: 99).

However, even this is staged. In order to understand the rhetoric of this staged authenticity, we need to pay attention to the settings used in tourism.

A setting is a crafted point of view initiated and facilitated by certain structures that are placed in certain positions so that the viewer can get particular views of the object. MacCannell suggests that there is a movement from the front to the back stage in any tourist setting.

Stage 1: This is the social space of the reception, of the very visible area which the tourist is convinced is only a façade.

Stage 2: Here the front region may carry some icons and details of the back regions as reminders of what is behind the set. Thus a piece of equipment from the farm may be placed in the front so as to convey a sense of the real.

Stage 3: Here the front region is organized to look like the back region. In this context the back region may actually be simulated, with live performances.

Stage 4: Here the back region is opened partially to tourists and visitors. Included in this stage are magazine and press coverage of celebrity lives, or the exposé of secret deals and negotiations within the corporate or state functionings.

Stage 5: Here the back region is *altered* to allow the tourist to 'look in'. The ship's interior, or sections of the factory may be 'revealed' through a tour.

Stage 6: Here the back region is opened up for the tourist to experience the 'real'.

What is important here is that the tourist always gets a staged authenticity. Even when the back regions are opened up to the tourist gaze, it remains a setting because the members in the back region are 'on their best behaviour', have been cleaned up—or the dirt and mess have been carefully scrutinized to see that they don't constitute a hazard—and altered for the moment. At the University of Hyderabad, where I teach, and student exchange programmes worldwide, foreign students have the option of staying with a local family. This is meant to provide access to the back region of another culture's family life. This is a good example of 'staged authenticity' because once again the host family is at its best, setting itself in such a way as to convey the best possible image to the foreigner.

Exoticization

One of the central modes of staging authenticity is exoticization. Exoticization can be defined as 'making strange'. The emphasis here is on presenting the object as a unique, singular instance. Exoticization is achieved through various means:

The exoticization of distance

In this mode the object is rendered strange and new by emphasizing its point of origin—which is very distant from that of the tourist. That is, the object is projected as something that hails from afar. Conversely, the tourist travels a great distance to see the sight. It is the distance—plus the dangers of travelling huge distances—that makes the object a tourism-worthy one. Tourist brochures frequently emphasize distance for this reason. The escape metaphor that haunts all brochures underlines the fact that people need to 'get away' from the everyday, go off elsewhere to rejuvenate themselves. The *Incredible!ndia* newsletter describes hotels as 'hideaways'. That is, a substantial distance must be put between the place of everyday life and the tourist spot (which are often, therefore, called 'getaways'). Distance is thus central to the attractiveness of the tourist spot. It is a 'welcome break from the usual' (*Incredible!ndia* newsletter). Or, in some cases, there are secret getaways in the heart of the city. Here distance is substituted with access, where it is not generally known that such places exist.

The exoticization of time

The Maharashtra Tourism brochure on Karla (2003) opens out into a visual of the Buddhist Karla caves. The first paragraph, set off in italics and divided from the rest of the printed material by a demarcation, concludes thus: 'The beautifully carved Chaityas and Viharas take you on a journey back in time, narrating stories of the past.'

Another way of rendering the tourist spot more attractive and exotic is to emphasize its temporal distance from the present (i.e., the tourist's own age/time). Nostalgia is integral to both exoticism and tourism. The idealized heritage industry is the perfect example of the marketing of nostalgia, as seen in the various tourist brochures in India. The high-lighting of antiquity is an attempt to underline this very distance, as in the *Karla* brochure. The *Garhwal Himalayas* brochure of UP Tourism uses the following catch-line under the opening visual on the front cover: 'Where time comes to a standstill.' Inside, under a massive visual of the Himalayas, is a text that describes the area as 'a storehouse of antiquity'. Rajasthan describes itself in one of its brochures as 'the Rajputana of yore'. Andhra Pradesh Tourism's *Warangal* brochure asks us to visit 'the ruins of the *once glorious* empire' (emphasis added). Karimnagar (Andhra Pradesh) stands for 'everlasting memories of a bygone era'. Several brochures and travel writings speak of 'glorious pasts' and 'mists of time' in order to create a mythology—what is from the past has a certain attraction for the present. The reclamation of memory—which is the purpose of museums and such tourist enterprises—is also an exoticization of the long-ago event. In fact, the staged world is rendered desirable precisely because they represent a world not present any more. Folk, for instance, is venerated because it represents non- or even pre-industrial labour and culture. This is the exoticization of time. Thus the retrieval (with the full awareness that this is false nostalgia, considering the impossibility of full or 'true' retrieval) of an ideal time (the past) is central to tourism.

The exoticization of difference

Difference is the key point of tourism: one travels to see (and admire, appreciate) difference. Tourism is a spectacle, a staging of difference. Even when the natural is staged—such as in animal shows or zoos—the audience is treated to a spectacle of difference: of species, in this instance. When folk or village culture is staged for the benefit of the tourist, it is done in such a way that the culture's difference from that of the tourist is highlighted. Karnataka Tourism advertises the state with the catch-line 'experience variety'. This in itself seems innocuous, until one notes the small print below. This states: 'Karnataka ... Theatre of Inspiration'. Both variety and inspiration are carefully staged, and presented as 'theatre' for a prepared audience. Jane Desmond (1999) proposes three models of staging difference in the case of cultural tourism, which showcases other cultures and peoples.

(*i*) In-situ staging: Here the animals and people are supposed to be themselves, with no spectators. Here the Other people (that is, the objects of the tourist gaze, the 'Others') go about their work as if no tourist were present (ibid. 171). This is particularly true of eco-tourism, which proposes to show the animals being 'natural'.

(*ii*) Out-of-situ: Here the animals or people perform behaviours that they would not perform in a natural state. Circuses and animal choreography (performing seals and such) are examples of this kind of staging of difference. Clearly the authenticity here is choreographed.

(*iii*) In-fake-situ: This is a slight improvement on the earlier stage. The animals and people are performing actions that they would be doing even in their natural habitats. However, even these are regulated and restricted. The entire range of behaviour—from fighting to mating—cannot be allowed in the tourist spot.

It is important to note here that the staging of difference through 'primitivizing' and 'naturalizing' discourses (Desmond: xvi, 8) is carefully plotted. Only certain kinds of differences can be staged or presented. One rarely sees the difference in mating habits being staged or highlighted, for instance. In the commodification of the tribal or the folk, what actually happens is a reiteration of the market-driven forces of unequal power relations between metropolis and periphery, rural and urban, rich and poor. There is a certain colonial appropriation of 'local' and 'native' cultures for the sake of (even postcolonial) tourism and marketing.

❏ CONSUMPTION AND PLEASURE

As noted earlier, tourism is about the consumption of places, objects and people. Pleasure is the primary motif of travel and tourism, though knowledge is also considered integral to the tourist experience. There are various consumption-related pleasures that are explicitly advertised in the tourist brochure or travelogue. This consumption of commodified places and things is ideological: the commodification of culture involves the transformation of traditional artifacts and practices into commodities which are then sold to tourists. This means that tourism and its impact is a two-way ideological and material process. Tourists, along with the community and its organizations (state or corporate/private), provide material support for particular aspects of local culture. Certain items get 'heritagized'. These items, recognized as such by both the tourist and the host, then get commodified into replicas, posters, and related products to be marketed. This means that the tourist interest in and interaction with the local product has definite social, economic and political effects.

Sensual or sensory pleasure

The *Incredible!ndia* programme of the Ministry of Tourism uses the following slogan-verse on its online fliers and promotional material:

It is a journey of mind and soul
It is a journey of the five senses
It is a journey of self-discovery
It is a journey of self-fulfillment.

Note the emphasis on the 'five senses' here. The *Chikhaldara* brochure of Maharashtra Tourism suggests that 'the nip in the air [will] send your senses tingling'. Andhra Pradesh Tourism declares that Prakasham district has 'everything to satiate the appetite' of the 'hungry-for-new' tourist.

Tourism is an attempt to satiate the senses, primarily the visual one. However, this does not mean that the other senses are not satiated. Tourist brochures often emphasize the sensory pleasures of places and activities. Spectacle and drama, integral to animal tourism, eco-tourism or even rural tourism, is meant to satisfy the visual cravings of the tourist. Thus *looking* at wildlife through the window panes of a tour bus or car, and, increasingly, capturing it through the 'window' of a digicam, is integral to the tourist experience.

The tourist brochure, even when highlighting nature, uses people as the key to the anticipation of pleasure. That is, the potential tourist anticipates her/his potential pleasure when s/he is shown people in various degrees of experiencing pleasure. Brochures use different kinds of people to suggest different kinds of sensory and other enjoyment. The address 'you' in these brochures is not gendered. The 'you' could be singular or plural. There are rare references to husbands or wives, and the only reference is to the 'family' as a unit. This assumes that families are about a heterosexual couple with one or two children. Family brochures invariably have pictures of nuclear families, mostly with young children. The *Karla* brochure of Maharashtra Tourism (2003) has a small visual inside it, depicting two adults and two children. The father—this is what

one presumes he is—is pointing to/at something in the distance, and the
children are staring intently at it. Just adjacent to the father is another
adult, a woman, presumably the mother. The brochure focuses on a
single family, with the adults portrayed in degrees of repose or activity,
but with active children alongside. Occasionally the parents are shown to
be pointing out a feature to the children, perhaps educating them, since
tourism is also a learning experience. The children are almost always in
close proximity to the parents. The woman traveller is invariably a part
of the family or a couple: she is almost never alone (women anyway constitute only 30.5 per cent of India's total international arrivals, according
to the 10th Five-Year Plan statistics, http://www.planningcommission.nic.in/
plans, 7.5: 820, 7 September 2004). This suggests a certain attitude
towards women—who stay circumscribed within relationships (and
under control?). The woman—her age, clothes, attitude, looks—is integral to such brochures because she appears to be defining the kind of
family itself. Thus, in the above *Karla* brochure, the 'mother' is dressed in
jeans and a shirt, with a backpack. The 'father' is in shorts and T-shirt,
with his own backpack. The Westernized clothing is meant to indicate a
'modern' family, not averse to dressing in non-traditional clothes.
Tourism and travel somehow expects this departure from traditional sartorial (and other) behaviour: you can wear what you want on travel. The
family, as in the Karla brochure, is rarely looking at the camera in such
brochures: they are busy having a good time, and have been photographed (supposedly without their knowledge) while at it. Senior
brochures—mainly advertising pilgrimage tourism—feature older couples (very rarely does one see singles here) who look healthy and active.
Youth market brochures—today the biggest draw is the young
professional—may be romantic (showing couples entwined around each
other, sharing a cosy moment), or adventurous (showing rapids, mountains). These also show couples or groups, and rarely solitary travellers.
The couples portrayed are almost always heterosexual—very rarely will
you find gay themes (on the marketing of queer identity itself as a tourist
attraction, see Rushbrook 2002)—especially in 'romantic destination'
brochures. In such brochures the couples face the camera and laugh or
smile. A certain image of idleness is also projected—with people reclin-
ing on couches and beach chairs. The (beautiful, young) woman in such
brochures may be a *constituent* of the potential pleasure that the holiday
offers (along with the sands, the food and the sport). Hotel visuals carry
a photograph of swimming pools, with women (and sometimes men) in
swimming costumes. The qualities of the natural 'setting' merge with the

qualities of the woman. Thus the *Rudraprayag* brochure of UP Tourism (1999) opens, as noted above, with two women in local costume. Somehow, the brochure seems to link the place with the women. Why is it that beach holidays in Western brochures (the scenes are rarer in Indian tourist brochures) require a *woman* in a swimsuit on the poster/brochure? Why does *Travel + Leisure*, announcing a special number on '50 Romantic Getaways', put a woman (alone) on the cover of the issue (February 2002)? Inside, advertising romantic hotels, the magazine shows photographs of hotels, mostly with a woman in the foreground. Is she, as pointed out earlier, associated with the romance, the pleasure (and/or cause) of 'getting away'? Is femininity a part of the aesthetic appeal of the place? Or is she the promise of pleasure?

Professional models are often used to represent tourists, and conform to the cultural ideals of the society: the sari-clad, married Indian woman (note Deepti Bhatnagar and other models going around Indian temples in the television serial, *Yatra*: dressed in carefully chosen silk saris, with *bindis*, groomed hair, a plate of flowers and offerings in her hands), the casually-dressed teenager, or the healthy youth river-rafting. The cultural politics of tourism and tourist brochures thus invariably function with a standard idea of the man or woman: young, slim, well-dressed and healthy. Ever seen brochures with fat, balding men or pregnant women, or physically challenged youth? Or, how many tourist brochures in India show dark-skinned (Dravidian) people travelling?

In each case the appeal is to the potential tourist's senses: see how much fun these people are having—why don't you go out and get some too?

Consumption, activity and metaphor

Tourist brochures speak of inhaling clean air, and 'taking in' the countryside. Metaphors of ingestion, assimilation and consumption abound in tourist writing. From nature to food, culture to architecture, tourism is intimately linked to consumption. However, in close conjunction with the gustatory metaphor is a set of images of activity. One of the key features of tourism today is the enormous burden of activity that is placed on the tourist. Even if s/he is just relaxing on a beach chair, s/he is asked to look at the sea and sky, to note the waves and the sand. Or else there is the imperative of relaxing by the pool and doing nothing. There can be no passive absorption of the atmosphere or surroundings. The tourist imperative, as I have termed it, is this enforced enjoyment of what is staged. This is the ideology of leisure itself, where the tourist on holiday does nothing but laze around and watch the world go by—with certain accessories (colourful umbrellas, soft drinks). An important element in this ideology is the work/labour that has to be done by the host in order to see that the tourist does nothing. Tourism involves the labour of some so as to keep someone else passive.

The tourist is supposed to have an entire range of sensory experience. This means that not only is the object of the tourist gaze staged, but also that the tourist's own body takes centrestage: consuming, perceiving, assimilating. We tend to see the tourist agenda as one-sided, where a spectacle is staged for the tourist's benefit. However, I want to emphasize here the enormous responsibility of the tourist to behave in certain ways in the presence of this spectacle. The tourist is an actant in the staging of the spectacle. Note, for instance, the chain of actions (and images of actions) recommended by the UP Tourism brochure:

> Holiday in a dozen hill stations, hunt or angle in Jungle and river teeming with game and fish, shoot with your camera in sanctuaries carbelt [sic., Corbett] bequeathed to the land, worship in a dozen pilgrim centers of different faiths, bathe in the Ganges at Varanasi, drink deep of history and legend in beautiful buildings ....

The Karnataka Tourism brochure categorizes the varieties of tourist spots, forms of entertainment and events thus: 'experience Bangalore', 'experience heritage', 'experience wildlife', 'experience adventure', 'experience romance', 'experience flavour', 'experience the coast', 'experience art', 'experience Mysore', 'experience cascades', 'experience divinity', 'experience festivity'. The emphasis is less on the place than on the *tourist's experience* of the place. Pondicherry describes itself thus: 'it's more than a place .... It's a feeling', thereby suggesting an embodied assimilation of the place into oneself, a cognitive, emotional and intellectual response to a place. The tourist is asked to 'explore', 'feel', 'touch', 'hear', 'learn', 'see', 'play', 'meet', 'discover' and 'wander'. Tourism is an embodied phenomenon because the tourist imperative is rooted in the body's actions, needs, perceptions and reactions. The tourist's body brings alive the staged spectacle in a kind of transaction (recall here that a tourist attraction is defined as an interaction between sight, marker and tourist).

It is important to note that pleasure, consumption and activity in the tourist brochure is linked to the facilities offered. Safety and hygiene are integral to the consumption of culture and the leisure activity. For instance, the Ministry of Tourism has issued a set of guidelines for tour operators, with effect from November 2003 (http://tourism.andaman. nic.in/guidelines). This states that for a tour operator to get recognition, the following are essential:

> The minimum office space should be of 250 sq. ft besides the office may be located in neat and clean surroundings and equipped with telephone, fax and computer reservation system etc. There should be sufficient space for reception and easy access to toilets. (p. 2)

The emphasis on infrastructure, convenience and safety/hygiene is very clear here. After 9/11, when tourism was severely affected the world over, *Travel + Leisure* ran a special feature (February 2002) on safety zones in tourist cities across the world, with particular attention paid to London, Paris, Hong Kong, Rome, Buenos Aires, Tokyo, Los Angeles and Washington, D.C.

Most brochures therefore show visuals of hotels and hotel rooms: the restaurant, the beds, the swimming pool (depending upon the 'class' of brochure). What is interesting is that the people are shown lying in the pool or beside it: rarely are they actually swimming! Ever seen a visual of the up-end hotel's kitchens, the air-conditioning plant or the bell-boys' rest area (if there is one)?

The ludic

Tourism involves a sense of the ludic. Tourist behaviour is meant to be about 'letting one's hair down', of being casual in a way that routine life does not allow. The ludic is this sense of the frivolous, of the casual that informs tourist behaviour. The entire experience of leisure and relaxation is meant to allow this freedom to be 'as one likes'. Surely it is significant that a lot of tourist photographs have tourists making funny faces or in 'joke poses'—poses they would not be seen dead in in their 'real lives'? The ludic element in tourism cuts across age boundaries too. Senior citizens and youth are both shown whooping it up in unusual places and poses. The ludic entails a certain element of the forbidden. Certain forms of behaviour, dress, conversation and even food habits that are unacceptable in their routine lives, are acceptable—indeed imperative—in the tourist situation (yet another element of the tourist imperative). The thrill of strange food, unusual behaviour or different costumes (beach wear, Hawaii shirts) is the ludic in tourism. As noted earlier, brochures offering visual 'evidence' of the pleasure of particular holidays—showing people enjoying themselves—often employ professional models for this purpose. The sense of play extends to the potential tourist's recognition that these are not actual tourists, but models. The play is in the self-reflexive recognition of the fact that her/his anticipated pleasure is staged by models in advance of the actual travel. Thus, when s/he travels, s/he is supposed to enjoy the holiday in similar ways.

❏ THE CULTURAL POLITICS OF TRAVEL

Tourism and its promotional literature demands that certain questions be asked: who identifies a site as 'heritage'? Who draws up the markers for the object to be gazed upon? What kinds of people do the actual gazing (their class, gender, racial affiliations, levels of income and education, and so on)? What politics govern the selection of tourism destinations of particular classes of people? Who controls the heritage product? What are the emphases in the promotional literature of a place? These questions address the cultural politics of tourism, and are significant because they treat tourism less as an industry in economic terms, and more as an industry of transculturation. As the above sections have demonstrated, there is a politics involved in every stage of tourism and its promotional culture.

Work in tourism involves retailing, accommodation and catering, selling, entertainment and transportation. When women generate products that are to be sold as cultural artifacts, do they gain significant economic mileage out of this work? Cultural commoditization and the woman's role in the production of saleable handicrafts have sometimes meant greater power for women in households (in the host community), though little change may be effected in the larger social field. Instances of local men befriending visiting tourists—both men and women—have frequently had local effects.

What this means is that the local social structure gets modified. People requiring jobs seek formal training, such as the ones recommended above. Tourism here directly affects literacy, social status, income and identity-formation in such societies, at both the micro and macro levels. The 10th Five-Year Plan states as its objective for tourism: 'its [tourism's] vast potential as an engine of growth and employment generator has remained largely untapped .... The 10th Plan objective is to integrate tourism with the socio-economic objectives of the Plan by creating 3.6 million jobs a year through the promotion of domestic and international tourism' (http://www.planningcommission.nic.in/plans, 7.5: 821, 7 September 2004). Tourism is thus directly linked to development and the economy. It is seen as encouraging more education and self-employment, and thus altering the structure of that society. International tourists affect rural destinations. Thus the Andhra Pradesh Tourism book (2002) declares, in bold print, separated from the rest of the text: 'Andhra Pradesh is now no more just Andhra or Telugu. Though the culture exists, it is now a global destination with no distinction between the visitor and the resident' (p. 9). The attempt here is to internationalize the place itself.

Then there is the segmentation of the tourist work itself. How many women are involved in the reception, ticketing, and such works in the Indian tourism industry? How many are actual tour guides? And how many work as janitors, cooks and other staff in hotels and establishments? Tourists are rarely aware of the (gendered) structures that smoothen (or roughen!) their travel. Back-end operations are almost always invisible to the tourist gaze. Issues of women's work—with related issues of hours of work, working conditions, wages and benefits—are central to understanding the gendered nature of tourism today.

The other non-tourist people in tourist brochures belong to two categories. They are either tourism workers, providing services to the holiday-makers, or they are the local inhabitants of the place. The first category is of the local working-class providing services. They are always, in brochures, smiling, young, well-dressed (at least cleanly dressed, which is not always the case), and endeavouring to convey the impression that this is not *work* at all. Everything seems to be smoothly done, with minimum effort. Such representations elide the material conditions of labour and work in the tourism *industry*. The smiling air-hostess at the airline, the cheerful travel agent, the grinning lift-operator and the pleasant waiter all convey this impression of *enjoying* what they do—just in case the tourist's enjoyment is mitigated by the knowledge that others toil for her/his pleasure.

The locals are either such service personnel or entertainers. Rarely does one see non-working locals as part of the scene. There is a subtle politics of leisure here: while the tourist can afford to relax, the local host community continues to either work away, or stops to entertain the visitor. Thus the *Chikhaldara* brochure of Maharashtra Tourism suggests that the tourist will be 'enchanted' by the 'genuineness of their [the tribals'] smiles' ('enchant', 'captivate', 'overwhelm', 'overpowering' are common terms in these brochures). Jharkhand Tourism assures us that the state's 'hills and numerous rivulets' will 'mesmerise' us. Rajasthan Tourism declares that Rajasthan is known 'not only for the sizzling heat and the dunes but also for the warmth in the hearts of the people'. These people somehow merge into the landscape, and are often part of the local 'experience'. However, this elides, like the conditions of labour, the conditions of tribal life itself. The 'genuineness' of the smiles may very well be 'designed' for the brochure and promotional material. The images of warmth, cheer and grace that brochures use are all metaphors, seeking to suggest an emotional, moral or ethical state.

I have suggested above that brochures signify countries and regions with iconic monuments. Andaman and Nicobar foregrounds its infamous Cellular Jail. The Jail is 'a place of pilgrimage for all freedom loving people'. The spiritualization of tourism is combined with a certain nationalist ideology to serve a commercial interest here. What is interesting is that these monuments and icons are invariably associated with the past, often with the very distant past. This is especially true of Asian tourist spots. India is noted for its ancient temples, Buddhist inscriptions and Mughal architecture, for instance. Rajasthan Tourism has the Victory Tower at Chitaurgarh on the cover of one of its brochures (1997). Inside, the catch-line goes: 'Rajasthan: The Reminder of Romance and Royalty .... The land synonymous with romance and chivalry. Immensely rich in culture, history and natural beauty ...' (p. 4).

Here the region/state is projected as nothing more than a mnemonic device of a glorious past. Such an image/metaphor posits the place as unchanging, frozen in time. The brochure suggests that one can revisit the past almost as though it were still alive. Much of Indian tourism projects this 'pastness' of India. On the other hand New York, Singapore or Hong Kong are signified by images of cities that are ultra-modern, even futuristic. As noted in the discussion on exoticization, it is the Asian *past* that is exotic, as is the 'First World' present and future (because even highly technologized cities are exotic in their difference). *Technological modernity defines the 'First World' and the tourist itself, just as tradition and labour define the Asian host.* This is why Andhra Pradesh Tourism's promotional material is interesting. It is one of the few that actually showcases a *contemporary* Indian city. In this case it is Hyderabad, with its Information Technology boom, and photographs of Cyber Towers in

'Hi-tech City' (2002: 21) sandwiched between photographs of pearls and heritage buildings! In another it describes the city as 'both contemporary and classic ... simultaneously historic and Hitech, a city where heritage and technological progress go hand in hand.' A third (2003) invites the tourist to 'experience a unique blend of the old dominion and rustic charm within the trappings of new age modernity'.

The word 'trappings' suggests the ornamental, the frivolous and the staged—conveying a sense of artificiality and performance. Nagarjunasagar is described in another brochure as 'a sight of modern Indian expertise. A glimpse of ancient Indian culture.' Aurangabad is described in one Maharashtra Tourism brochure as 'the fastest growing industrial town in India', a rare departure from standard brochure rhetoric of antiquity and tradition. Jharkhand Tourism has a separate leaflet on its industrial cities; however, the overall emphasis in Indian tourism has been on its spiritual/mystical aspects and history. Even here, though, it does not seek to present a completely technologized state. What the brochure does in a boxed introduction is a fascinating sleight-of-hand, shifting between mysticism and modernity, spiritualism and technology:

> Jharkhand is a state where Mother nature has poured life into every cranny and crevice. Where natural abundance forms a bedrock of progress on all fronts. Where people and resources combine to drive the engine to the future. Geography was kind enough to Jharkhand endowing it with enormous mineral resources around which high-growth industrial centers like Ranchi, Jamshedpur, Bokaro, Dhanbad have flourished.

The cultural politics of tourism causes a certain divide here. The past is Asian. It is always their unchanging, cultural features that come into focus. Contemporary India is not so much a tourist attraction—what is underlined is its past. The reality of everyday life in present-day India is jettisoned (or at least understated) in favour of the glorious past of kings and wealth. Thus Jaisalmer city describes itself as a 'golden fantasy', going on to highlight the past royalty and tales of valour. It concludes with a description of contemporary Jaisalmer:

> Today the desert city blooms with intricately carved havelis and old Jain temples [sic]. The landscape is compelling, and the sea of sand dunes has made it one of the most important tourist destinations in the country.

Even 'modern' India is notable only for its old temples, buildings and desert sands. Another Rajasthan city, Udaipur, describes itself thus:

> Udaipur is perhaps one of the most romantic and beautiful cities of India. In contrast to its desert neighbourhood it stands out with an enchanting image of white marble palaces, placid blue lakes, gardens, temples, surrounded by hills and mountains. It is like an oasis of colour in a stark and arid region …. Udaipur not only boasts a chivalrous past but also takes pride in its heritage, as a center for performing arts, paintings, crafts, culture and traditions.

Andhra Pradesh Tourism's *Vishakapatnam* brochure describes the place as a 'fantasy', before going on to speak, like the Udaipur and Jaislamer brochures, of the place as a 'city of valour'. Once again it is a 'glorious past' that is highlighted. The 'romance' is only this past.

In the case of 'First World' tourist destinations, of course, it is the heavily mechanized city that is focused on. This means that the tourist imperative is conditioned to see the West/'First World' as 'modern' and the Asian/African as 'traditional' through such condensation and selection. Kerala in India, for instance, is *condensed* to Ayurvedic medicine, Kathakali and the backwaters ('God's own country', thereby invoking a classic spiritual dimension that eschews any technologized modernity). *Incredible!ndia* declares this as a banner-ad on its online promotional newsletter: 'Maya, Tantra, Mantra. Our gurus were into special effects before Spielberg's great grandfather.'

This is just the beginning: *every* regional tourist brochure in India emphasizes spirituality over anything else, and almost every tourist brochure has a temple or ritual on its cover (AP Tourism's *Kurnool, Vijaywada, Srikakulam, Nizamabad, Warangal, Puttaparthi, Prakasham* brochures; Uttar Pradesh Tourism's *Garhwal and Kumaon, Chardham* brochures; Maharashtra Tourism's *Karla* brochures … the examples could be multiplied many times over).

UP Tourism's Hills Tourism brochure, *Fairs and Festivals of Garhwal and Kumaon Himalayas*, uses the following catch-line on its front cover: 'experience the mystique'. It even describes the natural landscape in similar terms: 'welcome to the celestial Garhwal Himalayas, the abode of the Gods'. The *Rudraprayag* brochure describes the place as 'where the gods choose to dwell'. Another brochure is simply titled 'heavenly hills'. The brochure from UP tourism for the entire state declares on its cover: 'Welcome to the Gateway of GODS.' This then goes on to suggest that visiting a place that provides 'a feel of heaven' can help 'purify one's soul'. Andhra Pradesh Tourism's brochure on Prakasham district announces on its cover: 'where faith thrives amidst the magic of nature', thus engaging the divine and the natural in a dialogue, each complementing the other: divine nature and a naturally divine. Andhra Pradesh Tourism's brochure on Kurnool uses the following catch-line: 'A trip through history. A tour of spirituality.' Such brochures select one aspect of the area—the temple, the religious rites/festivals—as its most significant feature, and projects it as the essence of the place in an act of condensation. In all these cases the brochure retains the image of a spiritual India, with no mention of any other India.

What such a cultural politics of tourism does is facilitate an instant recognition of a place through condensation and selection. The place is reduced to instantly identifiable stereotypes that *constitute* difference. There are two main types of people here.

(*i*)   There is the group that is clothed in the national or regional costume. Thus the UP Tourism brochure for Rudraprayag (1999) opens to a photograph of two women in traditional costume smiling into the camera in a close-up shot. This photograph *precedes* even the map of the area. *Fairs and Festivals of Garhwal and Kumaon Himalayas* has a woman in native costume as its opening visual. The Andaman and Nicobar tourist brochure opens to two small visuals positioned to the left of the text, following the map page. The visual on top is of a lush green landscape. The visual immediately beneath this shows a group of young women, dancing in the traditional costume. The two visuals set up a dialogue with each other here: the women are naturalized as the land, just as the landscape gets feminized in a semantic exchange where one reflects and refracts the other.

(*ii*) The second group shows people in local *work* conditions. We have stilt-fishermen in Sri Lanka, the Kerala fishermen throwing their nets, the tea picker in Assam, and so on. The brochure glosses over the conditions of labour here, the levels of poverty, the exploitation and the gender differentials. As noted above, the tribal or the aboriginal is always represented as a tribal, never as a lawyer or engineer. The technologized tourist, on the other hand, is a voyeur and consumer, while the local is worker and provider.

A final point to be kept in mind is that of rights. Organizations such as the Ecumenical Coalition on Third World Tourism (Hong Kong) and Tourism Concern (UK) have been advocating tourism policy reforms that take into account the rights of indigenous cultures in tourist spots/regions. As noted above, international tourism is skewed in the direction, 'First World' → 'Third World'. They suggest that there exists a correlation between the racialized, classed tourist gaze and the 'consumed', surveyed indigenous community put on show. What of destinations where human rights are violated on a regular basis by the state or by the business community (one has only to think of the sex tourism in South-east Asia)? Then, do indigenous communities such as tribals have the right to restrict their exhibition as 'cultural heritage' or 'native peoples' for tourists? Since debates about land rights in connection with tribals has been an old problem in India, what about the rights of visitation to their ancestral lands? Tourism and the foreign exchange it brings in is frequently tied to development. But do these notions of development find agreement with the indigenous people? When the government incorporates the territory of indigenous peoples into protected areas or tourist spots, the management of the area becomes a subject of dispute, especially if the government grants visitation rights to tourists. Some indigenous communities have developed their own tourism enterprises as a result of this problem (for example, the Cofan and Hoarani peoples in Ecuador).

❑ NOTES

1. I have mainly used brochures from State Tourism boards for my purposes. The arguments apply just as well, with minor variations and a greater emphasis on the promotional culture of capitalism, to private and corporate tourism brochures and guides such as the Mahendras or Thomas Cook or SITA.
2. Promotion crosses the line between advertising, packaging and design, and is an essentially persuasive communicative act.
3. The 300 largest TNCs control a quarter of the world's productive assets and system of global trade. About 90 per cent of them have their headquarters in the USA, Western Europe or Japan, with 180, 000 subsidiaries, and over \$6 trillion in worldwide sales. By the 1980s, TNCs represented 54 per cent of both US exports and imports.
4. For a brilliant reading of such examples of imaginative constructions of places and their connections to dominant socio-cultural ideas, see Gregory Woods' (1995) reading of island stories from Defoe's *Robinson Crusoe* to the hugely successful film, *The Blue Lagoon*.

❑ FURTHER READING

MacCannell, Dean. 1976. *The Tourist: A New Theory of the Leisure Class*. New York: Shocken.

Rojek, Chris. 1995. *Decentring Leisure: Rethinking Leisure Theory*. London: Sage Publications.

Ryan, Chris (ed.). 2002. *The Tourist Experience*. London and New York: Continuum.

Urry, John. 1998[1990]. *The Tourist Gaze*. London: Sage Publications.

BIBLIOGRAPHY

❑ COMIC BOOKS

Amar Chitra Katha

A Nation Awakes # 350
Abhimanyu # 533
Ananda Math # 655
Babasaheb Ambedkar # 611
Bhagat Singh # 234
Bikal the Terrible # 667
Birbal the Clever # 558
Bumper Issue, # 10: *The Story of the Freedom Struggle*
Chaitanya Mahaprabhu # 631
Dasha Avatar Special Issue # 10002
Dayananda # 624
Draupadi # 542
Ekalavya # 337
Ghatotkacha # 61
Guru Gobind Singh # 588
Guru Nanak # 590
Hanuman # 502
J.R.D Tata # 735
Jesus Christ # 10003
Kabir # 623
Kannagi # 666
Kochunni # 173
Krishna # 501 (also in *Pancharatna* Series)
Mirabai # 535
Narayana Guru # 403
Noor Jahan # 701
Rama # 504
Rani of Jhansi # 539
Savarkar # 309
Savitri # 511
Shakuntala # 530
Shankar Dev # 229
Shivaji # 564
Subramania Bharati # 708

Sultana Razia # 725
Tales of Sai Baba # 801
The Birth of the Indian National Congress # 348
The Call for Swaraj # 364
The Saga of Indian Revolutionaries # 360
The Salt Satyagraha # 368
The Sons of Rama # 503
The Tryst with Destiny # 372
(All from India Book House, Mumbai)

Others

Action Comics # 1 (1938)
Batman # 25 (2004)
Batman # 6 (2002)
Silver Surfer # 17 (2002)
Silver Surfer # 7 (2002)
Spider-man # 14 (2001)
Spider-man # 1 (2001)
Teen Titans # 2 (2004)
The Dark Knight Returns Special # 10 (2004 [1986])
The Man of Steel # 5
The Man of Steel # 22
The Ultimates # 2 (2003)
The Ultimates # 1 (2003)

❑ TOURIST BROCHURES AND PROMOTIONAL MATERIAL

Uttar Pradesh

Director Tourism (Hills)–Uttar Pradesh Tourism. *Chardham.* Dehradun: Director Tourism (Hills), n.d.
———. *Heavenly Hills.* Dehradun: Director Tourism (Hills), n.d.
———. *Rudraprayag.* Dehradun: Director Tourism (Hills), 1999.
———. *Garhwal Himalayas.* Dehradun: Director Tourism (Hills), n.d.
———. *Fairs and Festivals of Garhwal and Kumaon Himalayas.* Dehradun: Director Tourism (Hills), n.d.
Director Tourism. *Accommodation in Garwhal Himalayas.* Dehradun: Director Tourism (Hills), n.d.

Maharashtra

Maharashtra Tourism. *Karla*. Mumbai: Maharashtra Tourism Development Corporation Ltd, 2003.

————. *Chikhaldara*. Mumbai: Maharashtra Tourism Development Corporation Ltd, n.d.

————. *Tadoba National Park*. Mumbai: Maharashtra Tourism Development Corporation Ltd, n.d.

————. *Nagpur Orange City*. Mumbai: Maharashtra Tourism Development Corporation Ltd, 2002.

————. *Aurangabad*. Mumbai: Maharashtra Tourism Development Corporation Ltd, 2003.

Rajasthan

Rajasthan Tourism. *Tourist Guide Map of Rajasthan*. Jaipur: Dept. of Tourism, Government of Rajasthan, n.d.

————. *Tourist Guide Map of Jaisalmer*. Jaipur: Dept. of Tourism, Government of Rajasthan, n.d.

————. *Tourist Guide Map of Udaipur*. Jaipur: Dept. of Tourism, Government of Rajasthan, n.d.

————. *Discover Rajasthan*. Jaipur: Dept. of Tourism, Art and Culture, Government of Rajasthan, 1997.

Jharkhand

Jharkhand Tourism. *The Wild and the Beautiful*, n.d.

————. *Religious Places*, n.d.

————. *Industrial Cities*, n.d.

————. *Tamed and Untamed Waters*, n.d.

Andhra Pradesh

Andhra Pradesh Tourism. *Andhra Pradesh (Product Catalogue)*. Hyderabad: Andhra Pradesh Tourism Development Corporation, 2002.

————. *Prakasham*. Hyderabad: Andhra Pradesh Tourism Development Corporation, n.d.

————. *Kurnool*. Hyderabad: Andhra Pradesh Tourism Development Corporation, n.d.

————. *Vijayawada*. Hyderabad: Andhra Pradesh Tourism Development Corporation, n.d.

————. *Hyderabad*. Hyderabad: Andhra Pradesh Tourism Development Corporation, 2003.

————. *Warangal*. Hyderabad: Andhra Pradesh Tourism Development Corporation, 2003.

Andhra Pradesh Tourism. *Karimnagar*. Hyderabad: Andhra Pradesh Tourism Development Corporation, n.d.

———. *Srikakulam*. Hyderabad: Andhra Pradesh Tourism Development Corporation, n.d.

———. *Vishakapatnam*. Hyderabad: Andhra Pradesh Tourism Development Corporation, 2001.

———. *Nagarjunasagar*. Hyderabad: Andhra Pradesh Tourism Development Corporation, n.d.

Others

Himachal Tourism. *The Naldhera Golf Club*. Himachal Pradesh Tourism Development Corporation, n.d.

Jarrold's Guide to the University City of Oxford. Norwich: Jarrold, 1997.

Jarrold's Guide to the Historic City of York. Norwich: Jarrold, 2000.

Karnataka Tourism. *Karnataka*. Bangalore: Karnataka State Tourism Development Corporation, 2004.

Kerala Tourism. *Ayurvedic Health Holidays in Kerala*. Trivandrum: Kerala Tourism, 2004.

The Oxford Story (pamphlet). n.p.: n.p., n.d.

The Oxford Story Exhibition. (leaflet). 2000–2001.

Pondicherry Tourism. *Pondicherry*. Pondicherry: Pondicherry Tourism and Transport Development Corporation, n.d.

Westminster Abbey. (leaflet) London: Westminster Abbey, 2001.

York Minster. (leaflet) n.p.: n.p., 2001.

Victoria Coach Station Guide to London. London: Capital Publications and Victoria Coach Station. Winter 2000/2001.

❏ SECONDARY SOURCES

Abbott, Lawrence L. 1986. 'Comic Art: Characteristics and Potentialites of a Narrative Medium', *Journal of Popular Culture*, 19(4): 155–76.

Adam, Alison. 2002. 'The Ethical Dimension of Cyberfeminism', in Mary Flanagan and Austin Booth (eds), *Reload*, pp. 158–74. Cambridge, MA: MIT Press.

Adorno, Theodor and Max Horkheimer. 1992 [1944]. *The Dialectic of Enlightenment*. London: Verso.

Agamben, Giorgio. 1998. *Homo Sacer: Sovereign Power and Bare Life*. California: Stanford University Press.

Allen, Richard and Murray Smith (eds). 1997. *Film Theory and Philosophy*. Oxford: Clarendon Press.

Alpers, Svetlana. 1991. 'The Museum as a Way of Seeing', in Ivan Karp and Steven Levine (eds), *Exhibiting Cultures*, pp. 25–32. Washington and London: Smithsonian.

Altick, Richard. 1978. *The Shows of London*. Cambridge, MA: Harvard University Press.

Amar Chitra Katha. 2004. Catalogue.

Amin, Shahid and Dipesh Chakrabarty (eds). 1996. *Subaltern Studies IX.* Delhi: Oxford University Press.

Appadurai, Arjun. 2000a [1990]. 'Disjuncture and Difference in the Global Cultural Economy', in John Benyon and David Dunkerley (eds), *Globalization*, pp. 92–104. London: Athlone.

———. 2000b. 'Grassroots Globalization and the Research Imagination', *Public Culture*, 12(1): 1–19.

Appadurai, Arjun and Carol Breckenridge. 1992. 'Museums are Good to Think: Heritage on View in India', in Ivan Karp, Christine Mullen Kreamer and Steven D. Lavine (eds), *Museums and Communities*, pp. 34–55. Washington and London: Smithsonian.

Apple, Michael W. 2002. 'Pedagogy, Patriotism, and Democracy: On the Educational Meanings of 11 September 2001', *Discourse*, 23(3): 299–308.

Araeen, Rasheed, Sean Cubitt and Ziauddin Sardar. 2002. *The Third Text Reader on Art, Culture and Theory.* London and New York: Continuum.

Ashcroft, Bill. 2001. *Post-Colonial Transformation.* London and New York: Routledge.

Avadhani, V.V.S. 1976. *Guide Book to Victoria Jubilee Museum, Vijayawada.* Hyderabad: Government of Andhra Pradesh.

Babb, Lawrence A. and Susan S. Wadley (eds). 1995. *Media and the Transformation of Religion in South Asia.* Philadelphia: University of Pennsylvania Press.

Balamani, M. 2003. 'Personal Albums Revisited: Women, Ritual and Cultural Practices'. Paper presented at Forum on Contemporary Theory Conference on 'Rethinking Modernity', Jaipur, December 2003.

Barber, Benjamin. 1995. *Jihad vs McWorld.* New York: Times.

Barcan, Ruth. 2001. '"The Moral Bath of Bodily Unconsciousness": Female Nudism, Bodily Exposure and the Gaze', *Continuum*, 15(3): 303–17.

———. 2002. 'Problems without Solutions: Teaching Theory and the Politics of Hope', *Continuum*, 16(3): 343–56.

Barker, Martin. 1989. *Comics: Ideology, Power and the Critics.* Manchester: Manchester University Press.

Basa, K.K. 2001. 'Globalization and Cultural Heritage: Implications for Museum', in Ghoshmaulik and Basa (eds), *Understanding Heritage*, pp. 1–25. Bhubaneswar: Academic Staff College.

Baudrillard, Jean. 1999 [1985]. 'The Masses: The Implosion of the Social in the Media', in Paul Marris and Sue Thornham (eds), *Media Studies*, pp. 99–108. Edinburgh: Edinburgh University Press.

Baxandall, Michael. 1991. 'Exhibiting Intention: Some Preconditions of the Visual Display of Culturally Purposeful Objects', in Ivan Karp and Steven Levine (eds), *Exhibiting Cultures*, pp. 33–41. Washington and London: Smithsonian.

Baxi, Smita J. 1980. 'Role of Museum Exhibition', in Vinod P. Dwivedi (ed.), *Museums and Museology*, pp. 3–10. New Delhi: Agam Kala Prakashan.

Baxi, Smita J. and Vinod P. Dwivedi. 1973. *Modern Museum: Organisation and Practice in India.* New Delhi: Abhinav.

Beal, Timothy K. 2002. *Religion and its Monsters.* New York and London: Routledge.

Becker, Stephen. 1959. *Comic Art in America: A Social History of the Funnies, the Political Cartoon, Magazine Humor, Sporting Cartoon and Animated Cartoon.* New York: Simon and Schuster.

Bedekar, V.H. 1980. 'Using Natural Light for Museum Exhibition', in Vinod P. Dwivedi (ed.), *Museums and Museology*, pp. 11–24. New Delhi: Agam Kala Prakashan.

Bennett, Tony. 1999 [1995]. *The Birth of the Museum: History, Theory, Politics.* London and New York: Routledge.

Benthall, Jonathan. 1987. 'Ethnographic Museums and the Art Trade', *Anthropology Today,* 3(3): 9–12.

Benyon, John and David Dunkerley (eds). 2000. *Globalization: The Reader.* London: Athlone.

Berger, Arthur Asa. 1973. *The Comic-Stripped American: What Dick Tracy, Blondie, Daddy Warbucks, and Charlie Brown Tell Us about Ourselves.* New York: Walker and Co.

Béteille, André. 1996. 'Caste in Contemporary India', in C.J. Fuller (ed.), *Caste Today,* pp. 150–79. Delhi: Oxford University Press.

Bhabha, Homi K. 2000. 'On Minorities: Cultural Rights', *Radical Philosophy,* 100: 3–6.

Bharucha, Rustom. 2001. *The Politics of Cultural Practice: Thinking through Theatre in an Age of Globalization.* Delhi: Oxford University Press.

Bhatnagar, Anupama. 1999. *Museums, Museology and New Museology.* New Delhi: Sundeep Prakashan.

Bilgrami, Akeel. 1995. 'Secularism, Nationalism and Modernity', in Bilgrami and Nandy, *Paper No. 29,* pp. 1–29. New Delhi: Rajiv Gandhi Institute for Contemporary Studies.

Bilgrami, Akeel and Ashis Nandy. 1995. 'Secularism, Nationalism and Modernity' (Bilgrami) and 'The Politics of Secularism and the Recovery of Religious Tolerance'(Nandy). New Delhi: Rajiv Gandhi Institute for Contemporary Studies.

Booth, Ken and Tim Dunne (eds). 2002. *Worlds in Collision: Terror and the Future of Global Order.* Basingstoke, Hampshire: Macmillan.

Bourdieu, Pierre. 1999 [1989]. *Distinction: A Social Critique of the Judgement of Taste,* tr. Richard Nice. London: Routledge.

Brabazon, Tara. 2001. 'Buff Puffing an Empire: The Body Shop and Colonization by Other Means', *Continuum,* 15(2): 187–200.

Bradburne, James. 2000. 'The Poverty of Nations: Should Museums Create Identity', in J.M. Fladmark (ed.), *Heritage and Museums,* pp. 379–93. Shaftesbury, Dorset: Donhead.

Brown, Karen McCarthy. 1994. 'Fundamentalism and the Control of Women', in John Stratton Hawley (ed.), *Fundamentalism and Gender,* pp. 175–201. New York and Oxford: Oxford University Press.

Browne, Ray. 1996. 'Internationalizing Popular Culture Studies', *Journal of Popular Culture,* 30(1): 1–2.

Bruce, Steve. 2000. *Fundamentalism.* Cambridge: Polity.

Bruzzi, Stella. 1997. *Undressing Cinema: Clothing and Identity in the Movies.* London and New York: Routledge.

Butcher, Melissa. 2003. *Transnational Television, Cultural Identity and Change: When STAR Came to India.* New Delhi: Sage Publications.

Butler, Judith. 1993. *Bodies that Matter.* London and New York: Routledge.

———. 2002. 'Is Kinship always Heterosexual?', *Differences,* 13(1): 14–44.

Campbell, Joseph. 1949. *The Hero With a Thousand Faces.* Princeton, NJ: Princeton University Press.

Centre for Public Policy Research. 2002. 'Faith-Based Schooling and the Invisible Effects of 11 September 2001: The View from England', *Discourse,* 23(3): 309–17.

Chakrabarty, Dipesh. 2000. *Provincializing Europe: Postcolonial Thought and Historical Difference.* Princeton: Princeton University Press.

Chakravarty, Sumita S. 1989. *National Identity in Indian Popular Cinema, 1947–1989.* Austin: University of Texas Press.

Champalakshmi, R. and S. Gopal (eds). 2001 [1996]. *Tradition, Dissent and Ideology: Essays in Honour of Romila Thapar*. Delhi: Oxford University Press.

Chatrapati Shivaji Maharaj Vastu Sangrahalaya (Pamphlet). n.d. Mumbai: Chatrapati Shivaji Maharaj Vastu Sangrahalaya.

Chatterjee, Arun K. 2001. 'Museum in Safeguarding Tribal Art', in Ghoshmaulik and Basa (eds), *Understanding Heritage*, pp. 72–75. Bhubaneswar: Academic Staff College.

Chatterjee, Partha. 1986. *Nationalist Thought and the Colonial World—A Derivative Discourse*. Delhi: Oxford University Press.

——— (ed.). 1999 [1998]. *Wages of Freedom: Fifty Years of the Indian Nation-State*. Delhi: Oxford University Press.

Chatterjee, Partha and Pradeep Jeganathan (eds). 2002 [2000]. *Subaltern Studies XI: Community, Gender and Violence*. New Delhi: Permanent Black and Ravi Dayal.

Chen, Kuan-Hsing (ed.). 1998. *Trajectories: Inter-Asia Cultural Studies*. London and New York: Routledge.

Chow, Rey. 1998. 'Film and Cultural Identity', in John Hill and Pamela Church Gibson (eds), *The Oxford Guide to Film Studies*, pp. 169–75. Oxford: Oxford University Press.

Chowdhry, Prem. 2000. *Colonial India and the Making of Empire Cinema: Image, Ideology and Identity*. New Delhi: Vistaar.

Clare, Eli. 2001. 'Stolen Bodies, Reclaimed Bodies: Disability and Queerness', *Public Culture*, 13(3): 359–65.

Clover, Carol J. 2000 [1987]. 'Her Body, Himself: Gender in the Slasher Film', in Stephen Prince (ed.), *Screening Violence*, pp. 125–74. London: Athlone.

Cohn, Bernard S. 1997. *Colonialism and its Forms of Knowledge: The British in India*. Delhi: Oxford University Press.

Collins, Jim (ed.). 2002. *High-Pop: Making Culture into Popular Entertainment*. Oxford: Blackwell.

Connell, R.W. 1999 [1995]. *Masculinities*. Cambridge: Polity.

Corley, Sarah V. 1982. 'Women in the Comics', *Studies in Popular Culture*, 5: 61–71.

Cvetkovitch, Ann and Douglas Kellner. 1997. 'Thinking Global and Local', in *Articulating the Global and the Local*, pp. 1–30. Boulder, Colorado: Westview.

Dalmia, Vasudha and Heinrich von Stietencron (eds). 1995. *Representing Hinduism: The Construction of Religious Traditions and Religious Identity*. New Delhi: Sage Publications.

Dalmiya, Vrinda. 2000. 'Loving Paradoxes: A Feminist Reclamation of the Goddess Kali', *Hypatia*, 15(1): 125–50.

Dangle, Arjun (ed.). 1992. *Poisoned Bread: Translations from Modern Marathi Dalit Literature*. Hyderabad: Orient Longman.

Dash, Rabi Narayan. 2001. 'Heritage and Orissa State Museum', in Ghoshmaulik and Basa (eds), *Understanding Heritage*, pp. 33–53. Bhubaneswar: Academic Staff College.

Davenport, Christian. 1998. 'The Brother Might be Made of Steel, But He Sure Ain't Super … Man', *Other Voices*, 1(2). http://www.othervoices.org/1.2, 28 November 2004.

Day, Gary. 2001. *Class*. London: Routledge.

Der Derian, James. 2002. '*In Terrorem*: Before and After 9/11', in Ken Booth and Tim Dunne (eds), *Worlds in Collision*, pp. 101–17. Basingstoke, Hampshire: Macmillan.

———. 2003. 'Decoding the National Security Strategy of the United States of America', *Boundary 2*, 30(3): 19–27.

Derrida, Jacques. 2001. *On Cosmopolitanism and Forgiveness*, tr. Mark Dooley and Michael Hughes. London and New York: Routledge.

Derrida, Jacques. 2002. 'The University without Condition', in *Without Alibi*, tr. Peggy Kamuf, pp. 202–37. Stanford, California: Stanford University Press.

Deshpande, Satish. 1998. 'After Culture: Renewed Agendas for the Political Economy of India', *Cultural Dynamics*, 10(2): 147–69.

Desmond, Jane C. 1999. *Staging Tourism: Bodies on Display from Waikiki to Sea World*. Chicago and London: Chicago University Press.

Dhareshwar, Vivek and Tejaswini Niranjana. 2002 [2000]. '*Kaadalan* and the Politics of Resignification: Fashion, Violence and the Body', in Ravi S. Vasudevan (ed.), *Making Meaning in Indian Cinema*, pp. 191–214. Delhi: Oxford University Press.

Dickey, Sara. 2001. 'Opposing Faces: Film Star Fan Clubs and the Construction of Class Identities in South India', in Rachel Dwyer and Christopher Pinney (eds), *Pleasure and the Nation*, pp. 212–46. Delhi: Oxford University Press.

Dirks, Nicholas B. 2001. 'The Home and the Nation: Consuming Culture and Politics in *Roja*', in Rachel Dwyer and Christopher Pinney (eds), *Pleasure and the Nation*, pp. 161–85. Delhi: Oxford University Press.

Doane, Mary Ann. 1992 [1982]. 'Film and the Masquerade: Theorizing the Female Spectator', in John Caughie, Annette Kuhn and Mandy Merck (eds), *The Sexual Subject: A Screen Reader in Sexuality*, pp. 227–43. London and New York: Routledge.

———. 1999. 'Technophilia: Technology, Representation, and the Feminine', in Jenny Wolmark (ed.), *Cybersexualities*, pp. 20–33. Edinburgh: Edinburgh University Press.

Donald, James and Stephanie Hemelryk. 2000. 'The Publicness of Cinema', in Christine Gledhill and Linda Williams (eds), *Reinventing Film Studies*, pp. 114–29. London: Edward Arnold.

Dorfman, Ariel and Armand Mattelart. 1991 [1984]. *How to Read Donald Duck: Imperialist Ideology in the Disney Comic*, tr. David Kunzle. New York: International General.

Doyle, Julie and Kate O'Riordan. 2002. 'Virtually Visible: Female Cyberbodies and the Medical Imagination', in Mary Flanagan and Austin Booth (eds), *Reload*, pp. 239–60. Cambridge, MA: MIT Press.

Duncan, Carol. 1995. *Civilizing Rituals: Inside Public Art Museums*. London and New York: Routledge.

During, Simon (ed.). 1993. *The Cultural Studies Reader*. New York: Routledge.

———. 2000. 'Postcolonialism and Globalization: Towards Historicization of their Inter-Relation', *Cultural Studies*, 14(3–4): 385–404.

Dwivedi, Vinod. P. 1973. 'Acquisition and Registration', in Smita J. Baxi and Vinod P. Dwivedi (eds), *Modern Museum*, pp. 15–25. New Delhi: Abhinav.

———. (ed.). 1980. *Museums and Museology: New Horizons: Essays in Honour of Dr. Grace Morley on her 80th Birthday*. New Delhi: Agam Kala Prakashan.

Dworkin, Andrea. 1981. *Pornography: Men Possessing Women*. New York: Perigee.

Dwyer, Rachel and Divia Patel. 2002. *Cinema India: The Visual Culture of Hindi Film*. London: Reaktion.

Dwyer, Rachel and Christopher Pinney (eds). 2001. *Pleasure and the Nation: The History, Politics and Consumption of Public Culture in India*. Delhi: Oxford University Press.

Dyer, Richard. 1999 [1979, 1993]. 'The Role of Stereotype', in Paul Marris and Sue Thornham (eds), *Media Studies*, pp. 245–51. Edinburgh: Edinburgh University Press.

———. 2000 [1986]. 'Heavenly Bodies: Films Stars and Society', in Robert Stam and Toby Miller (eds), *Film and Theory*, pp. 603–17. Oxford: Blackwell.

Eck, Diana L. 1986. 'Darshan of the Image', *India International Centre Quarterly*, 13(1): 43–53.

Eco, Umberto. 1979. 'The Myth of Superman', in *The Role of the Reader: Explorations in the Semiotics of Texts*, pp. 107–24. Bloomington: Indiana University Press.

Edgar, Andrew and Peter Sedgwick (eds). 1999. *Key Concepts in Cultural Theory*. London: Routledge.

Estren, Mark James. 1987 [1974]. *A History of Underground Comics*. California: Ronin.

Everard, Jerry. 2000. *Virtual States: The Internet and the Boundaries of the Nation-State*. London and New York: Routledge.

Featherstone, Mike. 1991. *Consumer Culture and Postmodernism*. London: Sage Publications.

Featherstone, Mike, Scott Lash and Roland Robertson (eds). 1995. *Global Modernities*. London: Sage Publications.

Fiedler, Leslie. 1978. *Freaks: Myths and Images of the Secret Self*. London: Penguin.

Fladmark, J.M. (ed.). 2000. *Heritage and Museums: Shaping National Identity*. Shaftesbury, Dorset: Donhead.

Flanagan, Mary. 2002. 'Hyperbodies, Hyperknowledge: Women in Games, Women in Cyberpunk, and Strategies of Resistance', in Mary Flanagan and Austin Booth (eds), *Reload*, pp. 425–54. Cambridge, MA: MIT Press.

Flanagan, Mary and Austin Booth (eds). 2002. *Reload: Rethinking Women + Cyberculture*. Cambridge, MA: Press.

Forbes, Bruce David. n.d. 'Batman Crucified: Religion and Modern Superhero Comic Books'. World Association for Christian Communication, http://www.wacconline.org.uk/404.php, 28 November 2004.

Foucault, Michel. 1980. *Power/Knowledge: Selected Interviews 1972–77*, ed. Colin Gordon. Brighton: Harvester.

———. 1981. 'The Order of Discourse', tr. Ian McLeod, in Robert Young (ed.), *Untying the Text: A Poststructuralist Reader*, pp. 48–78. London: Routledge and Kegan Paul.

———. 1984 [1979]. *The History of Sexuality. Vol. 1: An Introduction*, tr. Robert Hurley. London: Peregrine-Penguin.

Franks, Mary Anne. 2003. 'Obscene Undersides: Women and Evil between the Taliban and the United States', *Hypatia*, 18(1): 135–56.

Franzen, Monika and Nancy Ethiel. 1988. *Make Way! 200 Years of American Women in Cartoons*. Chicago: Chicago Review Press.

Freitag, Sandra B. 2001. 'Visions of the Nation: Theorizing the Nexus between Creation, Consumption, and Participation in the Public Sphere', in Rachel Dwyer and Christopher Pinney (eds), *Pleasure and the Nation*, pp. 35–75. Delhi: Oxford University Press.

———. 2003. 'The Realm of the Visual: Agency and Modern Civil Society', in Sumathi Ramaswamy (ed.), *Beyond Appearances?*, pp. 365–97. New Delhi: Sage Publications.

Friedman, Jonathan. 1996 [1994]. *Cultural Identity and Global Process*. London: Sage Publications.

Frow, John. 1995. *Cultural Studies and Cultural Value*. Oxford: Oxford University Press.

———. 2002. 'Signature and Brand', in Jim Collins (ed.), *High-Pop*, pp. 56–74. Oxford: Blackwell.

Fullagar, Simone. 2002. 'Narratives of Travel: Desire and the Movement of Feminine Subjectivity', *Leisure Studies*, 21: 57–74.

Gabilliet, Jean-Paul. 1994. 'Cultural and Mythical Aspects of a Superhero: The Silver Surfer 1968–1970', *Journal of Popular Culture*, 28(2): 203–13.

Gaines, Jane. 2000. 'Dream/Factory', in Christine Gledhill and Linda Williams (eds), *Reinventing Film Studies*, pp. 100–113. London: Edward Arnold.

Garber, Marjorie. 1993. *Vested Interests: Cross-dressing and Cultural Anxiety*. London: Penguin.

Ghai, Anita. 2002. 'Disabled Women: An Excluded Agenda of Indian Feminism', *Hypatia*, 17(3): 49–66.

Ghoshmaulik, S.K. 2001. 'People as Curator: Participatory Museum', in Ghoshmaulik and Basa (eds), *Understanding Heritage*, pp. 63–71. Bhubaneswar: Academic Staff College.

Ghoshmaulik, S.K. and K.K. Basa (eds). 2001. *Understanding Heritage: Role of Museum*. Bhubaneswar: Academic Staff College.

Gilroy, Paul. 2002. 'Toward a Critique of Consumer Imperialism', *Public Culture*, 14(3): 589–91.

Giroux, Henry A. 1997. 'White Squall: Resistance and the Pedagogy of Whiteness', *Cultural Studies*, 11(3): 376–89.

———. 2000. 'Public Pedagogy as Cultural Politics: Stuart Hall and the "Crisis" of Culture', *Cultural Studies*, 14(2): 341–60.

———. 2004. 'Beyond Belief: Religious Fundamentalism and Cultural Politics in the Age of George W. Bush', *Cultural Studies/Critical Methodologies*, 4(4): 415–26.

Goodwin, Jeff and James M. Jasper. 2003. *The Social Movements Reader: Cases and Concepts*. Oxford: Blackwell.

Gopalan, Lalitha. 2001. 'Indian Cinema', in Jill Nelmes (ed.), *An Introduction to Film Studies*, pp. 360–87. London: Routledge.

———. 2002 [2000]. 'Avenging Women in Indian Cinema', in Ravi S. Vasudevan (ed.), *Making Meaning in Indian Cinema*, pp. 215–37. Delhi: Oxford University Press.

Goswami, B.N. 1991. 'Another Past, Another Context: Exhibiting Indian Art Abroad', in Ivan Karp and Steven Levine (eds), *Exhibiting Cultures*, pp. 68–78. Washington and London: Smithsonian.

Gramsci, Antonio. 1971. *Selections from the Prison Notebooks*. Selected and tr. by Quentin Hoare and Geoffrey Novell-Smith. London: Lawrence and Wishart.

Greenblatt, Stephen. 1989. 'Towards a Poetics of Culture', in H. Aram Veeser (ed.), *The New Historicism*, pp. 1–14. New York: Routledge.

———. 1991. 'Resonance and Wonder', in Ivan Karp and Steven Levine (eds), *Exhibiting Cultures*, pp. 42–56. Washington and London: Smithsonian.

Grewal, Inderpal and Caren Kaplan. 2001. 'Global Identities: Theorizing Transnational Studies of Sexuality', *GLQ*, 7(4): 663–79.

Gubar, Susan and Joan Hoff (eds). 1989. *For Adult Users Only: The Dilemma of Violent Pornography*. Bloomington: Indiana University Press.

Guha, Ranajit (ed.). 1999 [1982]. *Subaltern Studies I*. Delhi: Oxford University Press.

Gupta, Dipankar. 1999. 'Secularization and Minoritization: The Limits of Heroic Thought', in D.L. Sheth and Gurpreet Mahajan (eds), *Minority Identities and the Nation-State*, pp. 38–58. Delhi: Oxford University Press.

Gupta, S.P. 1985. *Masterpieces from the National Museum Collections*. New Delhi: National Museum.

Habermas, Jurgen. 2001. *The Postnational Constellation: Political Essays*, tr. and ed. Max Pinsky. Cambridge: Polity.

Hall, Stuart. 1980. 'Cultural Studies: Two Paradigms', *Media, Culture and Society*, 2(1): 57–72.

———. 1981. 'Notes on Deconstructing the Popular', in Raphael Samuel (ed.), *People's History and Socialist Theory*, pp. 227–40. London: Routledge.

Hall, Stuart. 1999 [1992]. 'The Question of Cultural Identity', in Stuart Hall, David Held and Tony McGrew (eds), *Modernity and its Futures*, pp. 273–325. Cambridge: Polity/Open University.

————. 2000 [1989]. 'Cultural Identity and Cinematic Representation', in Robert Stam and Toby Miller (eds), *Film and Theory*, pp. 704–14. Oxford: Blackwell.

————. 2002. 'Whose Heritage? Un-settling "The Heritage". Re-imagining the Post-Nation', in Rasheed Araeen, Sean Cubitt and Ziauddin Sardar (eds), *The Third Text Reader on Art, Culture and Theory*, pp. 72–84. London and New York: Continuum.

Hall, Stuart, David Held and Tony McGrew (eds). 1999 [1992]. *Modernity and its Futures*. Cambridge: Polity/Open University.

Hall, Stuart and Paul du Gay (eds). 1996. *Questions of Cultural Identity*. London: Sage Publications.

Hammonds, Evelynn. 1994. 'Black (W)holes and the Geometry of Black Female Sexuality', *Differences*, 6(2–3): 126–45.

Harpham, Geoffrey Galt. 1982. *On the Grotesque: Strategies of Contradiction in Art and Literature*. Princeton: Princeton University Press.

Harvey, Robert C. 1979. 'The Aesthetics of the Comic Strip', *Journal of Popular Culture*, 12(4): 640–52.

————. 1994. *The Art of the Funnies: An Aesthetic History*. Jackson: University Press of Missippi.

Hawley, John Stratton. 1994a. 'Hinduism: Sati and Its Defenders', in John Stratton Hawley (ed.), *Fundamentalism and Gender*, pp. 79–110. New York and Oxford: Oxford University Press.

———— (ed.). 1994b. *Fundamentalism and Gender*. New York and Oxford: Oxford University Press.

Hayles, N. Katherine. 1999. *How We became Posthuman: Virtual Bodies in Cybernetics, Literature, and Informatics*. Chicago: University of Chicago Press.

Hebdige, Dick. 1979. *Subculture: The Meaning of Style*. New York: Methuen.

Hides, Sean. 1997. 'The Genealogy of Material Culture and Cultural Identity', in Susan Pearce (ed.), *Experiencing Material Culture in the Western World*, pp. 11–35. London and Washington: Leicester University Press.

Hobson, Janell. 2003. 'The "Batty" Politic: Toward an Aesthetic of the Black Female Body', *Hypatia*, 18(3): 87–105.

Hoerder, Dirk. 2002. *Cultures in Contact: World Migrations in the Second Millennium*. Durham: Duke University Press.

Holmes, David (ed.) 1997. *Virtual Politics: Identity and Community in Cyberspace*. London: Sage Publications.

Hooper-Greenhill, Eilean. 1992. *Museums and the Shaping of Knowledge*. London and New York: Routledge.

Horn, Maurice (ed.). 1976. *The World Enyclopaedia of Comics*. New York: Chelsea House.

Huggan, Graham. 2001. *The Postcolonial Exotic: Marketing the Margins*. London and New York: Routledge.

Hunter, Ian. 1994. *Rethinking the School: Subjectivity, Bureaucracy and Criticism*. Sydney: Allen and Unwin.

Huntington, Samuel P. 1996. *The Clash of Civilizations and the Remaking of World Order*. New York: Simon and Schuster.

Hurley, Kelly. 1996. *The Gothic Body: Sexuality, Materialism and Degeneration at the Fin de Siecle*. Cambridge: Cambridge University Press.

Ilaiah, Kancha. 1996. 'Productive Labour, Consciousness and History: The Dalitbahujan Alternative', in Shahid Amin and Dipesh Chakrabarty (eds), *Subaltern Studies IX*, pp. 165–200. Delhi: Oxford University Press.

———. 1999 [1998]. 'Towards the Dalitization of the Nation', in Partha Chatterjee (ed.), *Wages of Freedom*, pp. 267–91. Delhi: Oxford University Press.

Inge, Thomas M. 1979. 'The Comics as Culture', *Journal of Popular Culture*, 12(4): 631–39.

———. 1990. *Comics as Culture*. Jackson and London: University Press of Mississippi.

Ivison, Duncan. 2002. *Postcolonial Liberalism*. Cambridge: Cambridge University Press.

Jain, Kajri. 2003. 'More than Meets the Eye: The Circulation of Images and the Embodiment of Value', in Sumathi Ramaswamy (ed.), *Beyond Appearances?*, pp. 33–70. New Delhi: Sage Publications.

Jancovich, Mark. 2002. 'Cult Fictions: Cult Movies, Subcultural Capital and the Production of Cultural Distinctions', *Cultural Studies*, 16(2): 306–22.

Jay, Martin. 2003. 'Drifting into Dangerous Waters: The Separation of Aesthetic Experience from the Work of Art', in Pamela R. Mathews and David McWhirter (eds), *Aesthetic Subjects*, pp. 3–27. Minneapolis and London: University of Minnesota Press.

Jayawardena, Kumari. 1986. *Feminism and Nationalism in the Third World*. London: Zed Books.

Jenkins, Henry. 1999 [1992]. '"Strangers No More, We Sing": Filking and the Social Construction of the Science Fiction Fan Community', in Paul Marris and Sue Thornham (eds), *Media Studies*, pp. 547–56. Edinburgh: Edinburgh University Press.

John, Mary E. and Tejaswini Niranjana. 1999. 'Mirror Politics: "Fire", Hindutva and Indian Culture', *Economic and Political Weekly*, 6–13 March.

Jordan, Glenn and Chris Weedon. 1995. *Cultural Politics*. Oxford: Blackwell.

Jordanova, Ludmilla. 1989. 'Objects of Knowledge: A Historical Perspective on Museums', in Peter Vergo (ed.), *The New Museology*, pp. 22–40. London: Reaktion.

Jorvik News. 2001. York Archaeological Trust, and operated by Heritage Projects Ltd, in association with the City of York Council.

Joshi, Svati (ed.). 1991. *Rethinking English: Essays in Literature, Language, History*. New Delhi: Trianka.

Kakoudaki, Despina. 2002. 'Spectacles of History: Race Relations, Melodrama, and the Science Fiction/Disaster Film', *Camera Obscura*, 17(2): 109–53.

Kapur, Anuradha. 1993. 'Deity to Crusader: The Changing Iconography of Ram', in Gyanendra Pandey (ed.), *Hindus and Others*, pp. 74–109. New Delhi: Viking.

Karp, Ivan. 1991. 'Culture and Representation', in Ivan Karp and Steven Levine (eds), *Exhibiting Cultures*, pp. 11–24. Washington and London: Smithsonian.

Karp, Ivan, Christine Mullen Kreamer and Steven D. Lavine (eds). 1992. *Museums and Communities: The Politics of Public Culture*. Washington and London: Smithsonian.

Karp, Ivan and Steven D. Lavine (eds). 1991. *Exhibiting Cultures: The Poetics and Politics of Museum Display*. Washington and London: Smithsonian.

Kasbekar, Asha. 1996. 'An Introduction to Indian Cinema', in Jill Nelmes (ed.), *An Introduction to Film Studies*, pp. 365–91. London: Routledge.

———. 2001. 'Hidden Pleasures: Negotiating the Myth of the Female Ideal in Popular Hindi Cinema', in Rachel Dwyer and Christopher Pinney (eds), *Pleasure and the Nation*, pp. 286–308. Delhi: Oxford University Press.

Katju, Manjari. 2003. *Vishva Hindu Parishad and Indian Politics.* Hyderabad: Orient Longman.

Kazmi, Fareed. 1999. *The Politics of India's Conventional Cinema.* New Delhi: Sage Publications.

Kempkes, Wolfgang. 1974. *International Bibliography of Comics Literature.* New York and London: R.R. Bowker.

Kesavan, Mukul. 2001. *Secular Common Sense.* Delhi: Penguin.

Khera, Rajesh. 2004. 'Khera's gay Abandon'. Interview with Vickey Lalwani, Entertainment and TV Guide, *Deccan Chronicle,* 14 February, pp. 8–9.

Khilnani, Sunil. 2004 [1997]. *The Idea of India.* New Delhi: Penguin.

Kimball, A. Samuel. 2002. 'Conceptions and Contraceptions of the Future: *Terminator 2, The Matrix,* and *Alien Resurrection', Camera Obscura,* 17(2): 69–107.

King, Margaret J. 1981. 'Disneyland and Walt Disney World: Traditional Values in Futuristic Form', *Journal of Popular Culture,* 15(1): 116–40.

Klein, Naomi. 2001 [2000]. *No Logo.* London: Flamingo.

Klock, Geoff. 2002. *How to Read Superhero Comics and Why.* New York: Continuum.

Kramer, Cheris. 1974. 'Stereotypes of Women's Speech: The Word from Cartoons', *Journal of Popular Culture,* 8(3): 624–30.

Kunzle, David. 1990. *The History of the Comic Strip in the Nineteenth Century.* Berkeley and Los Angeles: University of California Press.

Lang, Jeffrey S. and Patrick Trimble. 1988. 'Whatever Happened to the Man of Tomorrow? An Examination of the American Monomyth and the Comic Book Superhero', *Journal of Popular Culture,* 22(3): 157–73.

Legman, G. 1963. *Love and Death: A Study in Censorship.* New York: Hacker Art.

Lutgendorf, Philip. 2003. 'Evolving a Monkey: Hanuman Poster Art and Postcolonial Anxiety', in Sumathi Ramaswamy (ed.), *Beyond Appearances?,* pp. 71–112. New Delhi: Sage Publications.

MacCannell, Dean. 1976. *The Tourist: A New Theory of the Leisure Class.* New York: Shocken.

Macdonald, Amanda. 1998. 'In Extremis: Hergé's Graphic Exteriority of Character', *Other Voices,* 1(2), http://www.othervoices.org/1.2/amacdonald/herge.html.

MacDonald, Andrew and Virginia. 1976. 'Sold American: The Metamorphosis of Captain America', *Journal of Popular Culture,* 10(1): 249–55.

Madan, T.N. 1997. *Modern Myths, Locked Minds: Secularism and Fundamentalism in India.* Delhi: Oxford University Press.

Manion, Jennifer C. 2003. 'Girls Blush Sometimes: Gender, Moral Agency, and the Problem of Shame', *Hypatia,* 18(3): 21–41.

Mannur, Anita. 2000. '"The Glorious Heritage of India": Notes on the Politics of Amar Chitra Katha', *Bookbird,* 38(4): 32–33.

Manuel, Peter. 2001. *Cassette Culture: Popular Music and Technology in North India.* Delhi: Oxford University Press.

Margaroni, Maria. 2003. 'Jane Campion's Selling of the Mother/Land: Restaging the Crisis of the Postcolonial Subject', *Camera Obscura,* 18(2): 93–123.

Marris, Paul and Sue Thornham (eds). 1999. *Media Studies: A Reader.* Edinburgh: Edinburgh University Press.

Mathews, Pamela R. and David McWhirter (eds). 2003. *Aesthetic Subjects.* Minneapolis and London: University of Minnesota Press.

Mazumdar, Ranjani. 2002 [2000]. 'From Subjectification to Schizophrenia: The "Angry Man" and the "Psychotic" Hero of Bombay Cinema', in Ravi S. Vasudevan (ed.), *Making Meaning in Indian Cinema,* pp. 238–64. Delhi: Oxford University Press.

McCarthy, John D. and Mayer N. Zald. 2003. 'Social Movement Organizations', in Jeff Goodwin and James M. Jasper (eds), *The Social Movements Reader*, pp. 169–86. Oxford: Blackwell.

McKee, Alan. 2002. 'What Cultural Studies Needs is More Theory', *Continuum*, 16(3): 311–16.

McQuat, Gordon. 2001. 'Cataloguing Power: Delineating "Component Naturalists" and the Meaning of Species in the British Museum', *British Journal for the History of Science*, 34: 1–28.

McRobbie, Angela. 1997. 'The Es and the Anti-Es: New Questions for Feminism and Cultural Studies', in Marjorie Ferguson and Peter Golding (eds), *Cultural Studies in Question*, pp. 170–86. London: Sage Publications.

Menon, Nivedita. 1999 [1998]. 'Women and Citizenship', in Partha Chatterjee (ed.), *Wages of Freedom*, pp. 241–66. Delhi: Oxford University Press.

Merchant, Hoshang (ed.). 1999. *Yaraana: Gay Writing from India*. New Delhi: Penguin.

Merriman, Nick. 1989. 'Museum Visiting as a Cultural Phenomenon', in Peter Vergo (ed.), *The New Museology*, pp. 149–71. London: Reaktion.

———. 1991. *Beyond the Glass Cage: The Past, the Heritage and the Public in Britain*. Leicester, London, and New York: Leicester University Press.

Metz, Christian. 1982 [1975]. 'The Imaginary Signifier', tr. Ben Brewster, in *The Imaginary Signifier: Psychoanalysis and Cinema*, pp. 3–87. Bloomington: Indiana University Press.

Miah, Andy. 2000. 'Virtually Nothing: Re-evaluating the Significance of Cyberspace', *Leisure Studies*, 19: 211–25.

Michasiw, Kim. 1994. 'Camp, Masculinity, Masquerade', *Differences*, 6(2–3): 146–73.

Mitchel, Delores. 1981. 'Women Libeled: Women's Cartoons of Women', *Journal of Popular Culture*, 14(4): 597–610.

Mondello, Salvatore. 1976. 'Spider-Man: Superhero in the Liberal Tradition', *Journal of Popular Culture*, 10(1): 232–38.

Morley, Grace. 1981. *Museums Today*. Baroda: Department of Museology, M.S. University, Baroda.

Mukherjee, Rudrangshu. 1984. *Awadh in Revolt: A Study of Popular Resistance*. Delhi: Oxford University Press.

Mulvey, Laura. 1975. 'Visual Pleasure and Narrative Cinema', *Screen* 16(3): 6–18.

Museum of Modern Art. 1999. *MOMA Highlights: 325 Works from The Museum of Modern Art, New York*. New York: The Museum of Modern Art.

Nair, Bindu. 2002. 'Female Bodies and the Male Gaze: Laura Mulvey and Hindi Cinema', in Jasbir Jain and Sudha Rai (eds), *Films and Feminism*, pp. 52–58. Jaipur: Rawat.

Nandy, Ashis. 1995a. 'An Intelligent Critic's Guide to Indian Cinema', in *The Savage Freud and Other Essays on Possible and Retrievable Selves*, pp. 196–236. Delhi: Oxford University Press.

———. 1995b. 'Sati in Kali Yuga: The Public Debate on Roop Kanwar's Death', in *The Savage Freud and Other Essays on Possible and Retrievable Selves*, pp. 32–52. Delhi: Oxford University Press.

———. 1995c. 'The Politics of Secularism and the Recovery of Religious Tolerance', in Bilgrami and Nandy, *Paper No. 29*, pp. 30–64. New Delhi: Rajiv Gandhi Institute for Contemporary Studies.

———. 1998a [1994]. *The Illegitimacy of Nationalism: Rabindranath Tagore and the Politics of the Self*. Delhi: Oxford University Press.

Nandy, Ashis. 1998b. 'A New Cosmopolitanism: Toward a Dialogue of Asian Civilizations', in Kuan-Hsing Chen (ed.), *Trajectories*, pp. 142–49. London and New York: Routledge.

———. 1999. 'Coping with the Politics of Faiths and Culture: Between Secular State and Ecumenical Traditions in India', in Joanna Pfaff-Czarnecka, Darini Rajasingham-Senanayake, Ashis Nandy and Edmund Terence Gomez (eds), *Ethnic Futures*, pp. 135–66. New Delhi: Sage Publications.

———. 2001. 'Invitation to an Antique Death: The Journey of Pramathesh Barua as the Origin of the Terribly Effeminate, Maudlin, Self-Destructive Heroes of Indian Cinema', in Rachel Dwyer and Christopher Pinney (eds), *Pleasure and the Nation*, pp. 138–60. Delhi: Oxford University Press.

Narayan, Lala Aditya. 1980. 'The Display of Prehistoric and Protohistoric Materials in a Museum: Some Suggestions', in Vinod P. Dwivedi (ed.), *Museums and Museology*, pp. 26–30. New Delhi: Agam Kala Prakashan.

National Tourism Policy. 2002. Department of Tourism and Culture, Government of India.

Nava, Mica. 1987. 'Consumerism and its Contradictions', *Cultural Studies*, 1(2): 204–10.

Nava, Mica and Orson Nava. 1999 [1992]. 'Discriminating or Duped? Young People as Consumers of Advertising/Art', in Paul Marris and Sue Thornham (eds), *Media Studies*, pp. 766–74. Edinburgh: Edinburgh University Press.

Nayar Pramod K. 2004. *Virtual Worlds: Culture and Politics in the Age of Cybertechnology*. New Delhi: Sage Publications.

———. (forthcoming). 'Deleuze's Nietzsche: The Nomadic War Machine and the Martial Sublime', in Franson Manjali (ed.), *Nietzsche: Philosopher, Philologist, Culture Critic*. New Delhi: Allied.

Nayar, Sheila J. 2001. 'Cinematically Speaking: The Impact of Orality on Indian Popular Film', *Visual Anthropology*, 14(2): 121–53.

Negus, Keith. 2002. 'The Work of Cultural Intermediaries and the Enduring Distance between Production and Consumption', *Cultural Studies*, 16(4): 510–15.

Nelmes, Jill (ed.). 2001. *An Introduction to Film Studies*. London and New York: Routledge.

Newbold, Chris, Oliver Boyd-Barrett and Hilde Ban Den Bulck (eds). 2002. *The Media Book*. London: Arnold.

Nigam, M.L. 1985 [1966]. *Fundamentals of Museology*. Hyderabad: Navahind Prakashan.

Niranjana, Tejaswini. 1994. 'Integrating Whose Nation? Tourists and Terrorists in "Roja"', *Economic and Political Weekly*, 15 January: 79–82.

———. 2002 [2000]. 'Nationalism Refigured: Contemporary South Indian Cinema and the Subject of Feminism', in Partha Chatterjee and Pradeep Jeganathan (eds), *Subaltern Studies XI*, pp. 138–66. Delhi: Oxford University Press.

Nixon, Sean and Paul du Gay. 2002. 'Who Needs Cultural Intermediaries?', *Cultural Studies*, 16(4): 495–500.

Nye, Russel B. 1981. 'Eight Ways of Looking at an Amusement Park', *Journal of Popular Culture*, 15(1): 63–75.

Palumbo, Donald. 1983. 'The Marvel Comics Group's Spider-Man is an Existential Super-Hero; or "Life Has No Meaning Without My Latest Marvels"', *Journal of Popular Culture*, 17(1): 67–82.

Palumbo-Liu, David. 2002. 'Multiculturalism Now: Civilization, National Identity, and Difference Before and After September 11th, *Boundary 2*, 29(2): 109–27.

Pandey, Gyanendra (ed.). 1993. *Hindus and Others*. New Delhi: Viking.

———. 1995. 'The Appeal of Hindu History', in Vasudha Dalmia and Heinrich von Stietencron (eds), *Representing Hinduism*, pp. 369–88. New Delhi: Sage Publications.

Paranjape, Makarand. 2004. 'Balle Bollywood: Bombay Dreams and Postcolonial Realities', in Udaya Narayana Singh, N.H. Itagi and Shailendra Kumar Singh (eds), *Language, Society and Culture*, pp. 96–105. Mysore: Central Institute of Indian Languages and Mahatma Gandhi International Hindi University.

Pearce, Susan M. (ed.). 1997. *Experiencing Material Culture in the Western World*. London and Washington: Leicester University Press.

Perebinossoff, Philippe. 1975. 'What Does a Kiss Mean? The Love Comic Formula and the Creation of the Ideal Teen-Age Girl', *Journal of Popular Culture*, 8(4): 825–35.

Pernau, Margrit, Imtiaz Ahmad and Helmut Reifeld (eds). 2003. *Family and Gender: Changing Values in Germany and India*. New Delhi: Sage Publications.

Pfaff-Czarnecka, Joanna, Darini Rajasingham-Senanayake, Ashis Nandy and Edmund Terence Gomez (eds). 1999. *Ethnic Futures: The State and Identity Politics in Asia*. New Delhi: Sage Publications.

Philips, Robert C. 2003. 'The War against Pluralism', in James P. Sterba (ed.), *Terrorism and International Justice*, pp. 101–13. New York: Oxford University Press.

Pickering, Michael. 2001. *Stereotyping: The Politics of Representation*. Basingstoke, Hampshire and New York: Palgrave.

Pinney, Christopher. 1997. *Camera Indica: The Social Life of Indian Photographs*. London: Reaktion.

———. 2003. ' "A Secret of Their Own Country": Or, How Indian Nationalism Made itself Irrefutable', in Sumathi Ramaswamy (ed.), *Beyond Appearances?*, pp. 113–50. New Delhi: Sage Publications.

Plantinga, Carl. 1997. 'Notes on Spectator Emotion and Ideological Film Criticism', in Richard Allen and Murray Smith (eds), *Film Theory and Philosophy*, pp. 373–93. Oxford: Clarendon Press.

Pollock, Sheldon, Homi K. Bhabha, Carol A. Breckenridge and Dipesh Chakrabarty. 2000. 'Cosmopolitanisms', *Public Culture*, 12(3): 577–89.

Prasad, M. Madhava. 1998. *Ideology of the Hindi Film: A Historical Construction*. Delhi: Oxford University Press.

Pratt, Mary Louise. 1995 [1992]. *Imperial Eyes: Travel Writing and Transculturation*. London: Routledge.

Prince, Stephen (ed.). 2000. *Screening Violence*, London: Athlone.

Pritchett, Frances W. 1995. 'The World of Amar Chitra Katha', in Lawrence A. Babb and Susan S. Wadley (eds), *Media and the Transformation of Religion in South Asia*, pp. 76–106. Philadelphia: University of Pennsylvania Press.

Pugh, Judy F. 1986. 'Celestial Destiny: Popular Art and Personal Crisis', *India International Centre Quarterly*, 13(1): 54–69.

Pyle, Christian L. 2004. 'The Superhero Meets the Culture Critic'. Review of Richard Reynolds, *Super Heroes: A Modern Mythology*. http://jefferson.village.virginia.edu/pmc/text-only/issue.994/review-6.994, 27 November.

Rajadhyaksha, Ashish. 2002 [2000]. 'Viewership and Democarcy in Cinema', in Ravi S. Vasudevan (ed.), *Making Meaning in Indian Cinema*, pp. 267–96. Delhi: Oxford University Press.

Ramakantam, S. 1976. *State Museum, A Hyderabad: A Folder*. Hyderabad: Government of Andhra Pradesh.

Ramaswamy, Sumathi (ed.). 2003. *Beyond Appearances? Visual Practices and Ideologies in Modern India*. New Delhi: Sage Publications.

Rao, Sandhya. 2000. 'Amar Chitra Katha Comics: A Quick-Fix Culture Course for Kids', *Bookbird*, 38(4): 33–35.

Ray, Satyajit. 1983 [1976]. *Our Films, Their Films*. Hyderabad: Orient Longman.

Reddy, A.K.V.S. 1998. *Salar Jung Museum Guide Book*. Hyderabad: Salar Jung Museum.

Redhead, Steve, with Derek Wynne and Justin O'Connor (eds). 1997. *The Clubcultures Reader: Readings in Popular Cultural Studies*. Oxford: Blackwell.

Reynolds, Richard. 1994. *Super Heroes: A Modern Mythology*. Jackson: University Press of Mississippi.

Rheingold, Howard. 1992. *The Virtual Community*. New York: Simon and Schuster.

Richter, Linda K. 1989. *The Politics of Tourism in Asia*. Honolulu: University of Hawaii Press.

Robbins, Trina. 2002. 'Gender Differences in Comics', *Image and Narrative*, 4. http://www.imageandnarrative.be, 28 November 2004.

Robertson, Roland. 1992. *Globalization: Social Theory and Global Culture*. London: Sage Publications.

———. 1995. 'Glocalization: Time-Space and Homogeneity-Heterogeneity', in Mike Featherstone, Scott Lash and Roland Robertson (eds), *Global Modernities*, pp. 25–44. London: Sage Publications.

Robins, Kevin. 1998 [1995]. 'Cyberspace and the World We Live In', in Mike Featherstone and Roger Burrows (eds), *Cyberspace/Cyberbodies/Cyberpunk*, pp. 135–55. London: Sage Publications.

Robinson, Jerry (ed.). 1974. *The Comics: An Illustrated History of Comic Strip Art*. New York: G.P. Putnam.

Roy, Srirupa. 2001. 'Nation and Institution', *Interventions*, 3(2): 251–65.

———. 2003. 'Moving Pictures: The Postcolonial State and Visual Representations of India', in Sumathi Ramaswamy (ed.), *Beyond Appearances?*, pp. 233–64. New Delhi: Sage Publications.

Rushbrook, Dereka. 2002. 'Cities, Queer Space, and the Cosmopolitan Tourist', *GLQ: A Journal of Lesbian and Gay Studies*, 8(1–2): 183–206.

Sack, Robert David. 1992. *Place, Modernity and the Consumer's World: A Relational Framework for Geographical Analysis*. Baltimore and London: Johns Hopkins University Press.

Saraceni, Mario. 2003. *The Language of Comics*. New York and London: Routledge.

Sarkar, Tanika and Urvashi Butalia (eds). 1995. *Women and the Hindu Right*. New Delhi: Kali for Women.

Savage W. William, Jr. 1990. *Comic Books and America, 1945–1954*. Norman and London: University of Oklahoma Press.

Sayre, Shay and Cynthia King. 2003. *Entertainment and Society: Audiences, Trends, and Impact*. Thousand Oaks: Sage Publications.

Schuler, Douglas and Peter Day (eds). 2004. *Shaping the Network Society: The New Role of Civil Society in Cyberspace*. Cambridge, MA: MIT Press.

Schultheis, Alexandra W. 2004. *Regenerative Fictions: Postcolonialism, Psychoanalysis and the Nation as Family*. New York and London: Palgrave-Macmillan.

Searle-Chatterjee, M. and Ursula Sharma (eds). 1994. *Contextualising Caste: Post-Dumontian Approaches*. Oxford: Blackwell/Sociological Review.

Seidman, Steven and Jeffrey C. Alexander (eds). 2001. *The New Social Theory Reader*. London and New York: Routledge.

Sen, Ashish Kumar. 2004. 'From Brain Drain to "Brain Circulation"', *Span*, April: 6–7.

Sharma, Rajnish. 2002. 'Amar Chitra Katha's Westward Voyage', Little India.com, http://supra.websitewelcome.com/~little/may 2002.htm.

Sharma, Ursula. 2002. *Caste*. New Delhi: Viva.

Sherman, Daniel J. and Irit Rogoff. (eds). 1994. *Museum Culture: Histories, Discourses, Spectacles*. London: Routledge.

Sheth, D.L. 1999. 'The Nation-State and Minority Rights', in D.L. Sheth and Gurpreet Mahajan (eds), *Minority Identities and the Nation-State*, pp. 18–37. Delhi: Oxford University Press.

Sheth, D.L. and Gurpreet Mahajan (eds). 1999. *Minority Identities and the Nation-State*. Delhi: Oxford University Press.

Singh, Udaya Narayan, N.H. Itagi and Shailendra Kumar Singh (eds). 2004. *Language, Society and Culture*. Mysore: Central Institute of Indian Languages and Mahatma Gandhi International Hindi University.

Sircar, Sanjay. 2000. 'Amar Chitra Katha: Western Forms, Indian Contents', *Bookbird*, 38(4): 35–36.

Skinner, Kenneth A. 1979. 'Salaryman Comics in Japan: Images of Self-Perception', *Journal of Popular Culture*, 13(1): 141–51.

Smith, Charles Saumarez. 1989. 'Museums, Artefacts, and Meanings', in Peter Vergo (ed.), *The New Museology*, pp. 6–21. London: Reaktion.

Spiegelman, Art. 1986 [1973]. *Maus: A Survivor's Tale*, 2 vols. New York: Pantheon.

Spivak, Gayatri Chakravarty. 1988 [1985]. 'Subaltern Studies: Deconstructing Historiography', in Ranajit Guha and Gayatri Chakravarty Spivak (eds), *Selected Subaltern Studies*, pp. 3–34. Delhi: Oxford University Press.

Springer, Claudia. 1999. 'The Pleasure of the Interface', in Jenny Wolmark (ed.), *Cybersexualities*, pp. 34–54. Edinburgh: Edinburgh University Press.

Srilata, K. 1992. 'Children's Literature and the Formation of Subjectivity: A Study in the Indian Context'. Unpublished dissertation, University of Hyderabad.

Srinivas, S.V. 1997. *Fans and Stars: Production, Reception and Circulation of the Moving Image*. Unpublished dissertation, University of Hyderabad.

———. 2002 [2000]. 'Devotion and Defiance in Fan Activity', in Ravi S. Vasudevan (ed.), *Making Meaning in Indian Cinema*, pp. 297–317. Delhi: Oxford University Press.

Stam, Robert and Toby Miller (eds). 2000. *Film and Theory: An Anthology*. Oxford: Blackwell.

Sterba, James P. (ed.). 2003. *Terrorism and International Justice*. New York: Oxford University Press.

Stewart, Susan. 1984. *On Longing: Narratives of the Miniature, the Gigantic, the Souvenir, the Collection*. Baltimore and London: Johns Hopkins University Press.

Storey, John. 1998. *Cultural Theory and Popular Culture: A Reader*. Hemel Hempstead: Prentice-Hall.

———. 2003. *Inventing Popular Culture*. Oxford: Blackwell.

Strinati, Dominic. 1997 [1995]. *An Introduction to Theories of Popular Culture*. London and New York: Routledge.

Sukthankar, Aswhini (ed.). 1999. *Facing the Mirror: Lesbian Writing from India*. New Delhi: Penguin.

Sunder Rajan, Rajeswari. 2000. 'Women between Community and State: Some Implications of the Uniform Civil Code Debates in India', *Social Text*, 18(4): 55–82.

Taylor, Woodman. 2003. 'Penetrating Gazes: The Poetics of Sight and Visual Display in Popular Indian Cinema', in Sumathi Ramaswamy (ed.), *Beyond Appearances?*, pp. 297–322. New Delhi: Sage Publications.

Thapan, Meenakshi (ed.). 1997. *Embodiment: Essays on Gender and Identity*. Delhi: Oxford University Press.

Tharu, Susie and Tejaswini Niranjana. 1996. 'Problems for a Contemporary Theory of Gender', in Shahid Amin and Dipesh Chakravarty (eds), *Subaltern Studies IX*, pp. 232–60. Delhi: Oxford University Press.

Thomson, Rosemary Garland (ed.). 1996. *Freakery: Cultural Spectacles of the Extraordinary Body*. New York: New York University Press.

Thornton, Sue. 1997. *Club Cultures: Music, Media and Subcultural Capital*. Cambridge: Polity.

Uberoi, Patricia. 1997. 'Dharma and Desire, Freedom and Destiny: Rescripting the Man-Woman Relationship in Popular Hindi Cinema', in Meenakshi Thapan (ed.), *Embodiment*, pp. 145–71. Delhi: Oxford University Press.

———. 2001. 'Imagining the Family: An Ethnography of Viewing *Hum Aapke Hain Koun...!*', in Rachel Dwyer and Christopher Pinney (eds), *Pleasure and the Nation*, pp. 309–51. Delhi: Oxford University Press.

———. 2003. '"Unity in Diversity?": Dilemmas of Nationhood in Indian Calendar Art', in Sumathi Ramaswamy (ed.), *Beyond Appearances?*, pp. 191–232. New Delhi: Sage Publications.

Urry, John. 1998 [1990]. *The Tourist Gaze*. London: Sage Publications.

Valicha, Kishore. 1988. *The Moving Image: A Study of Indian Cinema*. Hyderabad: Orient Longman.

van Zoonen, Liesbet. 1996 [1994]. *Feminist Media Studies*. London: Sage Publications.

Varney, Wendy. 2002. 'Of Men and Machines: Images of Masculinity in Boys' Toys', *Feminist Studies*, 28(1): 153–75.

Vasudevan, Ravi S. 2000. 'The Politics of Cultural Address in a "Transitional" Cinema: A Case Study of Popular Indian Cinema', in Christine Gledhill and Linda Williams (eds), *Reinventing Film Studies*, pp. 130–64. London: Edward Arnold.

———. 2001. 'Bombay and Its Public', in Rachel Dwyer and Christopher Pinney (eds), *Pleasure and the Nation*, pp. 186–211. Delhi: Oxford University Press.

———. (ed.). 2002 [2000]. *Making Meaning in Indian Cinema*. Delhi: Oxford University Press.

Veblen, Thorstein. 1994 [1899]. *A Theory of the Leisure Class*. London: Constable.

Vishwanath, Gita. 2002. 'Saffronizing the Silver Screen: The Right-Winged Nineties Film', in Jasbir Jain and Sudha Rai (eds), *Films and Feminism*, pp. 39–51. Jaipur: Rawat.

Wallis, Brian. 1994. 'Selling Nations: International Exhibitions and Cultural Diplomacy', in Daniel J. Sherman and Irit Rogoff (eds), *Museum Culture*, pp. 265–82. London: Routledge.

Walsh, Kevin. 1992. *The Representation of the Past: Museums and Heritage in the Post-Modern World*. London and New York: Routledge.

Wearing, Stephen and Betsy Wearing. 2001. 'Conceptualizing the Selves of Tourism', *Leisure Studies*, 19: 143–59.

Weeks, Jeffrey. 1997 [1986]. *Sexuality*. London and New York: Routledge.

Wernick, Andrew. 1994 [1991]. *Promotional Culture: Advertising, Ideology and Symbolic Expression*. London: Sage Publications.

Wertham, Frank. 1954. *Seduction of the Innocent*. New York: Rinehart.

White, David Manning and Robert H. Abel (eds). 1963. *The Funnies: An American Idiom*. London: Free Press of Glencoe.

Williams, Jeff. 1994. 'Comics: A Tool of Subversion?', *Journal of Criminal Justice and Popular Culture*, 2(6): 129–46. Available online at http://www.albany.edu.scj/jcjpc/vol2is6/comics.html, 28 November 2004.

Williams, Raymond. 1976. *Keywords: A Vocabulary of Culture and Society*. London: Fontana.

Willis, Paul. 1978. *Profane Culture*. London: Routledge and Kegan Paul.

Wilson, E.O. 1975. *Sociobiology: The New Synthesis*. Cambridge, MA and London: Harvard.

Wolmark, Jenny (ed.). 1999. *Cybersexualities: A Reader on Feminist Theory, Cyborgs and Cyberspace*. Edinburgh: Edinburgh University Press.

Woods, Gregory. 1995. 'Fantasy Islands: Popular Topographies of Marooned Masculinity', in David Bell and Gill Valentine (eds), *Mapping Desire*, pp. 126–48. London and New York: Routledge.

Yinger, J. Milton. 1984 [1982]. *Countercultures: The Promise and Peril of a World Turned Upside Down*. New York and London: Free Press and Collier Macmillan.

Žižek, Slavoj. 1989. *The Sublime Object of Ideology*. London: Verso.

INDEX

ABOUT THE AUTHOR

Pramod K. Nayar teaches at the Department of English, University of Hyderabad. He was Fulbright Senior Fellow at Cornell University (USA) in 2005–2006; Charles Wallace India Trust–British Council Visiting Fellow at the University of Kent at Canterbury (UK) in 2001; and Smuts Visiting Fellow in Commonwealth Studies, University of Cambridge (UK) in 2000–2001.

Among his other interests are postcolonial literatures, Indian writing in English, the aesthetics of the sublime and cultural studies. His published books include an edition of Emily Brontë's *Wuthering Heights* (2005), *Virtual Worlds: Culture and Politics in the Age of Cybertechnology* (Sage 2004) and *Literary Theory Today* (2002). His forthcoming works are *Colonizing Aesthetics*, a study of English writings on India, a book on postcolonial literatures, *The 1857 Reader* and others.